THE CALL

THE SPIRITUAL REALISM OF SARGENT SHRIVER

JAMIE PRICE

SSPI PRESS

Paperback ISBN 979-8-9872726-0-2
eBook ISBN: 979-8-9872726-1-9
Audio Book ISBN: 979-8-9872726-2-6

Published by
SSPI Press
12400 Wilshire Boulevard, Suite 1275
Los Angeles, CA 90025

Book and cover design by Barbara Aronica-Buck
Cover painting by Lowell Boyers

Manufactured in the United States of America

for Sarge

CONTENTS

Foreword by Charles Hefling   vii

Introduction   xi

SPIRIT

1. Sarge Gets the Call   3

2. Differentiating Spirit   26

SPIRITUAL REALISM

3. Catcher   47

4. Flow   65

5. Logjam   89

6. Connect the Dots   115

7. Narrative Image   137

PRACTICAL IDEALISM

8. Chicago: On Releasing the Spiritual Power of the People   159

9. Peace Corps: Blessed Are the Peacemakers   204

Notes   231

Bibliography   289

Acknowledgments   311

About the Contributors   313

FOREWORD

Charles Hefling

All the wisest saints and sages tell us that if there is anything worth knowing it is ourselves. No knowledge is more valuable, and none is more difficult to acquire. To know who you are, in the most serious sense, is to know more than your name, more than the story of how you came to be all that you are. It is to know what you have been doing, and still do, in making the choices that made you and make you, that settle on you the character you have, that form and inform your identity, your self. It is to be aware of your own inclinations and attitudes and standards, the roles you enact, the motives you take account of in deciding what you do.

What it might be like to arrive at this sort of reflective knowledge can best be learned from those who, by paying attention to how the internal engine that propels them operates, have succeeded in discovering themselves in themselves. Such a one was Sargent Shriver, the principal character in this book. Shriver was a very public figure, perhaps best known for shepherding the Peace Corps into being. That and other notable achievements of his are essential ingredients in this book, but it is not a history book or a biography. The story of Shriver's life and deeds has been told, and well told, elsewhere. What has largely been left untold is why he did what he did, in the way he did it—how he discerned what could and should be done, and how he determined the way he would go about doing it. Shriver knew all that. He knew himself and knew what he was doing. This is a book about what he knew and about the deliberate, methodical approach he brought to bear on the issues he dealt with and the projects he undertook.

If this method, as he called it, were a set of impersonal bullet points or a recipe for turning out the same product time after time, it could be expounded without much ado. That is not what it is, and Jamie Price does not expound it. He exhibits it. Formally, what he has written is a dialog, which is to say a drama with a cast of two. Each of these characters speaks in response to what the other has spoken, which is to say their speaking is a conversation. As the verbal interaction goes forward, the reader is introduced not only to the topics under discussion but also, at the same time, to the characters as individuals. Moreover, while you as reader may choose simply to eavesdrop on the conversation, you may also find yourself engaging more personally with what is said, by taking on the roles of the speakers, adopting their attitudes, thinking their thoughts, and especially by asking for yourself the questions they ask. If that happens, so much the better. The conversation in this book is intimate, but not private. It invites sympathetic, imaginative participation. It invites you.

One of the *dramatis personae* in this drama is Sargent Shriver himself. Inasmuch as the other one, Didymus by name, is an invention, he and "Sarge" take part in what Price aptly calls a true conversation that never actually happened. Not all that Sarge is given to say is on record, but all of it is true in the way a portrait painted by a perceptive artist is true to life. As Price's extensive notes testify, no one is better equipped than he is, by friendship, experience, and scholarly labor, to paint the essential Shriver. That metaphor, however, fails in one respect. A painting is static, whereas what Price's words express is dynamic. He presents the workings of a mind and heart blessed with self-knowledge and with a willingness to share with Didymus—and anyone else who cares to listen—what he knew.

More particularly, what Shriver shares is his method. There is a name for it: spiritual realism. Not that the name matters, unless perhaps "spiritual" brings with it connotations that point away from what the name really refers to. Shriver makes no attempt to define the word for Didymus. Definitions are abstract. Spirit, or the spirit, is an objective reality. Didymus, who takes after his namesake Thomas the Doubter, is therefore right to insist on being shown that this reality *is* real. He requires evidence for what Shriver is talking about. And Shriver obliges him—not by arguing or even by reporting examples, but rather, in good Socratic fashion, by a kind of midwifery. He gently sets up the conditions for Didymus himself to experience himself as present both to himself and to the spirit. There is nothing spooky about this, nothing supernatural in that sense. It is the most natural thing in the world, provided you pay attention to it. Exactly how, then, does Sarge induce or elicit or enable what happens in and through the conversational drama?

For that, you will have to read the book. Like every real conversation, it roams. There are excursions—baseball is one of them—but no pointless detours. At the end, it returns to where it began: the genesis of the Peace Corps. As Price acknowledges, "To say that the Peace Corps was intentionally designed to harness the power of the spirit is to make a bold claim." But that is just what he does claim. And, together with his meticulous notes, the nine conversational episodes he sets out in *The Call* show how firmly founded his claim is.

Read those episodes slowly. They are nothing like the "conversations" on social media. Imagine them as spoken aloud. And pause from time to time, long enough to ask yourself what you have read, but also and especially to ask what you were doing as you were reading, and why you were doing it. The time will be well spent.

INTRODUCTION

The Call is a dialog, an extended conversation between Sargent Shriver and his friend Didymus about the role of the spirit in Sarge's efforts to build peace. Sargent Shriver (1915–2011) was one of the most innovative and accomplished American peace builders of the twentieth century—a fact widely recognized at the time though it is now slipping from popular memory. In the 1950s, Sarge was a major figure in business, education, and civil rights in Chicago. In the 1960s, he designed and ran the Peace Corps under President Kennedy, America's War on Poverty under President Johnson, and he hosted the first round of peace talks to end the Vietnam War as the US Ambassador to France. In 1972, he served as the Democratic Party's nominee for vice president and in subsequent years worked as a citizen diplomat to marshal interreligious peacebuilding in the Middle East, to foster detente with the Soviet Union, and to champion the No First Strike nuclear arms policy embraced by the American Catholic Bishops and key leaders in the US foreign policy establishment. In the final years of his professional life, Sarge teamed up with his wife, Eunice Kennedy Shriver, to globalize the reach of Special Olympics International, notably in China.

It was my privilege to get to know Sarge personally during the last twenty years of his life. It was also my good fortune to serve as the founding director of three programs dedicated to understanding and advancing Sarge's approach to leadership and peacebuilding: the Shriver Peaceworker Program at the University of

Maryland, Baltimore County (UMBC), the Sargent Shriver Program for Leadership in Public Service in the Institute of Politics at the University of Chicago, and the Sargent Shriver Peace Institute, launched in cooperation with what is now the Carter School for Peace and Conflict Resolution at George Mason University.

During this time I came to recognize—as many who worked closely with him also knew—that the good he sought to achieve in the world was the fruit of his distinctive approach to making program decisions. The approach was grounded not only in Sarge's personal, practical, and political wisdom as a leader, but also in his profound, conscious presence to the flow of the spirit in himself and human affairs more broadly. Of course, it is difficult to speak concretely about the spirit, not least because our capacity for spiritual experiencing transcends our ability to name it. Efforts to pin it down verbally lend themselves to airy abstractions, and as a result, spiritual texts are filled with cautionary reminders not to confuse the words and images that gesture toward our experience of the spirit with the experience itself. As a hedge against this tendency, this book unfolds in the form of a dialog rather than a treatise. This makes it possible to hear from Sarge directly and for the reader to correlate the experiences Sarge describes with their own inner conscious grasp of those experiences.

A further word about this dialog is in order. The Didymus who converses with Sarge in this book is an historical figure too, albeit from a different era and not a contemporaneous acquaintance of Sarge. "Didymus" is the Latinized form of the Greek word for "twin," and the given name of this particular twin is Thomas, one of Jesus's disciples. This disciple is commonly known by the epithet "doubting Thomas" because of the way his spontaneously empirical concern to verify the reality of Jesus's resurrected body is portrayed in the Gospel of John. Thomas insists on touching Jesus's wounds as a condition of his assent. But this Didymus is not an ideologically driven doubter. He is not a pugnacious debater with a penchant for taking the opposing side. He is questioning Thomas, curious Thomas. He really wants to learn about Sarge and himself, and over the course of their conversation he does.

So Didymus is a literary device in this conversation with Sarge, but he is not a fiction. Neither is their conversation. For as an historical matter, Sarge was drawn to this gospel story about Thomas and routinely invoked Thomas's presence in his daily meditative practice. And so it was that I felt drawn to choose Didymus as the symbolic interlocutor of Sarge's thoughts and deeds in this book. Didymus relies upon his empirical proclivities and presses Sarge to clarify the claims he makes—especially his spiritual claims—and to specify his reasons for thinking they might be so. The hope is that Didymus's curiosity will serve as prompt and carrier of the reader's curiosity too.

Like any real conversation, the flow of Didymus's dialog with Sarge is non-linear, though it possesses a form and structure of its own. Didymus opens the conversation by wondering about Sarge's engagement with the Peace Corps. His curiosity is piqued by Sarge's account of a highly significant telephone call with President Kennedy on the afternoon of January 21, 1961—a call in which the newly inaugurated president asks Sarge to lead the design and development of the Peace Corps. Didymus is struck by Sarge's matter-of-fact disclosure that despite having serious personal reservations about taking on the role, he felt spiritually called to do so. Didymus's effort to understand precisely what Sarge means by this declaration—and to pin down whatever experiential basis it may have—orients the rest of their ensuing conversation. It unfolds in nine episodes that progressively explore three distinct but related component parts or themes: experiencing spirit, modeling spiritual realism, and implementing practical idealism.

"Spirit" is the term Sarge typically uses to refer to the transcendent dimension of consciousness and reality. "Spiritual realism" refers to Sarge's efforts to categorize and model the relationship between spirit, human consciousness, and the natural world. It is a term coined by my friend and colleague, Tim Shriver, in the course of our many efforts together to pin down the role of the spirit in human living. "Practical idealism" is a term first used by Gandhi, but it was appropriated by Sarge to describe his efforts to put spiritual realism to work in the creation and design of the Peace Corps. As Sarge puts it, "in the early days of Peace Corps, we were looking for a formula for practical idealism."

In Part I—Spirit—Didymus seeks to understand both what Sarge means by his declaration that he discerned a spiritual call to lead the Peace Corps effort, and what experiential basis he might have for making this claim. Part I has two episodes: "Sarge gets the Call," and "Differentiating Spirit." In Part II—Spiritual Realism—Didymus wants Sarge to explain the relationship of spiritual experiencing to our other types of experiencing—namely sensory and conscious experiencing. This leads them to discuss Sarge's work both in Chicago and with the Peace Corps, and over the course of five conversational episodes, Didymus discovers that Sarge employs a model of spiritual realism that enables him to think critically about the role of the spirit in personal and institutional decision-making: "Catcher," "Flow," "Logjam," "Connecting the Dots," and "Narrative Image." In Part III—Practical Idealism—Didymus's grasp of Sarge's model leads him to ask about how Sarge puts it to use, which they explore in two conversational episodes: "Chicago: On Releasing the Spiritual Power of People" and "Peace Corps: Blessed are the Peacemakers".

The fact that Sarge is an active participant in this conversation raises the question of the historical authenticity of the things he says. In answer, I suggest that it's best to think about the exchange between Sarge and Didymus as a true conversation that never actually happened. It never happened in the simple sense that Sarge never actually sat down with a friend named Didymus to have this particular conversation—not until now anyway. At the same time, their conversation is true in the sense that all the people, the events, and many of the words Sarge speaks are historically accurate and verifiable.

Questions about the historicity of Sarge's words in his conversation with Didymus are addressed in the endnotes. These notes demonstrate in considerable detail that the thoughts and ideas espoused by Sarge in this conversation are properly attributable to him and do so by drawing upon four key sources. The first is the collection of well over one hundred public speeches that Sarge gave during the time period under discussion. Sarge was open and forthright in discussing the role of the spirit in his work, as these speeches clearly attest. A second source of Sarge's ideas is traceable to the work of philosophers and theologians that Sarge read carefully, knew well, and cited in his speeches. These include Thomas Aquinas, Jacques Maritain, and Teilhard de Chardin, among others. A third source of conversational verification comes from biographical accounts of Sarge's life and from histories of the Peace Corps, the Catholic Church, and race relations in Chicago. These historical sources testify to the fact that the events discussed by Didymus and Sarge took place as presented. A fourth source of information lies in the answers to questions I put to Sarge in the course of personal conversations I was fortunate enough to have with him during the last twenty years of his life. Finally, in compiling these notes, I am pleased to acknowledge that I have had the pleasure of working closely with my friend and colleague, Ken Melchin, whose unfailing intelligence, encouragement, and help have been indispensable.

The influence of Bernard Lonergan's thought on this work must also be acknowledged. Lonergan (1904–1984) was a contemporary of Sarge. He was a philosopher, theologian, and methodologist whom Sarge knew and read, but whose work had more of an influence on me in writing this dialog than it formally did on Sarge's thinking. As his conversation with Didymus makes clear, Sarge was rigorously methodical in his work, but unlike Lonergan, he was not a methodologist. In his various roles directing programs and serving the public, Sarge was understandably more concerned with implementation, action, and communication than he was with formally explaining how he did things and why. In this conversation with Didymus, however, Sarge has the time and opportunity to delve into these questions, and as the notes make clear, it is Lonergan's foundational method that has helped me to guide this aspect of the conversation.

While the historical veracity of Sarge's conversation with Didymus is admittedly important, the main line of inquiry raised in this book is not precisely historical. The main line of inquiry is philosophical, empirical, and ultimately theological. Did Sarge actually claim to be consciously present to the spirit during his high stakes, politically oriented phone call with President Kennedy about who should lead the Peace Corps? Yes, he did. Did Sarge's conscious presence to the spirit lead him to make certain key programmatic decisions rather than others when he was designing the Peace Corps? Yes, it did. But as important as these affirmative answers may be, the broader question raised by the dialog between Sarge and Didymus is ultimately this: Does the model of spiritual realism that Didymus and Sarge elucidate in the course of their conversation resonate with the inner conscious experience of the reader? I hope this proves to be so, for as readers enter into the conversation between Sarge and Didymus, they are invited to wrestle with the answer to this question for themselves.

The questions Didymus puts to Sarge serve to carry the reader's inquiry into the relationship of sensory, conscious, and spiritual experiencing. Sarge's performance in creating the Peace Corps and desegregating Chicago's Catholic high school system provides the locus for discovery. The dialogical structure of this conversation makes it possible not only to clarify what Sarge was thinking about the relationship of spirit and social action, but also to grasp how he was using his mind when he did so. In this way, the dialog between Didymus and Sarge invites the reader to try on the mindset of Sargent Shriver and to critically engage his approach to spiritual realism. That is a major aim of this book.

But the book also has a loftier aim, shared by Sarge, which lies in the broader cultural implications of his socially innovative approach to spirit and action. In the course of his conversation with Sarge, Didymus seeks to understand and empirically verify the model of spiritual realism Sarge used to infuse the spiritual values of compassion and service into the policies and programs he designed. And in this time of cultural and religious polarization it is worth noting that Sarge was able to implement this model without triggering the divisive, dominating effects of ratifying particular religious doctrines or traditions. The hope therefore is that engaging in this spirited conversation about Sarge's spiritual realism will be of practical help to aspiring leaders, innovators, and peace builders of all political, religious, and spiritual stripes. The hope is that by illustrating this model in action, Sarge's example will make it possible for contemporary peace builders to think more creatively and constructively about their own efforts to redress contemporary challenges to human dignity, welfare, and security.

For to enter critically into this conversation between Didymus and Sarge on the relationship of spirit and action is also to enter constructively into a broader conversation about one of the major political and spiritual conundrums of modern times. Weber called it "the disenchantment of the modern world." Lonergan refers to it as "the absence of God in modern culture." Whatever we may call it, the social and political clash between secular and religious factions in modern societies across the world are familiar to us all, and Sarge's model of spiritual realism makes it possible to imagine an alternative path. Sarge forthrightly claims that the Peace Corps exemplifies the way spiritual values can be infused into the institutional structures of secular affairs. He further claims that the way to make friends, build peace, and to transcend contemporary barriers of language, politics, and cultural difference is to release the spiritual power of people to transcend the limitations of self-interest and group bias. Didymus's line of inquiry openly invites Sarge to clarify how this might be so. By engaging in this conversation, you, dear reader, are cordially invited to ask your questions and to discover within yourself the model of spiritual realism Sarge used in his efforts to build peace.

SPIRIT

Sarge Gets the Call[1]

DIDYMUS: Good morning, Sarge. I appreciate your willingness to engage with me in this series of conversations.

SARGE: I'm looking forward to it.

DYD: I'd like to understand your approach to building peace and in particular, your involvement with the Peace Corps. I've done some homework, but I still have a lot of questions.

RSS: I'm quite fond of questions.

DYD: Are you?

RSS: It's better to have a head fully stocked with questions than a head filled with certainties. Bernard Lonergan once said something like that. I agree.[2]

DYD: Then take us back, if you will, to January 21, 1961—the day after your brother-in-law was inaugurated as the thirty-fifth president of the United States—and the first day of your formal involvement with Peace Corps. What was going on?[3]

RSS: That was a pivotal day—for me and for my family too.

DYD: By all accounts, you attended the inauguration ball in DC on the night of the twentieth and then flew back home to Chicago the next morning. That's where President Kennedy got in touch with you by phone.

RSS: That's right. We'd only been home an hour or two when the phone began to ring. The president called several times, but I was avoiding the telephone, so Eunice took his calls. Finally, she said to me: "You know, Sarge. Jack is the president now. You have to talk to him."

DYD: You were reluctant to take the call.

RSS: I was tired, frankly, and I was looking forward to just being at home. We'd been going full bore since April, when I joined Jack's campaign for the Wisconsin primary. And then, the day after the election, Jack put me in charge of our "talent hunt," so I was responsible for vetting and staffing the new administration—the cabinet, regulatory agencies, ambassadors, everything. For two months, Harris Wofford and I ran that 24/7 whirlwind out of the Mayflower Hotel.

DYD: You were tired of DC.

RSS: I was. So Eunice and I had tickets on the first flight out on the morning of the twenty-first, and I was relieved to touch down in Chicago.

DYD: Did you have any idea what the president might be calling about?

RSS: I had a hunch. Because of my involvement in the talent hunt, I knew every job we needed to fill and the people Jack wanted for each of them, and the Peace Corps was the elephant in the room. We hadn't formally discussed either what the program should be or who should head it up.

DYD: But you'd been thinking about it?

RSS: Not seriously, no. But I knew Jack's promise to create the Peace Corps was on his mind, a promise that both worried and tantalized him.

DYD: He was worried about it?

RSS: Back in November—right after the election—he wrote a letter to Walt Rostow at MIT, expressing his concern that sending young Americans to the developing world to build peace might be a mistake.[4]

DYD: Rostow was an advisor to President Eisenhower, wasn't he?

RSS: Right, a foreign policy advisor. Jack asked Walt to have Max Millikan draft a Peace Corps implementation plan. The two of them had been advising Eisenhower on foreign aid and economic development.

DYD: But Eisenhower ridiculed the president's Peace Corps idea as a juvenile experiment, didn't he?

RSS: He did. And it seems Millikan shared Ike's view of it. Either that, or he allowed Jack's misgivings to carry his thinking.

DYD: What makes you say that?

RSS: Millikan's proposal for the design and implementation of a Peace Corps was more concerned with minimizing the political risk of sending young volunteers into developing nations than it was with building peace with host country nationals.

DYD: So what became of it?

RSS: Jack's transition team released it to the press in late December, during the transition period. But nothing came of it.

DYD: Why not?

RSS: As I said, it captured Jack's worries about the Peace Corps well enough, but it completely missed America's spontaneous fascination with the program. Millikan's plan was so risk averse it would have undercut that enthusiasm instead of tapping into it.

DYD: What kind of enthusiasm are you talking about?

RSS: We received more letters of inquiry about the Peace Corps than we did for all the other jobs in the administration combined. Thousands of people were offering to volunteer for a program that didn't even exist! That enthusiasm was on Jack's mind too, and he spoke directly to it in his inaugural address.

DYD: "Ask not what your country can do for you . . ."

RSS: Exactly. A Gallup poll conducted just before the inauguration revealed that over 70 percent of Americans approved of the idea of creating a Peace Corps.

DYD: But let's bring this back to you. The day after the inauguration the president tries to get you on the phone. You suspect that he wants to talk to you about the Peace Corps job, so you're ducking his calls. What was your reluctance?[5]

RSS: I loved Chicago. It was home, and it had been for nearly fourteen years. When Eunice called me to the phone I was in the living room, looking out the window of our apartment. We lived on a top floor. Our building was eighteen stories tall, and we had a terrific view of Lincoln Park. I remember holding my son Timmy in the crook of my arm. He was only eighteen months old at the time and his arm was around my neck. We were looking out across the boat basin onto Lake Michigan. Did you know the lake is so big you can't see across it? It's a shimmering expanse of blue water stretching into the horizon.

DYD: You were content.

RSS: As I said, I loved Chicago, and I wasn't all that crazy about relocating to DC. I didn't need a job, you know. I liked my work at the Merchandise Mart.[6]

DYD: What did you like about it?

RSS: The Merchandise Mart was the world's largest building. We had ninety-three acres of floor space and over six miles of corridors to manage.

DYD: That's a lot to manage.

RSS: Yes, but it was an entirely fascinating challenge. When Ambassador Kennedy bought the Mart in 1945, the building was over half empty, and the occupied part was let to tenants with underperforming agreements. He hired me to fill up the building with blue chip tenants and turn it into a going concern.

DYD: A challenge indeed.

RSS: I was only thirty years old. Still, the ambassador saw something in me.

DYD: I should think so. You had a law degree from Yale, you'd been a gunnery officer on an aircraft carrier in the Pacific, and you were working as a journalist at *Newsweek*.

RSS: It's true. I had some experience, but none in business or commercial real estate.

DYD: You learned.

RSS: I had a great team to work with. Wallace Ollman was the general manager. Tom King was the advertising director. And I thoroughly enjoyed cultivating relationships with top executives in businesses like NBC, Western Electric, and Eastern Airlines.

DYD: So what experience did you pick up?

RSS: I learned how to negotiate contracts, close deals, and create the administrative systems we needed to support those agreements and keep our clients happy.

DYD: And you made it work?

RSS: The Mart became wildly successful, and in 1961 it still had plenty of potential for growth. I aimed to fulfill it.

DYD: As you say, when the president called you didn't need a job.

RSS: No. And beyond that, I was looking forward to working on the other things I had going in Chicago before I got involved in Jack's campaign.

DYD: What things?

RSS: I had to take a leave of absence from the Mart when I signed onto Jack's campaign full time, but I also had to step down as president of the Board of Education in Chicago.[7]

DYD: That sounds like a loss.

RSS: I was sorry to give up the role, yes. I had been entrusted as the leading voice in public education in Chicago, and I felt called to make sure every child in Chicago received the best possible education.

DYD: It was gratifying.

RSS: To help create a school system dedicated to forming thoughtful, curious, open-minded citizens? I should say so.

DYD: You're clearly drawn to major challenges.

RSS: And to the nitty-gritty work it takes to meet them.

DYD: So what did it take in the case of the School Board?

RSS: I got seriously involved in developing school policy. We raised school standards, encouraged educational experimentation, upgraded our school buildings and playgrounds, and made sure our teachers were fairly paid. I also got engaged in the political give and take with the city council, the mayor's office, and the state legislature in Springfield. I advocated for our programs.

DYD: And got them funded?

RSS: Yes. That was the best part. We ran a tight, scandal-free ship, which was a rarity in Chicago.

DYD: And I gather that along the way you were building political capital.

RSS: That too. My work with the School Board stirred up talk about standing for elective office, maybe a run for the US Senate in 1962, or for governor in 1964. That was appealing.

DYD: But to turn those political opportunities into realities, you'd have to be in Chicago.

RSS: That's right. But that wasn't my only reason for staying in Chicago. I was president of the Board of the Catholic Interracial Council in Chicago, and I was committed to that role too.

DYD: You got involved with the CICC before being appointed to the Chicago School Board. Am I right about that?

RSS: Yes. It was 1952—so I'd been involved a little more than eight years at that point—though I'd only been president for the last few of those years.

DYD: Tell me a bit about the Catholic Interracial Council. It was a national organization, wasn't it?

RSS: It was more of a national movement, actually. A Jesuit priest named John LaFarge launched the first Catholic Interracial Council in New York in the spring of 1934. His aim was to address problems of interracial justice in America's political culture by cleaning up problems of interracial justice in the Church. Over the next twenty years, nearly fifty Catholic Interracial Councils were established in cities across the country. Chicago joined in 1946.

DYD: So it was an idea whose time had come.

RSS: Yes, but the Catholic Interracial Council in Chicago was one of the smallest in the country. When Lloyd Davis, the new executive director, pointed that out to me, I thought it was scandalous.

DYD: Another challenge for you!

RSS: And a worthy one. The prospect of bringing the Church into the vanguard of interracial justice in Chicago was inspiring to me. Besides, Lloyd asked me to take charge of CICC's work in the realm of education. And he gave me free reign in program design.

DYD: Did you have a particular focus?

RSS: I did. The Diocese ran a large network of Catholic high schools in Chicago. Seventy-nine high schools, if you can believe it. But at the time Lloyd invited me to come on board, those schools were racially segregated.

DYD: Really? So that was your focus.

RSS: We wanted White and Black students in Chicago to have equal opportunities to go to Catholic high school—as well as the opportunity to go to school together. So we focused on making that possible. But beyond that, we wanted all our students to grapple seriously with the problem of racial justice in their school, the city, and their hearts.

DYD: A high aspiration.

RSS: Yes, but necessary. Once those students were admitted to their new schools, we knew we had to address the racial misunderstanding and mistrust in the hearts of everyone in those schools. The sin of racism, we called it.

DYD: So you wanted the students to flourish personally as well as academically.

RSS: Socially too. That's where the real work began.

DYD: How did you tackle that?

RSS: We sponsored clubs in each school that brought the students together voluntarily—Black students with White students—students who wanted to discuss the racial and civil rights problems they encountered in their classrooms, in the city, and in themselves.

DYD: You gave them the opportunity to work it out together, face to face.

RSS: And they did. The bonds created between those students were very strong, but the clubs themselves were invariably small. We discovered it was easy for club members to feel isolated and overwhelmed. They needed support.

DYD: So what did you do?

RSS: Two or three times a year we organized system-wide symposia on civil rights. We called them study days. We would bring together over a thousand club participants from across the schools to wrestle for a couple of days with the issues of interracial justice they were experiencing in their lives.

DYD: That sounds like a lot of organizing.

RSS: Yes, but the energy we released in those gatherings was fantastic.

DYD: And contagious, no doubt.

RSS: Absolutely.

DYD: So, you were looking forward to getting back to that work, to that energy, and to taking on the sin of racism.

RSS: For me, there could be no higher priority in Chicago, in the United States, or anywhere else in the world than to find practical answers to the number one question of the day. How can people of different religions, cultures, and races—White, Black, Yellow and Brown—come together in peace to advance the dignity and welfare of all?

DYD: And at CICC, you had created an applied lab for working out some of those answers.

RSS: Exactly.

DYD: So there you are. It's Sunday, January twenty-first, the day after the inauguration, and you're feeling glad to be back home. You have high-level aspirations and opportunities you want to pursue, and when the phone rings, you are reluctant to take the president's call.

RSS: I didn't want to be sidetracked.

DYD: You'd done your bit for the family. You had just dedicated nine months to electing and staffing the new president.

RSS: That's right. Besides, the prospect of becoming a federal bureaucrat running the Peace Corps out of some division buried in the State Department held absolutely no allure for me.

DYD: But as it happened, Eunice hands you the phone, you speak to the president, and two minutes later you're saying goodbye to Chicago and everything you were hoping to achieve either in public office or as president of the Catholic Interracial Council. Instead, you're saying yes to heading up the Peace Corps task force.

RSS: That's right.

DYD: That's astonishing, is what it is.

RSS: I guess it is. It certainly wasn't my plan when we touched down in Chicago that morning.

DYD: So what changed your mind?

RSS: Well, for one thing, Eunice was right. Jack was the

president, and as you can well imagine, it is very difficult to say "no" to the president. Especially if he's your brother-in-law, and you admire him, and you are keenly aware that your wife—his sister— would much rather be in the thick of things in DC than in Chicago.

DYD: But?

RSS: But when I picked up the phone, I was fully prepared to say no.

DYD: Yet, you didn't.

RSS: No I didn't. When the president offered me the role of leading a task force charged with designing the Peace Corps, I felt called to let go of my other plans and say yes to the challenge.[8]

DYD: What do you mean you felt called?

RSS: I mean I felt spiritually called.

DYD: Spiritually?

RSS: Yes.

DYD: That's surprising.

RSS: It always is.

DYD: Let me make sure I understand. You're saying that during your phone call with the president—and more specifically, when you heard him ask you to lead the task force—you experienced some sort of a spiritual call?

RSS: I am, and it wasn't "some sort of a spiritual call." It was an actual spiritual call, and I have Mary to thank for it.[9]

DYD: Mary? What would Mary have to do with it?

RSS: Well, to my mind, Mary is Our Lady of Spiritual Awareness. For me, she is the perfect image of spiritual openness.

DYD: She's an exemplar for you.

RSS: When the angel Gabriel appears to her in the first chapter of Luke, he announces that God has chosen her to be the vessel of his entry into the world, the physical vessel. Needless to say, this was surprising to her. And it had to be puzzling and troubling on any number of levels too.

DYD: Had to be.

RSS: But here's the thing. Mary remains centered in the face of her encounter with Gabriel. She maintains her equanimity. She doesn't turn away from Gabriel or shut him out. She doesn't resist the role she's been selected to play. If she's doubtful and afraid, there is no record of it. She has let that go. Her reply to Gabriel is extraordinary. "Be it done to me according to thy Word."

DYD: What does she mean by that?

RSS: You can't be more open to grace, more consciously present to the spirit, than Mary was at that particular moment.

DYD: "Consciously present?"

RSS: It's another way of saying "explicitly aware of"—though I think it's more accurate.

DYD: So, you're saying that, in the manner of Mary, you were consciously present to the spirit in your conversation with the president?

RSS: As we've discussed, I had plenty of good reasons to stay in Chicago, to get on with my life, and plenty of good reasons to reject the idea of going back to DC.

DYD: But you remained open to new possibilities. How so?

RSS: When I pray the Rosary—and I pray the Rosary every day—I pray the words Mary spoke to Gabriel. I ask for her help in being more like her. She is present to me in her words.

DYD: In the midst of your conversation with the president?

RSS: Yes.

DYD: So your daily practice of saying the Rosary—of praying to Mary—prepared you to be present to a spiritual call in your phone call with the president?

RSS: That's right.

DYD: It seems we've come a long way from that phone call in your apartment overlooking Lake Michigan.

RSS: Not all that far, really.

DYD: None of the other histories of the Peace Corps point to spiritual experience as a key factor in your decision to head up the Peace Corps.[10]

RSS: Then it's a good thing we're having this conversation.

DYD: You think so?

RSS: I do, though I realize there's risk involved.

DYD: How so?

RSS: I've been using devotional language to talk to you about my phone call with the president. Of course, that's fine with me, and that's where your questions carried my mind. But I know that talking this way has its risks. Communicatively.

DYD: What risks?

RSS: The risk that people will leap to conclusions—false conclusions.

DYD: What conclusions?

RSS: That I am either being uncritical or doctrinaire. Maybe both.[11]

DYD: I wasn't thinking about you that way.

RSS: Not everybody would, of course.

DYD: But some people, perhaps. And that concerns you.

RSS: It does.

DYD: So help me to understand. As soon as these people hear your report that you felt spiritually called to lead the Peace Corps task force, you're worried they will leap to what conclusion?

RSS: The conclusion that I am not being realistic—that my spiritual convictions have led me to surrender the critical use of my mind. That by claiming I was consciously present to the spirit in my conversation with the president, I surrendered any claim I might have to be taken seriously as an evidence-based thinker.[12]

DYD: Because . . .

RSS: Because they are convinced that whatever happened during my phone call with the president, it is best understood in explicitly secular, sensory terms, not in religious or spiritual terms.

DYD: But for you, it's not best understood that way?

RSS: No.

DYD: And you're concerned that because you discuss your experience in devotional terms, people will refuse to take you seriously.

RSS: That's right. My other concern is that my references to Mary and the spirit could come across as sectarian, exclusive.

DYD: As some sort of privileged speech . . .

RSS: As conversation-stoppers in their own right.

DYD: But that's not how you think of it.

RSS: I think of it as true, as right. But I also recognize that my devotional language is my brand of spiritual common sense. It's personal to me, of course, because I'm the one seeking spiritual openness. And it's culturally and religiously particular in the sense that it's guided and shaped by the worshiping community to which I belong.

DYD: And?

RSS: And frankly, I don't think anybody gets through the day without some form of spiritual common sense—some form of practical wisdom—whatever language they use, whatever cultural traditions inform them.

DYD: And as a result, you don't consider yourself doctrinaire.

RSS: I'm spiritual. I'm devout. I am Catholic. I go to Mass every morning. I say the Rosary, and I pray to Mary every day. But I'm not narrow or exclusive about it. I think my way of being devout is a good way, a self-transcending way—but it's not the only way.

DYD: It's the way you were given?

RSS: Yes. And it's the way I continue to choose. My conscious presence to the spirit has come into my life this way, and I am grateful for it. But being forthright about my devotion to Mary doesn't mean I've surrendered my intelligence or ceased to be realistic about the world. Nor does it mean I think my way of devotion is the only valid or authentic way of being engaged with the spirit.

DYD: Which raises another question. If you think there is more than one valid way, would it be fair to think of you a spiritual relativist? A relativist who just happens to be strongly devoted to your own particular path?

RSS: That's not it either. My way may not be the only way, but that doesn't mean I think all ways of thinking about the spirit or relating to the spirit are equivalently valid or authentic. I said I was devoted. I said I was appreciative of other ways. I didn't say I had surrendered my ability to raise questions or think critically.

DYD: Okay. Then what precisely are you saying?

RSS: It isn't really that mysterious, is it? People are conscious. We have minds and we use them. But we use them in the context of different religions, cultures, and national and group allegiances. We have different images, practices, and beliefs. Our spiritual common sense differs. It's a function of time and place. That's the main thing I'm saying. It comes with the territory.

DYD: What territory?

RSS: The territory of being a conscious human being. None of us can avoid thinking and feeling and speaking from personal, social, and cultural points of view. And that goes for my secular friends too, who regard the world and their place in it as completely secularized and disenchanted, and whose spiritual common sense explicitly excludes religious language or talk of the spirit.

DYD: But isn't that the problem? Differences in language and culture and tradition create barriers to mutual understanding. They generate entirely different worlds of meaning—spiritual and other-wise.

RSS: Yes. But do you really think that the sheer fact of cultural and linguistic difference can completely close someone off from the presence of the spirit?[13]

DYD: Well, I know there are many people who have reached precisely that conclusion. In any tradition you care to name—and that includes your own Roman Catholic Church—there are people who think differences in devotion, belief, language, and practice function as spirit-proof barriers—barriers that make the difference between salvation and damnation, intelligence and idiocy, scandal to the community and openhearted welcome.

RSS: Like I said, I'm not a spiritual relativist.

DYD: But you're not troubled by differences?

RSS: I'm much more troubled by the assumption that differences can't be transcended.

DYD: So you think that barriers rooted in personal, racial, cultural, and religious differences can be overcome, even transcended.

RSS: With the help of the spirit, yes, I do.

DYD: I presume then that for you as for John 3:8, "the spirit blows where it will"?

RSS: Of course it does. But here's the thing. The spirit not only blows where it will; you can count on the fact that it's blowing.

DYD: Count on the fact that it's blowing within us?

RSS: Whoever you are. Wherever you are. Whatever you are doing.

DYD: And it was blowing while you were on the phone with the president?

RSS: It was.

DYD: But how did you know?

RSS: Know what? Which way the spirit was blowing?

DYD: Yes.

RSS: I try not to jump to conclusions. I try to stay curious and open to further questions.

DYD: You question your experience of being called?

RSS: Of course I do. Until I don't have any more questions.

DYD: That's the standard of your knowing? That you've run out of questions?

RSS: What better standard is there?

DYD: I'm not sure, but don't you find this one to be rather precarious?

RSS: Of course it's precarious! I'm fallible. You're fallible. We're all fallible. That's why we have to keep asking questions. We're bound to be missing something.

DYD: What are you saying, that if we can learn to foster a sustained skepticism about our own certainties, we'll be okay?

RSS: Better than otherwise, yes. Of course, once your questions are asked and answered, you have to move beyond critique to commitment. That can be even harder. That's why I find Mary is so helpful.

DYD: Okay. But staying with critique for a moment, I can imagine someone wanting to question the spiritual claim you're making about your phone call with the president. What if someone were skeptical about that?

RSS: Skeptical in what way?

DYD: Well, what if they found themselves thinking that your sudden and unexpected decision to leave Chicago—to say "yes" to the president—might be explained more adequately in non-spiritual ways.

RSS: Such as?

DYD: By appealing to some combination of family pressure, political opportunism, or moral and political conviction on your part?

RSS: I would welcome that line of questioning.

DYD: You would?

RSS: Of course I would. If you are wondering whether I am alert to the possibility that my conscious presence to the spirit might have been distorted or influenced by factors like the ones you cited—ego, family, my own political agendas—then my answer is yes. I wondered that myself.

DYD: So you hold your certainty loosely? You're open to being questioned and potentially corrected?

RSS: Either way, it's all to the good. My only hope is that the person with questions and doubts is driven by curiosity and a desire to understand.

DYD: What would be the alternative?

RSS: The one I'm thinking about is an aggressive form of interrogation that seeks to discredit and refute rather than to understand.

DYD: Questioning that isn't really curious.

RSS: Questioning that is certainty masquerading as doubt.

DYD: Well, here's a genuinely curious question. How do you cultivate your openness to further relevant questioning?

DYD: That's where Thomas comes in.

DYD: Thomas Aquinas?

RSS: No, but you're right. His head was full of questions. But I mean Doubting Thomas.[14]

DYD: So tell me, how does Thomas fit into the picture for you?

RSS: Thomas is my model for spiritual curiosity and discernment. You know, don't you, that Thomas was one of Jesus's twelve disciples?

DYD: I'm familiar with the story of Thomas in the Gospel of John.

RSS: Then you know that after Jesus was crucified, he appeared first to Mary Magdalene, and then to the other disciples, but not to Thomas.

DYD: Yes, and that when the disciples told Thomas the news that Jesus had appeared to them, he had his doubts.

RSS: Thomas wasn't satisfied with taking the word of his fellow disciples. He had questions. He wanted evidence. He wanted to make the judgment of fact for himself.

DYD: Yes. John has Thomas on record as saying that he wants to see the wounds in Jesus's hands and touch them with his fingers.

RSS: Thomas was a man of empirical principles. That's how I think of it.

DYD: I see your point. But judging from the way Thomas is portrayed in John's gospel, it's clear that John was a bit chary about Thomas's empirical orientation. He insinuates that Thomas's faith is weak in some way.

RSS: True. But as the story plays out, it becomes clear that Jesus doesn't have the same problem with Thomas's questions.

DYD: Jesus appears to the disciples again, but this time Thomas is in the room.

RSS: And the first thing Jesus does is to approach Thomas, hold out his hands, and invite Thomas to touch his wounds.

DYD: But Thomas hesitates.

RSS: Well, it's an awkward moment, isn't it? Jesus is standing right there in front of Thomas, hands out. Under the circumstances, I'm sure Thomas's concerns about evidence no longer feel quite so seemly.

DYD: No.

RSS: But Jesus insists. He tells Thomas to touch his wounds.

DYD: Thomas does. And falls on his knees.

RSS: I would too.

DYD: Okay, so Thomas is empirical and Jesus backs him up. But in practical terms then, what does this do for you?

RSS: Well, the image of Thomas questioning the other disciples inclines me to remain curious about my presence to the spirit. He helps me to resist the temptation of a rush to certainty.

DYD: In your phone call with the president?

RSS: Right. Thomas helped me to question Jack's offer.

DYD: Seriously?

RSS: Of course I'm serious.

DYD: Okay. Let me see if I can put these pieces together.

RSS: Good.

DYD: It all begins when the president asks you to direct the Peace Corps task force.

RSS: Right.

DYD: And in your response to the president's request, Mary's example modeled a quality of openness and equanimity that enabled you to be in touch with the spirit.

RSS: Right.

DYD: And Thomas helps you how? To doubt your inclination to say yes?

RSS: I didn't exactly doubt. But the image of Thomas wanting to check out Jesus's wounds helped me stay on track.

DYD: Stay on track?

RSS: What if my discernment was off base? In particular, I wanted to make sure the role I was feeling called to embrace was actually the one on offer from the president.

DYD: As opposed to what?

RSS: As opposed to a false projection of my own aspirations and desires.

DYD: So, what did you do?

RSS: I said, "Mr. President, I don't know anything about a Peace Corps."

DYD: What were you going for?

RSS: I wanted to make sure the offer was genuine. I want to give Jack an opportunity to reconsider his decision and withdraw the offer.

DYD: But he had no concerns?

RSS: None. He said, "That's all right, Sarge. Neither does anyone else."

DYD: And that satisfied you?

RSS: It reassured me. If no one knew what the Peace Corps should be, the president included, then the scope and structure of the program was wide open. That's what I felt called to embrace. And that meant that the program would be open to whatever the spirit might be calling me to realize.

DYD: You weren't curious about that?

RSS: Not at that point. I was just trying to be open—to be clear—about what was being asked of me.

DYD: So your curiosity was satisfied?

RSS: Actually, I pushed back again.

DYD: About what?

RSS: I probed for any second thoughts the president might be having about tapping me for the job. I wondered if he might rather appoint one of his political friends to the post. I knew several people from the talent hunt who were likely to be interested and available. I was prepared to offer names right then, had he asked.

DYD: But he didn't?

RSS: He dismissed my question. He said, "Look, Sarge. Everyone thinks this Peace Corps idea might be a fiasco, and if it is, it would be easier to fire a relative than a political friend."[15]

DYD: Was he serious?

RSS: Oh, he was serious all right. He said it lightly, and we laughed, but he meant it. As I said earlier, Jack was ambivalent about the Peace Corps. He knew it was a high risk, high reward venture. The fact that he was willing to throw me to the wolves to hedge his political risk struck me as pretty funny.

DYD: You thought it was funny?

RSS: Spiritual gallows humor, I guess. At least I knew my ego wasn't driving the bus, and I found that to be quite consoling. So yes, it made me laugh, and I joked about it in public afterwards. But at the time, I figured that if I was wrong in my discernment of the call—or if the president changed his mind and decided to turn the leadership over to someone else once—I could always come back to Chicago and get on with my work.

Differentiating Spirit[1]

DYD: Sarge, let's pick up the conversation where we left off.

RSS: With me returning to DC to work on the Peace Corps?

DYD: No, I'd like stay for a bit with the telephone conversation you had with the president.

RSS: What are you wondering about?

DYD: It seems to me that getting a call at home on a Sunday afternoon from the president of the United States would be unusual under any circumstances.

RSS: Does it? Jack was my brother-in-law, remember. He's the uncle of my children. My wife is his sister.

DYD: Yes.

RSS: So in context . . .

DYD: Okay. Getting a call from this particular president may not have been unusual for you. Still, I'm struck by the way you engaged with it. For most of us, a phone call—even an unusual phone call—is a mundane, secular event. But you discerned a spiritual component in yours.

RSS: And you find that striking.

DYD: More than striking, actually. If I understand you correctly, this wasn't particularly unusual for you. You anticipate experiences like this; you actually prepare yourself for them.

RSS: That's true.

DYD: That's what I find unusual. You take a phone call from the president, discern a spiritual call "to be done to" according to his offer, and it's business as usual.[2]

RSS: Not business as usual. That phone call was game changing for me. I'd been away from my home and my family for the better part of a year, and now, to my very great surprise, I find myself being called away from my work in Chicago to do who knows what for who knows how long.

DYD: Granted. It was huge for you. But it was a phone call. There is no burning bush, no being struck blind on the way to Damascus, no being spat from the belly of a fish onto a beach in a strange land.

RSS: Not literally, no.

DYD: Literally, though, on Sunday afternoon, January 21, 1961, in your apartment overlooking Lincoln Park in Chicago, you spoke with the president on the telephone. You heard his voice. He offered you a role as leader of the Peace Corps task force. You registered your thoughts and feelings in response, and discerned a spiritual call to take on the role. You even questioned your discernment. But you said yes.

RSS: That's right.

DYD: That's really quite dramatic.

RSS: I suppose it is.

DYD: It reminds me of experiences I've had at the theatre. I'll be engaged in the play, when suddenly the lights come up on a darkened part of the stage. It's been in the shadows. I haven't been focusing on it. But now that the lighting is drawing my attention to it, I realize there is another character on stage, hidden by the shadows and therefore unseen—but a character who has been part of the proceedings all along, even though I didn't realize it.

RSS: You're saying that discerning the spiritual component of my phone call with Jack brings up the lights on the presence of the spirit?

DYD: Well, I do find myself wondering about my own "phone call" moments, so to speak. So yes, it raises the question for me. It leaves me wondering whether I've been overlooking something, ignoring something.

RSS: We've lit up your curiosity. That's a good thing. Where do you want to go with it?

DYD: It's simple. I'd like to know what you were doing spiritually when you discerned the spiritual component of your call with the president.

RSS: What I was doing spiritually?

DYD: Yes.

RSS: I wasn't doing anything spiritual when I was on the phone with Jack.

DYD: You weren't?

RSS: Mary wasn't doing anything spiritual either. Neither was Thomas.

DYD: Are you playing word games with me?

RSS: On the contrary, I'm being precise.

DYD: Okay. What am I missing?

RSS: Wind filling your sails as you near the start of the race; your hat blowing down the street on a windy day; your long fly ball carried over the fence for a home run.[3]

DYD: You're sounding Zen to me now.

RSS: So tell me. What do you think I'm getting at?

DYD: When you compare being present to the spirit with having your hat blown off your head?

RSS: You know it's a metaphor. What connections does the image help you make?

DYD: It sounds like you're riffing on John 3:8—that like the wind, the spirit blows where it will.

RSS: That's right.

DYD: Well, if I take your use of the word seriously, it suggests that just as we don't actually do anything "windy" to get the wind to fill our sails, we don't do anything "spiritual" when we're discerning the spirit either.

RSS: Exactly. Eunice loves sailing at the Cape. The winds fill her sails, but she's not *doing* the wind.

DYD: Okay, but she is sailing the boat. She takes her bearings. She pulls the sheets. She sets the sails. She has a major part to play.

RSS: That's right. The wind blows. She sets the sails. The wind fills them. The boat moves. And with Eunice at the helm, boats move swiftly. She competed against the boys when she was young and she won many races and trophies. She was a racing pioneer. She was fierce about it.

DYD: Her sails were full.

RSS: Indeed they were.

DYD: What's your point, then? That the spirit is an independent principle of action? That it does its own thing?[4]

RSS: Exactly. We can be ready for it, attuned to it, lifted up by it, swept along by it. But nothing we do accounts for it, any more than what we do accounts for the power and movement of the wind.

DYD: The spirit plays its part. We play ours.

RSS: And we need to be able to distinguish them clearly if we're going to understand our relation to the spirit.

DYD: Then let's be clear. In discerning your spiritual call to accept a role as leader of the task force, you were playing your part. No more no less.

RSS: I was not the only player.

DYD: No. The president played a part. You say the spirit played a part too. But strictly speaking, you're saying that "discerning a spiritual call" does not involve doing anything spiritual.

RSS: It does not involve doing what the spirit does, no.

DYD: The wind was blowing; you discerned it. You trimmed your sails; the wind filled them.

RSS: And I booked a flight back to DC for the next day.

DYD: The boat moved ahead.

RSS: You've got it.

DYD: But it's still a metaphor.

RSS: Yes. What's the problem with that?

DYD: The problem is that the spirit is not the wind and our minds are not sails. We are not sailboats and for the most part, we do not live our lives on water.

RSS: So the image of having your sails filled with the divine wind . . . that doesn't resonate for you?

DYD: It's not that. The image is evocative. It's illuminating.

RSS: What are you missing then?

DYD: Understanding. Explanation.[5]

RSS: This metaphor does what metaphors do. They don't explain; they illuminate. They bring up the lights on one thing by drawing attention to its likeness with another.

DYD: In that sense the metaphor works just fine. It draws my imagination to the associations I have of the wind filling a sail, and it prompts me to think of my relationship to the spirit along the line of those images . . . stretched to the full . . . carried along.

RSS: Exactly.

DYD: Thanks to you, the image helps me distinguish the sail and the wind—my part and the part played by the spirit. But I'm still tethered to those images, and they don't really help me to understand the experience itself.

RSS: Because you're not actually a sailboat.

DYD: Yes.

RSS: So it's clarity on spiritual experiencing you want.

DYD: I do.

RSS: Well I have to tell you, if your aim is to be experientially precise, you're really better off with silence, with saying nothing. It's better simply to remain open, present . . .

DYD: Open to? Present to?

RSS: You can't put a label on what can't be labeled.

DYD: No labels then. But surely you can help me pin down the experience. I want to be able to notice it—to identify it in myself. You clearly do.

RSS: It's not a sensory experience, you know.

DYD: How could it be? The spirit is not a sensory object.

RSS: And that means spiritual experiencing is not a matter of seeing, touching, tasting, smelling, or hearing.

DYD: Spiritual experiencing is an altogether different category of experiencing.

RSS: That's right.

DYD: So what kind is it?

RSS: It's a type of conscious experiencing.[6]

DYD: I'm not sure what you mean by conscious experiencing.

RSS: That's part of the difficulty. When I refer to sensory experiencing, you know exactly what I mean, don't you?

DYD: I would say so.

RSS: You could easily supply your own examples of seeing, tasting, and so on.

DYD: Yes—though I can't say the same for conscious experiencing.

RSS: So let's begin with what you already know and work toward what's less evident.

DYD: Okay.

RSS: First then, you know you're a sensory being, that you have five senses, that you use all five senses, that you experience a range of sensory experiences.

DYD: All the time.

RSS: Good. Second then, in addition to being a sensory being, you are also a conscious being.

DYD: Meaning that I have a mind?

RSS: That's right. You not only have a mind, but you use it. In fact, we use our minds in a variety of ways—and there's a range of conscious experiences associated with that.

DYD: And that experience would be?

RSS: It's hard to say. So let me turn the question back to you. Can you describe the taste of salt for me?

DYD: The taste of salt? Describe the taste in words?

RSS: Of course in words: words that would enable me to identify the taste of salt on the basis of your description.

DYD: I know very well what the taste of salt is, and I could pick it out in a lineup of other tastes. But no, I can't really describe it.

RSS: So I'd have to experience salt to actually know what it tastes like.

DYD: It seems so.

RSS: The same goes for conscious experiencing. I can't describe the experience for you. The best I can do is direct your attention to it.

DYD: Direct my attention to the way I'm using my mind?

RSS: Or to the very fact that you're using it. It's a simple matter of catching yourself in the act—of becoming explicitly aware you are using your mind.[7]

DYD: Okay. Direct my attention.

RSS: So when was the last time you remember becoming consciously present to your mind?

DYD: Sorry, but how am I supposed to answer that question when I am still not sure of the experience you're talking about?

RSS: Well, we frequently become consciously aware of the way we're using our minds when our performance lets us down—when we recognize a breach in the way we've been using our mind.

DYD: A breach? You mean, when we've screwed up?

RSS: Exactly. It doesn't have to be a major breach, of course, just big enough to notice.

DYD: I think I understand.

RSS: So tell me then, when was the last time you remember screwing up in the way you were using your mind?

DYD: I'd say it was this morning.

RSS: What was the breach?

DYD: Well, I realized that I had misplaced my keys.

RSS: Were you aware of feeling anything particular in response?

DYD: Yes. I was distressed.

RSS: You'd put them somewhere. You didn't remember where. You couldn't find them immediately. You were distressed that . . .

DYD: Actually, I was distressed that I might be late. I had my appointment to meet with you. I needed to get going. I didn't want to keep you waiting.

RSS: What else did you notice going on in your mind?

DYD: I remember being explicitly aware of talking to myself, "Didymus, where in the world have you put your keys?"

RSS: So you were asking yourself a question, and you were aware of asking.

DYD: Yes, though it wasn't really as verbal as all that.

RSS: You were focused on the keys. You were also consciously present to yourself—aware you were asking yourself where they might be.

DYD: Yes, both. I was searching for them—in my jacket pocket, on the kitchen table, in my briefcase—and sort of talking to myself at the same time.

RSS: But not exactly in words.

DYD: No.

RSS: Did you find them?

DYD: Yes, dangling from the lock on the door to my apartment.

RSS: Ha! It seems you were more consciously present to yourself and to your keys in searching for them this morning than when you entered your apartment last night.

DYD: Clearly.

RSS: And what was your felt response to discovering them?

DYD: Of course, I was annoyed at myself for being so absentminded. Still, I was glad I had found the keys.

RSS: So, there you go. Conscious experiencing. Being present to your mind at work.

DYD: That's all it is?

RSS: That's all it is. It's mundane, I know—as mundane as taste and touch.

DYD: Except that you can't taste and touch your mind at work.

RSS: Though you can be consciously aware of tasting.

DYD: Okay. Sensory and conscious experiencing are different.

RSS: Yes. And spiritual experiencing is different yet again.

DYD: Which means that in addition to being conscious beings and sensory beings, we are also spiritual beings?

RSS: Spiritual in the sense that we have the capacity to experience the presence of the spirit, yes.[8]

DYD: That's the experiencing I've been wondering about.

RSS: I know. And once you pin it down, it will be as clear and present in its own right as any sensory or conscious experience you care to name.

DYD: Then help me pin it down.

RSS: The thing to keep straight is that we don't have experiences "of" the spirit.

DYD: What do you mean?

RSS: I mean that it's tempting to think of spiritual experiencing as a special type of sensory experiencing. But spiritual experiencing is not like sensory experiencing. The spirit is not a supersensory object that we have an experience "of."

DYD: How should we think of it then?

RSS: It's better to think of it in its relation to conscious experiencing, but again, I can't describe it. I can only help you attend to it.

DYD: Attend how?

RSS: You have to notice it in the doing.

DYD: Doing what?

RSS: You know what it is to aspire to something, right?

DYD: Sure. To aspire is to hope for, to hanker for, to aim for, to intend . . .

RSS: And to be consciously present to yourself aspiring?

DYD: To be explicitly aware that I'm hankering, aiming, hoping?

RSS: Good. So here's the thing. It's in connection with our conscious capacity for hoping, hankering, aspiring that we can become consciously present to the spirit.

DYD: In what sense?

RSS: Metaphorically, in the sense the wind fills a sail.

DYD: Expanding it? Opening it? Tugging it?

RSS: Yes.

DYD: And those would be metaphors too. Being expanded, opened, tugged?

RSS: It's very difficult to avoid metaphorical language when we talk about the spirit.

DYD: But when it comes to spiritual experience itself?

RSS: When it comes to the experience itself, I'm consciously aware that my aspiring—my hankering, my hoping—for a particular situation is being tugged to reach beyond my own pleasure and pain, beyond my own advantage and disadvantage, to my highest aspirations for that situation.[9]

DYD: So it's the conscious experience of being inspired, called, tugged—to perform, to carry out—your highest and noblest thinking, aspiring, hoping, valuing, loving.

RSS: Right. Though I am clearly using the word *tug* as something of a descriptor. The same goes for *call*.

DYD: Descriptors of the conscious experience involved.

RSS: Yes.

DYD: The author of 1 Kings refers to experiencing a "still, small, voice," don't they?

RSS: Elijah's encounter with the Lord is striking, isn't it? And as a descriptor, it's very precise—a voice so small, so still, that it's literally not a voice you can hear. It's not a sound at all, really.

DYD: To repeat the obvious, then, the tug you experienced in your phone call with the president wasn't a physical tug.

RSS: No.

DYD: It was connected somehow to your aspiring.

RSS: Yes. It's the conscious tug—the impetus, the call—by which I notice myself hankering to commit to my noblest aspirations.

DYD: So, if I want to get a handle on my own spiritual experiencing, I have to catch myself in the act of being called or tugged in that way.

RSS: That's the way I think of it.

DYD: But this isn't the only way to talk about spiritual experiencing, is it?

RSS: Not at all. But whatever terminology you use to pin it down—spiritual claims to being called, tugged, elevated, inspired, self-transcending—must always come with a caveat.[10]

DYD: What's the caveat?

RSS: The caveat is the recognition that it's very easy to misread the tug, to get it wrong.

DYD: So there's always a need to question.

RSS: Yes.

DYD: Question what?

RSS: The integrity of your aspiring, your loving. There's a sense of ultimacy that comes with feeling called to reach for your noblest aspirations. It's an ultimacy that we readily confuse with certainty.

DYD: The kind of certainty that doesn't entertain evidence to the contrary, that has no room for serious doubt?

RSS: And the kind of certainty that manifests as uncritical zeal for a particular course of action.

DYD: Which is where Thomas comes in for you?

RSS: That's right. The spirit has no truck with uncritical zeal.

DYD: Now that's a claim many find it easy to doubt.

RSS: Yes. Religious institutions have a lot to answer for. But all the great spiritual traditions warn in one way or another against the temptation to pride, certainty, and control.

DYD: Well, the Gospel of Matthew has Jesus fasting in the wilderness and wrestling with the devil for forty days at the outset of his ministry.

RSS: And my favorite is Jesus's struggle in the Garden of

Gethsemane toward the end of his ministry: "Father, if it be possible, let this cup pass from me. Nevertheless, not my will but thine."

DYD: With a nod to Thomas then—and to serious doubt—let me make sure I understand what you've been saying.

RSS: Good.

DYD: First, it would seem safe to say that experiencing a spiritual call to lead the Peace Corps task force was not an auditory experience for you. It was a conscious experience. You were present to your aspiring as tugged—consciously tugged to go beyond your plans in Chicago and to commit to the Peace Corps, wherever that might mean.

RSS: Good so far.

DYD: Second, this means you heard no words to the effect of "Sarge, let go of your work advancing Catholic interracial justice in Chicago. Let go of your aspirations for political leadership in Illinois. Commit yourself to the challenge of leading the Peace Corps task force."

RSS: Well, I did hear words to that effect.

DYD: Literally?

RSS: The president said words to that effect.

DYD: Well, yes. But sensory experiencing is one thing; conscious experiencing is another; spiritual experiencing is a third.

RSS: They're different, yes. But they're related too.

DYD: Related?

RSS: How could it be otherwise?

DYD: I don't really know. I've never thought about it.

RSS: Our encounters with the spirit are concrete and so are our calls to self-transcendence.

DYD: You're saying that the spirit does not elevate us to abstract states of self-transcendence?

RSS: Exactly. We're called at particular times, in particular places, in particular ways.

DYD: On the afternoon of January 21st, in your apartment in Chicago, by telephone.

RSS: Right.

DYD: You have a much more nuanced approach to spiritual experiencing than I was imagining.

RSS: Nuanced in what way?

DYD: Nuanced in the sense that at one and the same time—or maybe in one and the same conscious event—you were able to differentiate your sensory experience of the president's words on the one hand, your conscious response to the president's request for your service on the other, and your presence to the spirit for a third.

RSS: Just to be precise. When you suggest that I was able to "differentiate" those three components . . .[11]

DYD: I'm just trying to capture the complexity of your experience. We *discern* something when we register or notice it: sensory things like the president's words to you on the phone, or conscious things like your presence to the spirit.

RSS: Okay.

DYD: We *distinguish* those things when we recognize that they are not the same, that sensory experiencing and spiritual experiencing are different kinds of experiencing.

RSS: Right.

DYD: But we *differentiate* them—you do, in this particular

case—when we realize the things we are distinguishing are not simply different, but also related to each other as component parts of a whole.

RSS: So yes. I was able to differentiate the words the president was speaking, the conscious flow of my thoughts and feelings in response to his request, and my conscious presence to the tug of the spirit.[12]

DYD: All three components, at the time of the call—at that moment.

RSS: Yes.

DYD: Not just in retrospect?

RSS: What do you mean?

DYD: Well, it seems to me that the degree of difficulty is very high. Experiences like the one you had on the phone with the president happen so quickly—and are so packed with significance—that I have trouble imagining how you could be consciously on top of it all in the moment. I'm quite sure I couldn't do it. I'm not sure I could even reconstruct it after the fact.

RSS: Well, the three components are always present, always operative. So why not be on top of them?

DYD: Why not indeed. There's just the tiny matter of being prepared and practiced enough to discern and differentiate them the way you do.

RSS: That's right.

DYD: One last time, then, for differentiation's sake, if not for Thomas's. The experience began when you picked up the phone and you heard the president's voice. That was the sensory component of the event.

RSS: Yes, but remember: I was ambivalent about the call, so I was already in a heightened state of self-awareness when I took the phone from Eunice.

DYD: So when you heard the president say he wanted to talk about the Peace Corps, you not only heard the words he spoke, you were consciously present to yourself.

RSS: I was aware of his words, and I was also aware of my thinking and feeling in response, yes.

DYD: So what came up for you?

RSS: It was a mix. I felt resignation, apprehension, and weariness when I heard him mention the Peace Corps—but I was also interested and curious about what he'd have to say.

DYD: So it was complex for you. And in the midst of that, you were also consciously present to the spirit?

RSS: Once Jack asked me to run the task force, yes. I remember resting on my breath and consciously wrapping myself in the mantle of Mary.

DYD: The mantle of Mary?

RSS: "Be it done to me according to thy word."

DYD: I'm still not sure what you're saying.

RSS: It's what Mary said.

DYD: I know.

RSS: What I'm saying is that as I heard Jack's request I spontaneously reached out to Mary. I wanted to replicate in myself the conscious presence to the spirit manifest in her words.

DYD: You were seeking to be done to according to the spirit?

DYD: I was seeking to be open, to stay open. Yes.

DYD: So you're saying Mary's words were spontaneously available to you at that moment?

RSS: Yes.

DYD: I know you pray them every day.

RSS: I try to pray them all the time, whether I explicitly verbalize them or not, whether I have a Rosary in my hand or not.

DYD: Even as we speak?

RSS: All the time.

DYD: And that's what you mean by wrapping yourself in the mantle of Mary?

RSS: That's what I mean.

DYD: And that's what you were going for when you were on the phone with the president, to be wrapped in her mantle.

RSS: In response to his request, yes.

DYD: Again I have to say: that's a highly differentiated response.

RSS: It is. But it's not special to me.

DYD: No. I suppose not. It strikes me that Mary's response to Gabriel was differentiated in that way too.

RSS: What are you thinking?

DYD: I'm thinking that in her reply to Gabriel, Mary differentiated the sensory, conscious, and spiritual components of her experience.

RSS: Say more.

DYD: Well, when she says, "Be it done to me according to thy word," the "it" Mary is referring to is clearly Gabriel's message to her—the announcement that she was with child. She received that fact—"heard" it in some sense or another.

RSS: Okay.

DYD: So "be it done to me" is Mary's conscious response to that message—her acceptance, her acquiescence. When she adds "according to thy word," it seems to me she is expressing her conscious openness to the spirit.

RSS: Yes, she experiences a call to transcend herself—her own personal hopes and fears.

DYD: It seems that threefold differentiation is basic to the quality of Mary's spiritual openness.

RSS: It helps carry my own.

DYD: You've said this is a devotional matter for you.

RSS: It is.

DYD: But we haven't really been speaking devotionally, or using explicitly devotional language to talk about this.

RSS: No.

DYD: So how would we correlate Mary's reply to Gabriel with the terms you've been using to help me understand it?

RSS: You're interested in transposing Mary's words into the more explicitly experiential and explanatory language we've been using?

DYD: I am.

RSS: Are you thinking it might make the experience more accessible?

DYD: I don't know. More accessible to me, maybe.

RSS: So give it a go.

DYD: Well, instead of "Be it done to me according to thy word," might we say: "Lead me to the heights of my aspiring"?

RSS: Nicely said. Though it still sounds devotional to me.

SPIRITUAL
REALISM

CONVERSATION 3

Catcher

DYD: I'd like to stay with your notion of spiritual experiencing—to understand it more fully.

RSS: By all means. What are you missing?

DYD: It strikes me that the spiritual openness you cultivate in your devotion to Mary is particularly complex.

RSS: Is it?

DYD: It's differentiated, nuanced, action-oriented.

RSS: In practice it's simple enough. Simplifying, actually.

DYD: I'm curious about what you mean by that, because there seems to be a major difference between your devotional practice and meditation practices that call for letting go of sensory objects and other mental content.

RSS: What mental content do you mean?

DYD: Phone conversations, elevated aspiring, commitments to serve—the mental content you've been talking about.

RSS: Are you thinking about meditation practices that cultivate mystical states of consciousness? States in which the operation of your mind is totally stilled, like the "cloud of unknowing," or Theresa of Avila's "prayer of quiet"?[1]

DYD: No. I'm actually being much more prosaic. I'm talking about meditation practices that are organized around repeating a mantra, or watching your breath, or walking mindfully.

RSS: That's what I do when I walk my fingers around the beads of my rosary.

DYD: You're practicing mindfulness?

RSS: It seems to me the point of mindfulness practice is to cultivate a steady state of conscious awareness. Generally speaking, I'd say mindfulness practice focuses us more on our part as conscious beings than on the part played by the spirit. The authors of mystical texts pay more explicit attention to our relation to the spirit.

DYD: Yes. The core teaching calls for returning gently to your breath or your mantra when you discover your attention has become caught up in thinking about the details and responsibilities of life.

RSS: I take it then, that you're familiar with the problem of getting lost in your thoughts and needing to recover your conscious presence to yourself?[2]

DYD: That's how I lost track of my keys.

RSS: There you go.

DYD: Still, the mindfulness practices I'm familiar with don't really emphasize reaching for our noblest aspirations, or being consciously present to a sense of being tugged or called. Not the way you do, anyway.

RSS: I think it depends on the particulars of the practice and the devotional tenor of the language. For example, I'd say the practice we've been talking about has a lot in common with the spiritual exercises of St. Ignatius Loyola.[3]

DYD: As I understand it, those exercises are based on a series of meditations on scripture, and stories about Jesus in particular.

RSS: That's right. Mindfulness practice cultivates our conscious presence to the mind. Practices like the spiritual exercises orient us to our lived relationship to the spirit.

DYD: I want to make sure I follow. Are you saying mindfulness is not about the spirit? That it's just about consciousness?

RSS: What makes you say "just"? Do you know anyone who likes being mentally scattered or emotionally off balance?

DYD: So you regard mindfulness as a basic skill that we all should cultivate?

RSS: Don't you think we could all agree—no matter what tradition we follow—that if we haven't cultivated our conscious presence to ourselves, it's going to be very difficult to be mindful of the flow of our conscious operations—let alone to be consciously present to any aspirational tug or call?

DYD: Would you say Mary was mindful?

RSS: Of course she was. And anybody seeking to emulate her spiritual openness will be cultivating mindfulness too.

DYD: As in becoming consciously present to oneself?

RSS: It's the part we're called to play.

DYD: You're saying everyone needs a meditative practice?

RSS: Need. Want. I'm not sure what the verb should be. But don't you think that at some level we're all drawn to be more mindful? To be more centered?

DYD: If you're asking me whether I think that we're all drawn to practice mindfulness, then I'd have to say no. I don't see the evidence for it.

RSS: I'm not talking about formal meditation practice. I'm talking about the practical need we all experience, in certain circumstances, to be more centered, more focused, more mentally balanced. I'm talking about the fact that in some of our roles we actually need to cultivate it.

DYD: For instance?

RSS: I'm sure you recognize the way baseball players are drawn to batting practice.[4]

DYD: Batting practice?

RSS: You need a sharp eye to play baseball. As a batter, you have to pick up the pitch as it leaves the pitcher's hand. You have to read the spin on the ball as it approaches the plate. You have to coordinate your swing with what you see. It's a complex skill. It takes practice, focus; you have to cultivate it.

DYD: Is that what you're doing when you go to Mass every day? Taking spiritual batting practice?

RSS: That's certainly part of it. Being consciously present to the spirit is every bit as exacting as hitting a fastball—more exacting, in some ways. A fastball reaches home plate in about half a second, you know.

DYD: I didn't, actually. But that means—what? That batters have about a quarter of a second to swing at a pitch?

RSS: That's right. If you break it down, you have about a tenth of a second to get a visual on the pitch; another tenth of a second to identify the spin, speed, and likely trajectory of the ball; and less than half that—about fifty milliseconds—to decide whether to swing the bat and where to swing it. If your concentration breaks, the ball whizzes past you and into the catcher's mitt. You have to be mindful, attentive, focused, ready.

DYD: How do you know this stuff?

RSS: I was a catcher. I had to know this stuff.

DYD: To be a mindful catcher, you had to know the science of hitting a fastball?

RSS: Not exactly that. But to fulfill my role as a catcher, I had to be mindful of all the factors in the game. And to be mindful of those factors, I had to have a good working model of the game in my mind.

DYD: So, the mindfulness you're talking about is multifaceted.

RSS: Consciousness is multifaceted, so yes, mindfulness is too.

DYD: And the mindfulness you practiced as a catcher is analogous to the mindfulness you were practicing in your phone call with President Kennedy?

RSS: Analogous, yes.

RSS: Help me understand that.

RSS: You know the basic play in a baseball game, right?

DYD: You mean, the pitcher throwing a pitch to a batter?

RSS: I mean the catcher calling that pitch in the first place.

DYD: Okay. The catcher initiates the action. The catcher has to be on top of things.

RSS: Exactly. You have to be mindful of the game as it unfolds. You have to be aware of how the key factors in the game come together in the present moment of play. You have to understand what that implies for the pitch you should call next—a curve ball low and away, let's say, rather than a fastball high and inside.

DYD: What key factors are you referring to?

RSS: What's the score? What inning are we in? How many outs are there? What's the ball-strike count on the batter? How many runners are on base? Which bases are full? What are the strengths of the runners? What's the chance they will try to steal? What are the strengths of the batter? Is he a pull hitter? What are the strengths of the pitcher? Does he have control of his curve ball today? How is the defense lined up? Is the right fielder too deep? Is the third baseman hugging the line closely enough? Factors like that.

DYD: The key factors are questions?

RSS: Good point. No, they're actually the answers to those questions. The task is to raise the relevant questions and to correlate the answers.[5]

DYD: To connect the dots.

RSS: That's right. The dots are identified by the questions.

DYD: And when you're done correlating the factors?

RSS: After you've put the pieces together, you can respond to the situation. You've put yourself in a position to choose, to decide, and to act. As a catcher, that's what you want.

DYD: Still, that's quite a string of questions to master.

RSS: They're not distracting, if that's what you mean.

DYD: Though I can imagine they could be. If you're not sure of them, you might have to recite them aloud in your mind, or tick them off on your fingers, or refer to a cheat sheet. It could get cumbersome.

RSS: That's true. But once you've put the pieces together and mastered the relevant questions, you don't really have to think about them. In fact, you think *with* them. It's fast, nonverbal. It feels spontaneous.

DYD: Like going on autopilot?

RSS: That's the tendency, of course. But as a catcher, you can't let that happen—not to yourself, or to your teammates.

DYD: The temptation is strong?

RSS: Mindfulness is precarious, you know. So it's easy to get distracted and overlook a key factor—to lose track of the runner on second, to forget what out it is—so then, when the play comes to you, you throw to the wrong base and your mistake allows the runner to score.

DYD: So the key is to be mindful—to make sure you're on top of the game and asking the relevant questions—all of them.

RSS: Yes. Missing a question—asking an irrelevant question— will derail your thinking and your decision-making.

DYD: What would count as an irrelevant question?

RSS: In baseball? "What's the price of a beer?" "How many cars can the parking lot hold?" It could be anything.

DYD: Surely beer and parking are relevant factors in baseball.

RSS: For the fans, yes; for the people in marketing, maybe; but not for a catcher in the middle of play. Not for any ballplayer.

DYD: So the relevance of a particular question is directly connected to your role?

RSS: That's right. The role we inhabit sets the range of relevant questions—the horizon for things that matter.[6]

DYD: In your role as catcher, then, beer and parking are outside that horizon?

RSS: Until after the game is over.

DYD: And your role shifts.

RSS: And a new horizon of relevant factors opens up, raising a new set of relevant questions.

DYD: Okay, but how do you know what questions to ask?

RSS: If you're involved in baseball in some way—regardless of your role—you'll be operating with a model of the game in mind.[7]

DYD: And what do you mean by model?

RSS: I mean your understanding of the game, the way you put the pieces together.

DYD: And that model is the source of your relevant questions?

RSS: The model guides the way we put the pieces together at any given moment. We use the model to think with—to guide and direct our curiosity. We couldn't formulate our questions without it.

DYD: For instance?

RSS: Let's say you're a fan. If you didn't have a working model of the game in your mind, how could you fulfill that role? Why would you want to?

DYD: Okay.

RSS: But having a model of the game in your mind means you recognize that there are nine innings in a baseball game and that your team will remain at bat in an inning until three batters make an out. So when you want to catch up on the state of play, you ask your friend, "How many outs are there?"

DYD: And the reason I can ask that question is because I'm thinking with a model.

RSS: That's the point.

DYD: I get the point. But you're not talking about anything we can see or touch. You're talking about a conscious process.

RSS: Right. To get a handle on how models work, you have to heighten your awareness to using one.

DYD: So I'd have to be in a role, drawing on a model to raise a relevant question, and notice what I was doing?

RSS: Exactly. Let's do it.

DYD: Right now?

RSS: Right now. Imagine you're in the role of a ballplayer coming up to bat in a ballgame. I'll be the catcher.

DYD: You want me to imagine myself in a batter's box?

RSS: That's right. Take on the role.

DYD: Okay. I'm stepping up to the plate, getting into my stance.

RSS: Good. Notice that as you take on that role, the horizon of what you're wondering about tracks with it.

DYD: What should I be noticing?

RSS: Just pay attention to where your mind takes you in your role. What are you wondering about? What are you concerned about?

DYD: Well, I'm actually a little self-conscious about playing this role. I haven't had a bat in my hand for a while.

RSS: I'm talking about your role as a batter, not as a role player. What are you wondering about as a batter?

DYD: As a batter, I guess I'm wondering about the pitcher. The pitch he'll throw. What I want to do with it.

RSS: Good. So you're not thinking about frying an egg or sewing a button on your jacket.

DYD: How random is that?

RSS: Random for your role as a batter, yes, but not for a short order cook or a tailor.

DYD: And if I were a tailor or short order cook, I wouldn't be concerned about getting my bat around on a fastball in a quarter of a second.

RSS: Exactly.

DYD: Okay. Point taken. My role as batter comes with a particular horizon of interest and concern. I'm focused on that. And inside the horizon, questions arise. What inning is it? How many outs are there? Is anybody on base?

RSS: Right. Good questions. So let's specify the key factors. It's a tie game in the bottom of the ninth. There's one out, the bases are loaded, and you've run the count to full—three balls and two strikes. You've fouled off the last two pitches.

DYD: It's a high stakes situation.

RSS: It's a dramatic moment.

DYD: I could end the game right here and send the crowd home happy.

RSS: That's what you're aiming for?

DYD: Of course. A hit or a sacrifice fly will end the game.

RSS: A walk will end it too.

DYD: Right. Ball four and the runner on third base is forced home. Game over.

RSS: Step out of your imagined batter's box for a moment and tell me: Did you notice that you were thinking with your model of the game just then?

DYD: I'm not sure I did. I noticed we were talking about baseball and the possibilities for ending the game.

RSS: Yes, but since we're also talking about mindfulness, I'm wondering about yours. You're clearly aware of *what* you're talking about—of your mental content, as you put it earlier.

DYD: So, what else are you asking about?

RSS: Two other factors. First, were you aware you were using your mind when you were talking about ways to end the game?

DYD: I wasn't focusing on it, but I was aware I was thinking, yes.

RSS: Good. So here's question two. When you were thinking

about ways to end the game just then, were you explicitly aware there was a model of the game guiding and directing your thoughts?

DYD: This is tricky.

RSS: Once you differentiate the three components, it's not so tricky. It becomes commonplace.

DYD: The three components being the flow of my mind, the model guiding that flow, and the specific things I was thinking?

RSS: Yes.

DYD: Then your question is: was I explicitly mindful of the relationship between my mind and the model? Was I consciously experiencing the correlation of the two?

RSS: Were you?

DYD: I can't honestly say that I was. But I understand the distinction. It's logical. How could I be thinking of various ways to win the game without having a model of some sort in my mind?

RSS: I'm not asking you to affirm the logic of the correlation.

DYD: No. You're asking me about my conscious experience of it.

RSS: It's a matter of posing the relevant question. What's guiding the flow of my mind as I'm thinking these things?

DYD: And all I can say is, I'll try to be more mindful going forward.

RSS: Let's return to the batter's box. The factors are the same. The count is full. The bases are loaded with one out. The game is still tied. Tell me, what questions do you find yourself asking?

DYD: I'm wondering: what pitch I should I be expecting? Where I should try to hit it?

RSS: And what answers are you coming up with?

DYD: Well. I've just fouled off two fastballs, but I'm thinking I might see a third fastball anyway. Of course, it could be a change-up, to throw off my timing. But either way, your pitcher can't afford to walk me, so I should be getting a pitch to hit. I'll be looking to get a good swing on it and to hit the ball in the air deep enough to drive in the winning run.

RSS: Good. And I can tell you, as the opposing catcher, that my concern is to counter your efforts. I'll be calling for a pitch I think you're more likely to hit on the ground—a two-seam fastball on the inside of the plate.

DYD: You're hoping I'll hit into a double play and get you out of the inning.

RSS: If we don't force the runner at the plate or strike you out, yes.

DYD: I can't say I like any of those outcomes. So if I get a pitch I don't think I can handle, I'll try to foul it off, and we can go through this again.

RSS: So step out of the batter's box once more.

DYD: Okay. It definitely helped to have the distinction in mind. I was aware I was using a model of the game to think with.

RSS: What did you notice?

DYD: When you asked me what I was wondering about, I became explicitly aware I was asking questions—and asking questions only a batter would ask.

RSS: You were aware of your role.

DYD: Yes. And, as a batter, that my questions were guided by my understanding of the game.

RSS: By your model.

DYD: Okay. Yes. But it was not as though I was conscious of a full-blown, abstract model of the game. It was more a tacit understanding of how batting and pitching would be related in that particular situation.

RSS: You had your baseball thinking cap on.

DYD: Right. I was thinking concretely, in terms of baseball stratagems, not first principles.

RSS: You were hoping for a deep fly ball.

DYD: If I was going to drive in the run, that seemed the most likely way to achieve it.

RSS: You had aspirations and a plan for realizing them.

DYD: I wasn't aiming to hit into a double play or to strike out, if that's what you mean.

RSS: Let's move forward then. You're in the batter's box. I signal for the pitch, and the pitcher delivers. The pitch is over the plate more than I'd like, so you swing away—but the slider has pretty good movement on it, and you get your bat under the ball too much and pop it up high on the infield. I wave off the second baseman, signal the shortstop to make the catch, and he makes the catch. It's out number two. The crowd groans its disappointment.

DYD: And I slam my bat into the ground in frustration. The play would have ended differently if I'd been in charge of the narrative, I can tell you that.

RSS: Just stay in your role a moment longer. You miss the ball and slam your bat. It seems you are aware of the feelings that are coming up for you.

DYD: I'm frustrated, yes. As you tell the tale, I did not achieve what I was going for in that at-bat.

RSS: You were hoping to drive in the winning run.

DYD: I wanted to come through for my teammates and the fans. I wanted to walk off the field a winner, to be the hero of the game. I certainly wasn't hankering to pop out to short.

RSS: So what's guiding and directing the flow of your thoughts right now?

DYD: I'm not sure what you're referring to.

RSS: Events have moved on, and your mind has moved on. You're no longer thinking about the next pitch.

DYD: No, I'm thinking about my failed at-bat.

RSS: You're feeling your way into the significance of that at-bat—what it means for you, for yourself, for the fans.

DYD: And the question is, what's guiding my thinking?

RSS: That's the question.

DYD: Well, now that you mention it, it seems I had kind of a hero image going on there.

RSS: Very good.

DYD: So now I'm thinking with an image?

RSS: As we live into our roles, we think with models and images both. Metaphors too.

DYD: It's going to take some practice to get on top of this.

RSS: So here's something else to wonder about. Were you consciously present to being tugged or called to reach for your highest aspirations during your at-bat?

DYD: Are you talking about spiritual experiencing now?

RSS: You know the spirit is always blowing.[8]

DYD: Yes. But even in a role-play?

RSS: The Rosary is a role-play.

DYD: I don't know. I got into the role. I can say that. I felt anticipant and determined as the batter. I wanted to make solid contact with the ball, not to undercut it. I wanted to come through for my team and the fans. But present to the spirit? I don't think so.

RSS: As the batter, you were imagining yourself at your best, weren't you?

DYD: Sure I was. I wanted to be the hero. But I can't say I was explicitly mindful of being tugged to transcend myself.

RSS: Well, that's something to pay attention to then.

DYD: Is it? It seems to me the aspiration to drive in the run—to be the hero of the game—was mine alone. I was the one thinking with the model. I was the one operating with my hero image.

RSS: Yes, that was all yours. That was you doing your part. But hankering to be the best batter you could be at that particular moment? Wanting to come through for the people who had a stake in the game? That might not have been all you.

DYD: Maybe so. But we can drive a coach and six horses through that "might not" of yours, can't we? I was the one swinging the bat. I was the one who popped out to short.

RSS: Success isn't the issue. The spirit engages us where we are, as we are.

DYD: All I can say is that I wasn't explicitly aware of the experience.

RSS: Okay. What do you make of the fact that baseball players—athletes in general—consistently reach for their highest and noblest aspirations as athletes?

DYD: You mean do I recognize they aspire to get a base hit rather than to pop out—to do everything they can to succeed?

RSS: To be their best selves as athletes, yes.

DYD: Sure, but the role of the athlete is structured that way. The game orients you toward playing your best.

RSS: And that's one of the happy things about sports. It's no coincidence that so many athletes are so thankful, so grateful, so personally elevated by their performances. Some athletes are even explicitly devotional about it.

DYD: Are you talking about athletes who make the sign of the cross, as they get ready to shoot a free throw, or thank Jesus for their touchdown catch?

RSS: Yes I am.

DYD: There are plenty of ways to explain that.

RSS: There are. Yes. And that brings us back to models, doesn't it? To the way we put the pieces together?

DYD: But what makes you think the spirit is at play?

RSS: You mean, what model of the spirit do I have in mind? What model leads me to think it might be relevant to ask about the role of the spirit in any given conscious act?

DYD: More basically, what is it about athletic performance that leads you to think the role of the spirit is relevant in the first place?

RSS: Well, it's a case-by-case thing.

DYD: So you're saying there are clues?

RSS: Of course there are clues.

DYD: But you'd have to pick up on these clues in the sensory component of an athlete's performance, wouldn't you?

RSS: Good point. Watching an athlete's physical performance can only tell you so much about its inner conscious and spiritual components. But all three components are related.[9]

DYD: So the physical performances that we see and hear are also manifestations of the athlete's consciousness and spirit?

RSS: That's it. I find there's often enough evidence to come to a reasonable suspicion of self-transcendence.

DYD: Reasonable suspicion? That's not knowledge.

RSS: No, it's not. But speaking as a lawyer, to come to a reasonable suspicion is to form a hypothesis.

DYD: A hypothesis that remains to be verified.

RSS: Yes. In the role-play, you came up with the reasonable suspicion that the next pitch you'd see would be a fastball.

DYD: Right. And I didn't know that for sure that would be the case.

RSS: No. Not until the pitcher actually threw the pitch. But that didn't invalidate your hypothesis, did it? Or suggest that the baseball thinking cap you were wearing was unsound.

DYD: So we're talking about a spiritual thinking cap, and the hypotheses you generate when you wear it.

RSS: We're talking about the relevant questions it enables me to ask, yes.

DYD: Okay.

RSS: So tell me, why do you think the friends and family members of Special Olympics athletes—general spectators even—spontaneously and unaccountably find themselves weeping with joy when their athlete crosses the finish line? Even when their athlete happens to come in seventh, or ninth, or last?[10]

DYD: Are you suggesting those are spiritual tears?

RSS: It's a reasonable suspicion, isn't it? The self-transcendence of those athletes is almost palpable, whether they come in first or last. Their joy certainly is. So much so, in fact, that their athletic performance is spiritually elevating to anyone watching.[11]

DYD: How so?

RSS: *Cor ad cor loquitur*. Heart speaks to heart. It is unspeakably moving.

DYD: Wait. Are you saying a conscious presence to the spirit can be awakened within us when we witness self-transcendence in another person?

RSS: That's exactly what I'm saying.

DYD: And we can be consciously present to it?

RSS: Sometimes it can't be ignored.

DYD: In athletics in particular?

RSS: Not exclusively. In my early years as director of the Peace Corps, I made it a practice to visit Peace Corps Volunteers in their service placements. I visited them in scores of countries of mixed politics and belief, and everywhere I went, I witnessed the self-transcending deeds of the Volunteers—daily, difficult deeds of compassion and service—shattering barriers of politics, culture, economics and creed.[12]

DYD: You were mindful of the spirit at work in them? Resonating in your conscious presence to yourself?

RSS: Not only the Volunteers, the host country nationals too.

DYD: So you're a catcher of the spirit as well.

RSS: Not literally, of course. No one catches the spirit.

Flow

DYD: Sarge, let's pick up where we left off.

RSS: By all means.

DYD: In baseball, it's clear you've mastered the key factors and relevant questions. The same seems to be true when it comes to discerning the spirit—be it in a phone call from the president, a Special Olympics event, a Peace Corps service placement.

RSS: It takes practice.

DYD: And a good model.[1]

RSS: That too.

DYD: So, help me with the model. I'm not clear about the key factors or how you relate them—especially the part played by the spirit.

RSS: What have you got so far?

DYD: I know you distinguish the sensory, conscious, and spiritual components of particular situations and events.[2]

RSS: Yes. The model helps us to think about how those experiential components are different and how they're related.

DYD: How the three components are linked to each other.

RSS: How they are linked in the flow of our experience, yes.

DYD: So we're talking about an experiential flow with sensory, conscious, and spiritual components.

RSS: Right. And once you distinguish the three experiential

components, it becomes evident that the flow has a twofold pattern to it—a sort of double movement linking the three components.

DYD: And that twofold pattern is?

RSS: The first part of the pattern is defined by the relationship of sense and consciousness—and in particular by our conscious response to a concrete situation. The second part of the pattern is the presence of the spirit to our conscious response.

DYD: That's the model?

RSS: It's the core pattern defined by three of the factors in the model, yes.

DYD: Just so I'm clear, those three factors are?

RSS: Why don't you tell me?

DYD: Well, they seem to be the concrete situation, our conscious response to it, and the presence of the spirit to our response.

RSS: Very good.

DYD: That's it?

RSS: No. There are other key factors involved, but it's important to start simple, and to verify the relations as we go.

DYD: Verify how?

RSS: By paying attention to our experience of those relations.

DYD: By becoming conscious of the twofold pattern?

RSS: Exactly. We begin by noticing that we are consciously responding to our experience of concrete situations.

DYD: That's the first part of the pattern.

RSS: Right. And in our responding, we can also become consciously present to the presence of the spirit. That's the second part.

DYD: We're talking at a very generalized level here, aren't we?

RSS: Yes, but all good models are generalized. In this case, the range of our sensory and conscious experience is vast. And the spirit blows in surprising and unpredictable ways. The model has to account for that generality.

DYD: Okay. But can we bring this down to earth? I think that would help.

RSS: Absolutely. So let's go with the role-play. Try to identify the twofold pattern in the factors as you experienced them.

DYD: You're talking about the baseball role-play?

RSS: That's the one.

DYD: Okay, let me think.

RSS: Take it factor by factor.

DYD: Well, the first factor is the concrete situation. In my case, I swung at the pitch and popped out to short. I definitely had a conscious response to that performance. That's the second factor.

RSS: You felt frustrated at not driving in the run.

DYD: I felt frustrated at letting my team down, the fans down, at not becoming a hero.

RSS: Heroes often fail.

DYD: True enough. But what about the third factor? The spirit is somehow present to my frustration?

RSS: That's right.

DYD: I'm drawing a blank here.

RSS: Yes, the first link is easier to identify. At first anyway.

DYD: What makes it easier?

RSS: There's a temporal element in the link between the first two factors. You noticed it, didn't you?

DYD: You're talking about the temporal sequence involved? I swung at the pitch, popped it up, left the bases loaded, felt like a failure, and slammed my bat on the plate. That sequence?

RSS: Exactly. Focusing on the sequence makes it easier to correlate the sensory and conscious components of the situation.

DYD: It's easy enough to pick out now that you've told me what to look for. But I can't say I'm usually mindful of the distinction. I wouldn't say I was explicitly mindful of it during the role-play.

RSS: No. It takes practice. But here's the thing. There's no temporal element in the second link.

DYD: There is no temporal lag between my conscious response and the presence of the spirit?

RSS: Right.

DYD: The spirit is simply present to me? [3]

RSS: Blowing where it will, yes.

DYD: What are you saying? That the presence of the spirit is simply an experiential given?

RSS: Like sense and consciousness, yes.

DYD: But without a temporal link between them?

RSS: Right.

DYD: Which is why you say that being consciously present to the spirit is more exacting than hitting a fastball.

RSS: Precisely.

DYD: We don't have even a quarter of a second to see the spirit coming, do we?

RSS: There's nothing to see. There's nothing coming. It's already present.

DYD: Not to put too fine a point on it, but I certainly wasn't aware of that presence during the role-play.

RSS: That's not unusual.

DYD: But it's also a problem.

RSS: Is it?

DYD: Of course it is. If I'm not aware of that presence, how do I know—how can I say—it was actually present?

RSS: Fair point.

DYD: I don't think I can infer that presence either.

RSS: What do you mean?

DYD: I'm talking about my response to the situation. I'm talking about my felt sense of frustration, about slamming my bat on the plate. I don't discern any self-transcendence there.

RSS: You don't discern any tug to self-transcendence in that response?

DYD: I can't say I do. Besides, feeling frustrated at leaving the bases loaded—at failing to drive home the winning run—all that is my part, isn't it? Not the spirit's?

RSS: The spirit isn't doing your feeling for you, if that's what you mean. Imagining yourself as the hero is your part too, yes.

DYD: Then what is going on? What's the link between the spirit and my response?

RSS: The spirit is present to your aspiring, to your frustration, to your image of yourself as a hero.

DYD: Present how?

RSS: Present as a call to recognize and transcend your blind spots . . . present as a tug to reach for your noblest aspirations . . . present as an invitation to be your best self.

DYD: Present as a still small voice I can't actually hear?

RSS: Still? Definitely. Small? Up to a point.

DYD: Up to what point?

RSS: Up to the point of assuming that just because you can't see it or hear it—or because you may not be paying explicit attention to it—that the voice that's calling you is inconsequential, *de minimis*, absent.

DYD: Again, if I can't see it or hear it—and if I'm not consciously present to it—how am I supposed to affirm it?

RSS: You keep paying attention. You keep practicing.

DYD: I don't know.

RSS: What don't you know?

DYD: I don't really understand the second link—the second part of the pattern. But I think I need to change the example. I don't think the role-play has the data on the link to the spirit I need. Or if it does, then I'm the problem. I can't access it.

RSS: That's candid. What example would you like to explore instead?

DYD: Well, your decision to tackle the problem of segregation in Chicago's Catholic high schools strikes me as a potential example of self-transcendence.[4]

RSS: You want to shift the focus to me?

DYD: At this point, I think I'm better with questions than answers.

RSS: So what are your questions?

DYD: I have many. But one, I'm wondering how I would use the model to think about the relationship of sense, consciousness, and spirit in this particular case. And two, I'm wondering what the presence of the spirit had to do with your decision to commit to CICC.

RSS: Those are good questions, but first I have to return the focus to you. What is striking you as particularly self-transcending about my decision to work with the Catholic Interracial Council?

DYD: Well, the evidence is circumstantial, but I know you had a demanding, full-time job at the Merchandise Mart.

RSS: I did, yes.

DYD: Which means you had to be willing to take on a large and daunting challenge in your spare time—presumably without pay.

RSS: True.

DYD: And I'm guessing your spare time was at a premium too—that you were already a busy man, with many worthy and pleasurable things on the go.

RSS: Yes.

DYD: So, it's easy to imagine you turning down the opportunity to get involved with the Chicago Interracial Council. In fact, I imagine most people would turn it down, and I'd probably be among them. I think it would be a stretch for anybody.

RSS: So based on the logic of your argument—the fact that the challenge was big and that I was already busy—you suspect my decision to say yes was an act of self-transcendence?

DYD: I suspect your decision was more self-transcending than self-interested, yes.

RSS: But you don't know that for sure?

DYD: No. I'm speculating. But I'd like to know for sure.

RSS: Because there are other ways to argue the case, aren't there? Ways that would challenge your supposition of self-transcendence?

DYD: And that's the point. Perhaps you said yes to your role with CICC to better position yourself in a run for governor. Maybe you were more concerned with your own political advancement than you were with advancing racial justice in the Catholic high school system.

RSS: You mean, maybe I just wanted to cultivate the Catholic vote, and that I was more politically self-interested than self-transcending?

DYD: Right. Or maybe you just wanted to impress the boss's daughter with prima facie evidence of your devotion to the social justice causes of the Church. Taking a role with CICC would be a grand gesture.

RSS: For a grand lady.

DYD: Indeed. But how do we sort this out?

RSS: You mean, how do we know what is in fact the case?

DYD: Yes. How do we move beyond speculation and opinion to something closer to knowledge?

RSS: We need to get at the relevant data, don't we?

DYD: Which is where the model comes in.

RSS: Yes. We need a model that enables us to think critically about the sensory, conscious, and spiritual components of my decision to tackle segregation in the high schools.

DYD: And in particular, how those factors are related.

RSS: So let's do that. How would you suggest we begin?

DYD: How would *I* use the model?

RSS: Who else?

DYD: You, of course.

RSS: Come on. You can do this. Begin by thinking with the key factors.

DYD: Well, if as you say, the key factors are actually the answers to questions, I should begin by asking you about the situation—about the concrete context—in which you made your decision.

RSS: Very good. And in this case, I can tell you it was a very enjoyable event. I'm sure you can imagine yourself having dinner in a nice restaurant.

DYD: Yes.

RSS: So imagine this: you're sitting across the table from a new acquaintance whose name is Lloyd Davis. He's just been named executive director of the Catholic Interracial Council in Chicago. The food is good. The wine is good. The conversation is good. You're talking about race relations in the Church, when suddenly Davis surprises you by redirecting the conversation. He asks you to team up with him at the Catholic Interracial Council. He suggests you take a seat on the Board, and in that role spearhead the efforts of CICC's Education Committee to address the problem of segregation in Chicago's Catholic high schools.

DYD: And if I were you, I'd say yes.

RSS: Yes you would.

DYD: But I'm not. So how do I connect the key experiential components? How do I use the model to think this through?

RSS: What do you know about each of those components at this point?

DYD: Based on the account you just gave? Not much at all. On the sensory level, I can imagine the sorts of things Eyewitness News would have picked up if they'd been on the scene with their cameras and microphones. On the level of your conscious response, it seems you appreciated the conversation, the wine and the food, and that you were surprised by Davis's offer. Spiritually? I don't know anything. I know you said yes to Davis, which suggests self-transcendence to me. But I don't know anything about your conscious presence to the spirit or the spirit's presence to you.

RSS: Yes. There's much to discover. But you've distinguished the three main components, which is a start. Now the task is to relate them.

DYD: And to verify the relations.

RSS: That's how empirical models work.

DYD: Okay. So the model would suggest that the spirit is present to your response, and that you are consciously responding to a concrete situation. That means if I want to understand the spiritual component of your response to Davis, I have to understand the sensory component too.

RSS: You have to understand the situation, yes.

DYD: And what's involved with that?

RSS: That's not the real mystery here, is it? You want to understand the concrete context of my response to Lloyd, so you'd have to ask the same set of questions every journalist, lawyer, and historian worth their salt asks when they carry out an investigation.

DYD: You mean, "Who?" "What?" "When?" "Where?"

RSS: Exactly. Those are the key factors in the realm of the senses.

DYD: And their relation to the spirit?

RSS: First things first. The spirit blows not just where it will—but when it will, with whom, and with regard to what. So it's crucial to get those answers straight.

DYD: Okay, I think I can work with those questions—though

you've already outlined what you did. I take it that Davis asked you for the meeting?

RSS: He reached out to me, yes. But it was my suggestion to meet for dinner.

DYD: When was this?

RSS: I don't remember the exact date, but it would have been in the fall of 1952. It was cold outside and I was still living at the Ambassador East. Eunice and I were still engaged. We got married on May 23rd the following spring.

DYD: So late fall 1952. Where did you meet for dinner?

RSS: The Pump Room at the Ambassador East. We sat at my usual table, Booth One.

DYD: You'd been living at the Ambassador East for a while by that point?

RSS: For over five years. Ambassador Kennedy kept an apartment in the building, and he was kind enough to let me live there after I went to work for him. It's a grand building, close to the lake, only about a thirty-minute walk from the Merchandise Mart.

DYD: A good location.

RSS: It was. And Holy Name Cathedral is right on the way, on North Wabash, so it was easy for me to get to morning Mass too. I liked living in that part of Chicago. In fact, after Eunice and I got married, we moved to an apartment on East Walton Street, just a few blocks away. We needed a bigger place once Bobby, Maria, and Timmy were born, so we moved a bit north to Lincoln Park.

DYD: Which is where you took the call from the president the day after the inauguration.

RSS: Yes.

DYD: But to return to the evening in question, I'm curious about Lloyd Davis himself, who he was. I take it you didn't know him very well at that point?

RSS: Not well at all. Lloyd was new to his job at CICC, and he was making the rounds. We'd never had an opportunity for a long conversation.

DYD: But you'd met him before.

RSS: Some friends from the Cathedral introduced us after Mass earlier that fall. Lloyd was born and raised in the Bronzeville neighborhood on the south side. But he had just returned home from his tour of duty in the military when I met him.

DYD: He was in the navy too?

RSS: No, the army, stationed at Fort Leonard Wood in southern Missouri. He was never deployed to Korea, thank God. But he served in the battle on the home front to implement President Truman's executive order.

DYD: Which executive order was that?

RSS: Executive Order 9981. The president signed it in the summer of 1948 to a lot of fanfare, so I remember the number. It mandated equality of opportunity and treatment for everyone in the military, regardless of their race or national origin.

DYD: So in one fell swoop, the president banned all Jim Crow activity in the military. A dramatic deed.

RSS: President Truman wanted to end racial discrimination in the armed forces, so there was plenty of drama, that's for sure. Many people loved him for it. I know I did. But here's the thing— and Lloyd and I discussed this at length that night—when you order people to change deep-rooted behaviors, and you then rely on a chain of command to enforce your orders, you'll get some compliance of course, but there's going to be resistance too. You're going to kick up quite a fuss.

DYD: Resistance from the people who resented the order?

RSS: People who tried to subvert it. Still do.

DYD: And Davis got pulled into that?

RSS: Like every other person of color, yes. Lloyd's experience in the army taught him some important lessons about what works and what doesn't work when you try to change the habits and patterns of interracial relations in a large institution. In particular, he came to understand the limitations of using mandates to drive institutional change. I appreciated his insight.

DYD: I imagine those lessons were hard won.

RSS: They were. But Lloyd also found himself drawn to the work. So when the position at CICC came to his attention, the idea of working to improve race relations in another large, complex, mission-driven organization appealed to him.

DYD: CICC was part of the Church?

RSS: No. Good question. CICC wasn't a large or complex organization either. But it had its own governing structure, and it worked closely with the diocesan office. More importantly, it had the backing of Cardinal Stritch.

DYD: So CICC had the ear of Church leaders on interracial matters.

RSS: Though we couldn't tell them what to do.

DYD: No mandates.

RSS: No mandates. Any time CICC sought to improve race relations in a Church-related institution, we had to rely on communication and cooperation to bring it about.

DYD: And that suited you.

RSS: It suits the spirit too.

DYD: So you and Davis had an interesting conversation that night.

RSS: We closed down the Pump Room, yes.

DYD: Discussing racial justice and the Church.

RSS: We talked about the trouble spots of concern to the CICC, the Catholic hospital system among them. But Lloyd was particularly concerned about segregation in the diocesan high schools. I told you there were seventy-nine Catholic high schools operating in the diocese at the time, didn't I?[5]

DYD: You did, yes. Were all of them White?

RSS: Over seventy of them were. There were some Black Catholic schools on the south and west sides. Not many.

DYD: They were segregated too?

RSS: Both the boys' and the girls' high schools, yes.

DYD: And when you first heard from Davis about the segregation in the high schools, how did it strike you?

RSS: That's a very good question. Before I answer it, though, I have one for you.

DYD: Okay.

RSS: Were you aware that you just asked me about my conscious response?

DYD: Your mean the link between the situation and your conscious response to it?

RSS: Yes.

DYD: Actually, yes. I was aware of it. I had the key factors in mind—though it took me a while to figure out exactly what situation you were responding to.

RSS: Very good. Carry on.

DYD: Okay. So you and Davis discussed the segregation of the Catholic high schools, and I'm curious about your felt response to that?

RSS: I was profoundly dismayed. Shocked too.

DYD: What shocked you?

RSS: I wasn't surprised by the fact of segregation. It was the extent of it. Part of me had trouble believing the Church could be so off-kilter. In fact, one of my first acts at CICC was to survey the racial composition of every Catholic high school in the city.

DYD: And?

RSS: I regret to say that we confirmed what Lloyd had said. The schools were completely segregated.

DYD: This may seem like an odd question, and maybe I should be expected to know the answer on the face of it. But can you tell me what you found so dismaying about the segregation in the schools?

RSS: It's not an odd question. It's important. How could you expect to know what my response would be without asking me about it?

DYD: So what was so dismaying?

RSS: Well . . . you couldn't live in Chicago in 1952, one of the hubs of the great southern migration, and not be struck by the tumult in race relations in the city—by the public displays of fury and fear, by the demagoguery in City Hall, by the crushing conditions on the south side, the Black-owned homes set on fire.

DYD: So all the racial strife in the city . . .

RSS: Was extremely distressing, yes.

DYD: And the Church segregating the high schools?

RSS: That profoundly dismayed me too. How can you face down your fear of another person, if you have no genuine opportunity to understand the person you're afraid of?

DYD: What are you saying? That if we don't live or worship or go to high school with each other . . .

RSS: That's the point. A Catholic high school system should be on the front lines of healing and improving race relations, not legitimating the divide, reinforcing obstacles. How can anybody possibly transcend their fury if they have no occasion to question its legitimacy?

DYD: That's what dismayed you?

RSS: Yes. I was dismayed to realize just how deeply the sin of racism had penetrated the institutional fiber of the church.

DYD: So your dismay was your grasp of the situation? Your recognition that the sin of racism had penetrated the institutional fiber of the Church?

RSS: Right.

DYD: Then that's the conscious response you were talking about, isn't it? Davis informs you that the Catholic High schools in Chicago are totally segregated, and your response is profound dismay.

RSS: That's the first link, yes.

DYD: So your dismay is your grasp of a gap—a discrepancy—between your expectations for the Church and its actual performance in the schools.

RSS: That's what sin is—distortion, a gap, a failure to hit the mark. So yes, in my dismay, I was grasping the distortion, the failing in the Catholic high school admissions process.

DYD: And your response is the locus of the second link too, right?

RSS: Yes.

DYD: The spirit is somehow present to you in your felt sense of dismay.

RSS: Very good.

DYD: Except that I have no idea where to go with that.

RSS: What have you got?

DYD: All I've got is you telling me the spirit is consciously present to us as a tug or a call to transcend ourselves.

RSS: There you go.

DYD: But where?

RSS: What are you wondering about?

DYD: I'm curious about how a call to self-transcendence fits into this.

RSS: So, ask about it.

DYD: Well, I'm wondering about the flipside of the gap—the discrepancy—you were discerning. What were you actually expecting or hoping for from the Church—the high school system?

RSS: Now that's a good question. And my answer is pretty straightforward. I would expect the Church to be doing its level best to live into the aspiration St. Paul held up to the early Christian communities in Galatia.[6]

DYD: St. Paul and Galatia? That's a straightforward answer?

RSS: Sure it is. You know Galatia. In present-day Turkey?

DYD: I don't, actually.

RSS: Well, Paul established a group of Church communities there early in the first century, and after a decade or so, they began to splinter. The communities began to divide into factions—to segregate themselves into a set of cliques divided along traditional lines of ethnicity, social status, gender.

DYD: So Paul wrote them a letter.

RSS: Yes, he did. He wrote specifically to remind them that in their dealings with each other—and I quote him now—"There is neither Jew nor Gentile, neither slave nor free, nor is there male and female."

DYD: Tell me then. What would you say Paul was going for when he wrote that?

RSS: I think he wanted to awaken their conscious presence to the spirit.

DYD: I don't understand.

RSS: Evidently, the Galatians were no longer aspiring to be the sort of community they were originally called to become.[7]

DYD: So Paul was trying to refresh their way of thinking about each other?

RSS: Exactly. He was calling on them to pay more explicit attention to the way they were valuing each other, relating to each other.

DYD: He was calling on them to be mindful of their conscious responses to each other?

RSS: That was a big part of it. But he was also providing them with a narrative image that would help them.

DYD: A narrative image? Help them how?

RSS: Help them by providing a guide—a standard—an image of self-transcendence.

DYD: To carry their conscious presence to the spirit?

RSS: In fact, yes.

DYD: So what narrative image would you say they were using instead?

RSS: Oh, some version of "you're better if you're circumcised than not; you're better if you're male than female; you're better if you're a free citizen than an enslaved person."

DYD: And Paul was offering an alternative?

RSS: Not just an alternative. An alternative that would help them heed the call to transcend themselves.

DYD: Because they had drifted away from the spirit?

RSS: In a manner of speaking, yes.

DYD: In what manner of speaking? Are you suggesting the spirit is only present to us if we're thinking with certain models, metaphors, and narrative images?

RSS: Not at all. The spirit is always present, always blowing. We're the ones who need metaphors, models, and narrative images to carry our presence to ourselves and to the spirit.

DYD: So the spirit is present to us regardless.

RSS: That never changes.

DYD: Inspiring us, calling us to transcend our blind spots and limitations.[8]

RSS: Yes. We're the ones who change.

DYD: So certain models, metaphors, and narrative images are what? More compatible? More open to the spirit?

RSS: To the degree they enhance the likelihood of our self-transcendence, yes.

DYD: And that's what Paul's narrative image does?

RSS: Neither male nor female? Neither slave nor free? Don't you think so?

DYD: I think it's a fascinating claim.

RSS: Endlessly fascinating, yes. And here's the corollary. Left to our own devices—that is to say, out of touch with the spirit—we tend to lock into models, metaphors, and narrative images that orient us toward self-reference, group bias, and a preference for the way things are.

DYD: And so it was that the Galatian community splintered into factions?

RSS: And why the Catholic Church allowed its high schools to become segregated by race—all seventy-nine of them.

DYD: I take it then you had Paul's words in mind when you were registering your dismay at the segregation of the Catholic high schools?

RSS: Adjusting those words, of course, from the concrete realities of first-century Galatia to the situation in twentieth-century Chicago.

DYD: Adjusting how?

RSS: "There is neither Black nor White in Catholic high school admissions."

DYD: Okay. But tell me. What's the aspiration here? To be color blind?

RSS: No, not color blind. Self-transcendence does not blind us.

On the contrary, the aspiration is to differentiate the person and the color of their skin.

DYD: Because a student is a student.

RSS: That's right. Skin color is not a role.

DYD: But to recognize that, to discern that, to treat each other like that . . .

RSS: We need the spirit to lift us beyond our self-referenced aspirations, and beyond our own group interests and affiliations.[9]

DYD: And for that we need images and models that incline us to be present to the spirit.

RSS: And to transcend ourselves, yes.

DYD: Okay. So let's talk about your presence to the spirit in your conversation with Davis.

RSS: What's your question?

DYD: When did your awareness become explicit that night?

RSS: As I said earlier, I became consciously present to the spirit when Lloyd offered me the role with CICC.[10]

DYD: When he made his pitch: "How about joining the Board at CICC and spearheading the work of our Education Committee?"

RSS: That's right.

DYD: I can't help but notice the similarity to your phone call with the president. What was going on for you?

RSS: Lloyd surprised me, you know. Intrigued me too.[11]

DYD: What was surprising?

RSS: I'd never imagined myself involved in high school race relations. I was dismayed by the problem. But this was a bolt out of the blue.

DYD: So when Davis offered you the role . . .

RSS: It threw me back on myself. I experienced myself being put in play in a new way.

DYD: In what way?

RSS: The role on offer from Lloyd opened me up to a new horizon of concern. Were I to take it on, I would be a person charged with actually doing something about racial segregation in the Catholic high school system.

DYD: And that threw you back on yourself?

RSS: Yes. It made me explicitly conscious of myself as a person who could be engaged in this new possibility.

DYD: And you felt drawn to that?

RSS: I did. I felt drawn to being the person I might become in that role—the person I might want to be.

DYD: A person engaged in improving race relations and advancing racial justice in the Catholic high schools.

RSS: Right.

DYD: Okay. I understand you felt consciously drawn to possibility. But what is the spiritual component of your experience of being drawn? I still don't see it.

RSS: Are you looking for some sort of sensory analog?

DYD: Perhaps I am.

RSS: Better to think of the role—the possibility—as a sail.

DYD: And spiritual experiencing is a conscious awareness of being filled?

RSS: Called to reach for the possibility, yes.

DYD: May I take another run at this?

RSS: By all means.

DYD: Davis made you the offer and your conscious response

included a heightened awareness of yourself in that new role—a role that intrigued you, and that you aspired to fill because it would enable you to engage directly in reversing the gap, the distortion, in Catholic high school admissions.

RSS: Yes. It was a new role with a new horizon of concern. It was a big change.

DYD: And you said it was a big surprise too. What role were you in when Davis made this game-changing offer to you?

RSS: When? During dinner, you mean?

DYD: Yes.

RSS: That's an interesting question. And I'm not sure of the exact answer. But I'd have to say I was shifting in and out of a number of roles during dinner. They would have included being a resident of the Ambassador East, a regular in the Pump Room, a conversation partner with Lloyd Davis, a son of the Church, an executive at the Merchandise Mart . . .

DYD: Your roles shifted with the flow of the conversation?

RSS: Depending upon the subject and focus, yes. We all do that.

DYD: But none of those roles put you in play to grapple with the sin of racism in the Catholic high schools.

RSS: Not in the same way, no. In my role as his dinner partner, Lloyd and I obviously talked about racial issues in the Church, in the city, in the military. But there's a big difference between decrying the problem of racial bias in Chicago's Catholic high schools over dinner and addressing that problem in a role that explicitly calls upon you to help turn it around.

DYD: Your professional horizon of concern was different too, wasn't it?

RSS: Before Lloyd offered me the role at CICC, I was professionally engaged in the challenge of bringing blue chip companies into the Merchandise Mart. Suddenly, I find myself contemplating the challenge of ensuring there is neither Black nor White in Catholic high school admissions.

DYD: And to go back to the model now. In that very moment of registering the challenge involved in the offer—with no temporal lag—you found yourself consciously present to the spirit?

RSS: I did.

DYD: Concurrent with being thrown back on yourself, you experienced a call—an inner tug—to take on this new role, to transcend yourself in this particular way.

RSS: Yes. Though as we've discussed, it wasn't a matter of hearing words.

DYD: No. So how did it manifest in your conscious awareness?

RSS: That's a good question! I'd say it was manifest in the conscious pressure of a question I found myself asking and needing to answer.

DYD: What question?

RSS: Will I commit? Will I say yes?

DYD: Will I commit to taking on this role, to embracing its horizon of concern?

RSS: Yes.

DYD: I know your answer to that question, don't I?

RSS: I'm sure you do.

DYD: Be it done to me according to thy word.[12]

RSS: There you go.

Logjam[1]

DYD: When we last met, we wound up our conversation by discussing the spiritual component of your response to Lloyd's offer.

RSS: Right.

DYD: I'm beginning to have a sense of that now, so I find myself curious about what happened next—about what you did in your pursuit of that call.

RSS: To undo racial segregation in Catholic high school admissions?

DYD: Yes. You knew the admissions system was seriously jammed up. What did you do about that?

RSS: Concretely, we did lots of things. But overall, our aim was to release the spiritual capacity of the people involved in the admissions process. It was a tall order. It took a while to get things moving.

DYD: Your aim was to release the spiritual capacity of the admissions system?

RSS: Of the people who had roles in the system, yes.

DYD: That's an unusual approach to systems change.[2]

RSS: I can't imagine overcoming racial bias in a system without the help of the spirit. Can you?

DYD: In all honesty, I'd have to say yes. I've never thought about systems change as a spiritual issue before.

RSS: Why not?

DYD: Why indeed. I guess I just assume that if a system needs to be changed or improved, we're the ones who have to do it.

RSS: Yes of course. But do it on our own? Without the help of the spirit?

DYD: It's clear you don't think so.

RSS: I don't. But it's important to raise the question of the spirit. Everyone should wrestle with it.

DYD: Maybe so, but obviously not everyone does . . . or even can. I know most people have trouble imagining what the role of the spirit might be in the workings of a system. I'm not alone in this.[3]

RSS: It's a big problem. We should all be able to think clearly and realistically about this.[4]

DYD: But it's a vicious circle, isn't it? Questions like, "What's the role of the spirit here?" or "How do we release the spiritual capacity of this system?" only come up if the spirit is somehow relevant to the way we're thinking about building or improving our systems. And that relevance is far from clear.

RSS: True enough. So it's a good thing that the spirit is actually present to us no matter what system we're in, and no matter what shortcomings we have identifying it or being present to it.

DYD: That's what fascinates me about you. No shortcomings in that regard.

RSS: We all have shortcomings. I have many.

DYD: But if the key is to think clearly and realistically about the spirit, what were you thinking as you tackled the problem of racial bias in Catholic high school admissions?

RSS: Would you like me to answer that with a metaphor, or in more technical terms?

DYD: I'd be happy with either one.

RSS: Metaphorically then, we were aiming to foster the growth of the mustard seeds in the admissions process.[5]

DYD: Mustard seeds? You're referring to the image in the Gospel parable—the little seeds that grow into large trees?

RSS: It's my understanding that they grow into bushes about five feet tall.

DYD: Metaphorically though, it's a parable about the kingdom of God.

RSS: Yes, though I find it more helpful to imagine the world of the spirit than the kingdom of god. The kingdom metaphor has never been all that resonant for me.

DYD: So by tending to the mustard seeds in the Catholic high school admissions process, you hoped to help bring about the world of the spirit?

RSS: In technical terms, we wanted to enhance the probability that the persons with key roles in the admissions process would make increasingly more self-transcending decisions, and increasingly fewer biased ones.[6]

DYD: You're talking about the high school principals?

RSS: Not just the principals, all the key players in the system: parents, students, local pastors, teachers.

DYD: So the principals and the other players were your mustard seeds?

RSS: Yes.

DYD: And the emergence of these players as mustard trees . . .

RSS: Would be marked by the self-transcendence of their decision-making.[7]

DYD: That's an interesting mix of metaphorical and technical terms. What model were you thinking with in your approach to the admissions process?

RSS: What model do you think? The one we've been discussing.

DYD: We've been focusing on individuals so far, not systems. In fact, we've been focusing mainly on you. We've discussed your presence to the spirit and your connection to Mary and Thomas. We've discussed the sensory, conscious, and spiritual components of key decisions you made on the phone with the president and at dinner with Lloyd Davis. We haven't talked explicitly about systems.

RSS: That's true.

DYD: But now you're talking about releasing the spiritual capacity of an admissions system in a Catholic high school.

RSS: Seventy-nine Catholic high schools.

DYD: That seems like a major shift in focus to me.

RSS: Does it? It seems to me we've only widened our horizon a bit.

DYD: I don't follow.

RSS: You draw a strong contrast between individuals and systems.

DYD: I suppose I do, but individuals and systems are different.

RSS: Just tell me, what notion of system do you have in mind when you distinguish individuals and systems that way?

DYD: Are you asking me to be mindful again?[8]

RSS: I am.

DYD: You want me to bring to mind the notion—the model—that carries my thinking about systems?

RSS: That's right.

DYD: Well, I haven't actually thought much about that.

RSS: And now it's time. You think about systems, don't you?

DYD: Of course I do.

RSS: Then there's a notion of systems you're using to think with.

DYD: Well, then it's mostly nonverbal.

RSS: I'm sure it is.

DYD: Though now that you've called my attention to it, I'd say the model I use is based on a fairly standard notion of what a system is.

RSS: And if you were to put it into words?

DYD: I'd say that when I think of a system, I'm thinking about an organized collection of parts. A patterned network of activity. Something like that. Another thing is that systems are created for a particular reason—to accomplish particular things, like admitting students into high school or providing dinner at the Pump Room.

RSS: Would it be fair to say you're thinking of systems as entities in their own right?

DYD: I'm not sure. In what sense do you mean?

RSS: In the sense that they're distinct from any individuals who might be involved with them—a factor you haven't mentioned yet, by the way.

DYD: That is an interesting omission. Still, now that you point it out, it's clear that individuals drive the activity in a system. To admit a student to a high school—to achieve the particular aims of any system—a certain set of tasks has to be carried out. Individuals perform those tasks.

RSS: Unless you can get a machine to perform them instead.

DYD: Yes. There's that.

RSS: So in a system, you've got individuals correlated with the tasks they perform, and the tasks sequenced into the patterns needed to get the job done.

DYD: I'd say that's right.

RSS: And I'd say that's a pretty good model, as far as it goes.

DYD: There's somewhere else to go?

RSS: Well, your model limits your horizon of inquiry quite a bit.

DYD: My horizon of inquiry?

RSS: You know what I mean. Models are sets of key terms that set the horizon of the questions we ask. Your model limits the range of your curiosity in distinct ways.

DYD: I'm limited if I think about systems in terms of individuals carrying out sequences of tasks to accomplish particular aims?

RSS: It's not wrong, mind you. Just limited.

DYD: Limited in what way?

RSS: It's best if you answer that for yourself.

DYD: And how do I do that?

RSS: You pay attention to the way the key terms of your model carry your mind.

DYD: That's pretty abstract.

RSS: It's actually concrete. But let's say you want to understand the admissions process in a Catholic high school. And let's say you're thinking with the set of key terms you've just identified.

What would you want to know? What questions would you find yourself asking?

DYD: You don't make this easy, do you?

RSS: Being mindful this way isn't easy. Just try.

DYD: Well, if my focus were a Catholic high school admissions system, the first thing I'd want to know would be its aims and outcomes. So my questions would be, what are the admissions targets for this year? Did we meet them? How does that compare to last year?

RSS: Good. That's what systems do. They generate outcomes on a recurring basis.

DYD: Year by year, in the case of admissions systems.

RSS: Right. So now let's say you want to understand the process used to achieve those outcomes. What questions would you want to ask?

DYD: In that case I suppose my questions would be, what are the basic tasks in the process? How are they sequenced? Who does which task? When do they do it? Where do they do it? With whom do they do it?

RSS: Good. And if you actually had the answers to those questions, what would you be expecting to know?

DYD: Beyond the outcomes? I'd expect to understand the key steps in the admissions process. I'd expect to know who's accountable for what. I'd expect to be able to chart the flow of activity in the system.

RSS: From applications to admissions.

DYD: Exactly.

RSS: Good.

DYD: What more do I need to know?

RSS: Let me answer that by asking you two further questions. One, what is the conscious component in the sequence of tasks you've charted?

DYD: I've never really wondered about that before.

RSS: Two, in what ways would you say the spirit becomes a factor?[9]

DYD: I don't know how to answer that question either.

RSS: If you can't answer the first question, you'll never get a good handle on the second.

DYD: If I don't account for the conscious component of a system, I'll never get a handle on the spiritual component?

RSS: That's the point.

DYD: So what are you suggesting? That the way I think about a system is focused primarily on its sensory component?

RSS: Isn't it?

DYD: Well, I'm focused on what the tasks are, who performs them, how they are sequenced, and what results they produce.

RSS: Eyewitness News could report on any of those particulars quite nicely.

DYD: Okay. Point taken. Now that you've directed my attention to it, it's obvious that the individuals who carry out the tasks in the system are conscious people. So are the people who created the system. They have minds. They use them. They're not robots.[10]

RSS: Right.

DYD: Even so, I'm not sure about the relevance of accounting for the conscious component of a system—a high school admissions system in our case. Or how the question of the spirit even comes up.

RSS: What's the difficulty?

DYD: What role would the spirit be playing? We create the high school admissions systems we use, not the spirit. We design the systems, sequence the tasks, carry them out . . .

RSS: True.

DYD: And it doesn't matter what system we're talking about either. It could be a Catholic high school admissions process or a supply chain for the manufacture of jet engines. I don't see how the spirit could be a component part of any system.

RSS: No more than the wind could ever be a component part of a sail.

DYD: Yes, wind and sail are distinct, but it's also clear they're related. The sail catches the wind, enabling the boat to move.

RSS: So that's the question. Isn't it? What key factors enable us to understand the relation of spirit and system?

DYD: And?

RSS: And we've been talking about persons in roles all along.

DYD: That's the factor? How does thinking about a person in their role help us to understand the function of the spirit in a system?

RSS: It enables us to inquire about the conscious component.

DYD: And if I don't have a handle on the conscious component of a system, I can't understand the role played by the spirit.

RSS: Very good.

DYD: Except that I don't understand.

RSS: Do you remember our discussion of the role Lloyd offered me that evening in the Pump Room?

DYD: Of course I remember. I know the offer was pivotal for you. Davis offered you a place on the Board of the Catholic

Interracial Council with the role of leading their interracial justice work in the high schools.

RSS: Yes. That offer changed things for me.

DYD: You said it put you in play in a new way.

RSS: Right. The offer of the role opened up new possibilities—new opportunities for tackling the problem of racial bias in Chicago's Catholic high schools that were simply not available to me in my role at the Merchandise Mart.[11]

DYD: I can see that.

RSS: As you can well imagine, it was one thing to be dismayed about racial segregation in Chicago's Catholic high schools as head of sales for the Chicago Merchandise Mart, and quite another to be dismayed about it as the head of education initiatives for the Catholic Interracial Council of Chicago.

DYD: The horizons of concern were different in the two roles, weren't they?

RSS: Very good. What are you noticing?

DYD: Well, in your role as head of sales at the Merchandise Mart, I can't really imagine you calling up the principal of Mayor Daley's alma mater—De La Salle Institute in the Bridgeport neighborhood—to talk about the racial make-up of the student body.

RSS: Why not?

DYD: It doesn't really fit the concerns of the role, does it? If your primary concern is to fill office space in Merchandise Mart with blue chip companies, would the idea of calling the principal of De La Salle Institute even come up for you?

RSS: It wouldn't, no. Not for that purpose anyway.

DYD: It's much easier to imagine you calling the marketing

director of Eastern Air Lines to talk about leasing office space in the Mart.

RSS: Yes, Eastern Airlines was a good client for us. But being director of sales at the Merchandise Mart didn't mean I had to leave my concerns for racial justice on the side of the road.

DYD: I wouldn't think so. I imagine you'd feel dismayed by the sin of racism wherever you discerned it, the Merchandise Mart included.[12]

RSS: Yes, though it was obviously different at the Mart. It was never a question of who gets a place in next year's freshman class and who doesn't.

DYD: So, what were the questions?

RSS: Oh, who gets hired, who doesn't? What kind of public relations training do we give the security staff? Who gets to eat in the executive dining room, and who's not welcome?

DYD: Whites only?

RSS: It wasn't posted on the wall, but it was an unwritten, socially enforced rule.

DYD: A situation that dismayed you.

RSS: Yes.

DYD: So how did you deal with it?

RSS: I resisted by example. I invited my Black friends and colleagues to eat lunch with me in the executive dining room.

DYD: Causing a stir, I presume?

RSS: Consternation. Umbrage. Complaint. Approval too. But my lunch partners had to be willing to deal with all that, so we always discussed it in advance. If they didn't feel comfortable, we ate somewhere else.

DYD: In your own mind, then, were you explicitly committing these acts of institutional disobedience in your role as a senior official at the Merchandise Mart?

RSS: That was the point. My official title was Assistant General Manager. I was number two at the Merchandise Mart. I had a good deal of authority in that role, and I felt I had a responsibility to use it.

DYD: In pursuit of your aspirations for racial justice.

RSS: That's right.

DYD: So when you say our roles put us in play, that's what you mean?

RSS: Roles set the horizon of our options and opportunities, yes.

DYD: Which means that roles function much like models and metaphors.

RSS: Yes. But what are you noticing?

DYD: It strikes me that both guide the way we use our minds—the difference being that we use models and metaphors to think with, and our roles to act with.

RSS: Right. Models guide our thinking. Roles guide our acting.

DYD: Which isn't to say they're totally distinct.

RSS: Not at all. Thinking leads to acting, and we choose the models, metaphors, and narrative images we think with in the course of exercising our roles.

DYD: So Davis offered you a new role to act with.

RSS: It put me in play, yes. It gave me the opportunity to engage in the problem of segregation in the Catholic high school system.

DYD: And more specifically, it opened up the opportunity for you to bring your model of the spirit to bear on the racial bias you discerned.

RSS: It did.

DYD: Okay. All this makes sense to me as a reconstruction of what was going on for you. But I have to ask. Were you really aware of all these factors at the time? Roles, models, thinking, acting? Explicitly aware of them?

RSS: Are you doubtful?

DYD: Not exactly. But I am struck by how intricate the key factors there are, and how technical our discussion is.

RSS: Our discussion is technical. But using a model isn't the same as explaining it or trying to illustrate it. At the time, I didn't need to be as verbally precise as we're being here.

DYD: Because you were thinking with the model, not talking about it.

RSS: That's the point. So to answer your question, yes. I was mindful of the key factors involved. I was aware of being put in play, of the opportunities opened up by the new role, and of being drawn to affirm that role.

DYD: And by "drawn," you mean you were consciously present to the spirit drawing you.

RSS: That's right.

DYD: So that's another evidence-based claim. I keep wondering about the possibility of verifying them.

RSS: Once you know what factors to attend to, it's not so difficult to pin down their relations in your conscious experience.

DYD: Isn't it? I'd say that most of us aren't even aware of the experiential data you apparently attend to as a matter of course.

RSS: You think that's true?

DYD: I think most of us are simply embedded in our roles. We aren't specifically aware of being carried by them or the horizons they open up, let alone the models we use or which way the spiritual wind is blowing. I'd say most of us just drift from role to role and back again.

RSS: Now who's making an empirical claim?

DYD: Fair point. But we all drift. I know I do.

RSS: We all get embedded in our roles. They carry our use of our minds without our being aware of it. Which is why I pointed to the unexpectedness of Lloyd's offer—the newness of the role for me. It heightened my awareness of being put in play.

DYD: It threw you back on yourself, as you said. I presume President Kennedy's offer did too?

RSS: The offer to head up the Peace Corps? That was less surprising. But the point is the same. We all have the capacity to become consciously present to ourselves in that way—whether we make a practice of it or not.

DYD: Then let me roll this back a bit. What if Davis hadn't made you the offer? Or better, what if he made you the offer, but it didn't throw you back on yourself? Or wait, even if it did, what if your conscious presence to being put in play was fleeting and you didn't really pay attention to it?

RSS: That's too many questions. What are you asking me?

DYD: I'm asking if you think you'd have been consciously present to the spirit if you hadn't been consciously present to yourself.[13]

RSS: That's a good question. What do you think?

DYD: I think it's probably less likely.

RSS: It is less likely.

DYD: And if you hadn't been consciously present to the spirit, do you think you might have said no to Davis's offer instead?

RSS: I don't know. I might have. If I hadn't been consciously present to the spirit, maybe tackling racial bias in Catholic high schools admissions would have seemed like too much to take on.

DYD: But the spirit would have been tugging, calling, inspiring you to reach for your highest aspirations.

RSS: Of course it would have. The question is, was I sufficiently attentive to notice and respond?

DYD: As it happened, you were.

RSS: I'm grateful to say, I was.

DYD: But these outcomes seem so uncertain, so contingent.

RSS: They are uncertain. But notice the contingency is all on our side of the equation, not the spirit's.

DYD: There's cold comfort in that.

RSS: It makes things complicated, yes.

DYD: But let me make sure I understand what was going on for you.

RSS: By all means.

DYD: Lloyd Davis offered you a role in a system—the Catholic Interracial Council of Chicago—and he wanted you to go to work on another set of systems—the admissions systems of the Catholic high schools.

RSS: Right.

DYD: There are obviously sensorily perceptible tasks and

results associated with that role, but in response to the offer, you became consciously present to yourself—both as engaged in a new horizon of concern and as aware of asking yourself, "Will I commit to this?"

RSS: But there's more. In that same moment, I was also present to the spirit calling me to commit.

DYD: So the spirit was present to you. And in responding to Davis, you were consciously aware of its presence.

RSS: I was.

DYD: It was one conscious moment, but you differentiated two components—one spiritual, one conscious.

RSS: There was a sensory context too.

DYD: Yes. But in your response, Mary was carrying your presence to the spirit and modeling your response?

RSS: Of course she was. But as my Hindu friends might have said, "Ganesh is here."[14]

DYD: Seriously? The god of beginnings?

RSS: The remover of obstacles, yes.

DYD: Obstacles to spiritual openness?

RSS: Among others.

DYD: That makes Booth One quite a special place. A sacred place of a sort.

RSS: It was more than a physical booth; it was the place Lloyd offered me the role. The place I said yes to the offer.

DYD: The place where you were present to the spirit.

RSS: Yes.

DYD: And in honor of that presence, your Hindu friends might have suggested reupholstering the seats in orange.

RSS: Brightly, tastefully of course.

DYD: We're no longer talking about a system as a set of tasks and results, are we?

RSS: Not in the simple sense, no. Booth One provided the sensory context for a nexus of persons, systems, spirit, and consciousness unfolding in the Pump Room that winter night in late 1952.

DYD: Including a place for devotional language.

RSS: Devotional language can be tricky. But there's no reason to leave it completely behind.

DYD: Because we are persons in roles, conscious and open to the spirit?

RSS: Yes. And because we are not replaceable parts in a linked set of tasks and action steps.

DYD: Although sometimes we are.

RSS: Yes.

DYD: All too often, that's exactly what we are.

RSS: There's the rub.

DYD: So, what then?

RSS: So let me ask you again: Can you imagine improving the operation, the outcomes, or the structure of a personally truncating system without seeking to release the spiritual capacity of the persons in their roles?

DYD: Well, your question makes sense to me now—though I still can't imagine how you would actually do that.

RSS: Can't you?

DYD: I know you focused your attention on the decision-making of the principals.

RSS: And the other key players too. Their combined

decision-making generated a segregated school system year after year after year.

DYD: Tell me then, how do you get a principal to change their habit of making racially biased admissions decisions?

RSS: You can't. They have to change it for themselves.

DYD: All right. Then what do you do to facilitate that change?

RSS: What do you think?

DYD: Do you always have to be so Socratic about this?

RSS: I do. How else are you going to learn to think with the model?

DYD: But I'm just fumbling in the dark.

RSS: You're not fumbling. You have a good sense of it. How would you think this through?

DYD: I honestly don't know. Identifying a racially biased decision and recognizing it needs to change is one thing. Knowing how to facilitate that change is quite another.

RSS: Just begin with what you already know.

DYD: Well, I know you facilitated change, but you didn't do it by trying to force or compel the principals into changing their minds.

RSS: That's true. I didn't make any threats. I didn't issue any mandates or executive orders. I didn't sue anybody. I didn't crack any heads. But I wasn't in a role that would have tempted me to choose any of those options anyway.

DYD: And presumably you weren't in a position to pay anybody off, either.

RSS: Hardly.

DYD: So that clarifies some of the ways you didn't go, but it doesn't really illuminate what you did.

RSS: Let's make the question a bit more precise. What would you say I was aiming for?

DYD: Your aim? Well, you said that you wanted to release the spiritual capacity of the admissions system—to enhance the probabilities that the principals would make more self-transcendent decisions.

RSS: Good. So how would you imagine going after that?

DYD: Well, if you wanted to release the spiritual capacity of the principals in their roles, I imagine you'd want to enhance their spiritual awareness.

RSS: No. That's not it either.

DYD: Really?

RSS: As we've discussed, being consciously present to the spirit is a fairly high-level spiritual attainment.

DYD: Yes. It's more exacting than making contact with a 90-mile-an-hour fastball. And it takes practice.

RSS: Which is why I'm always happy when I find myself working with someone who is spiritually conscious and open. And why I always do my best to keep working with such people. But it's not something you can really count on, or make happen in another person.

DYD: Because that's the part played by the spirit?

RSS: Exactly. It's not on us to pour the spirit into the minds and hearts of other people.

DYD: Or to fill their sails.

RSS: Right. We can't expect to flip a switch and bring up the lights of spiritual awareness in another person. In the end, everyone has to work out their relationship to the spirit for themselves.

DYD: So what do you do instead?

RSS: Use the model to think it through.[15]

DYD: Point by point?

RSS: That's a good way to go at it.

DYD: Okay. Point one: the principals are persons in roles. Point two: in the role of principal, they are engaged in a particular horizon of concern—one that among other tasks involves them in recruiting, selecting, and admitting students to their high school. Point three: in performing those activities, I presume they aspire to recruit the best class of students they can. And point four: they must be using some sort of model or image to carry their aspirations and to think through what that best class would be.

RSS: Very good.

DYD: Point five: the spirit would be present to the principals in the conscious exercise of their roles—tugging, calling, inspiring them.

RSS: That's key. The spirit is already present to them.

DYD: Though whether they are consciously present to the spirit is a separate question.

RSS It is.

DYD: As is whether they are consciously present to themselves, which is point six.

RSS: That's a key variable too.

DYD: It would seem that self-transcendence is not exactly a defining characteristic of the decisions the principals were making.

RSS: Not with regard to race, diversity, and high school admissions, no.

DYD: So if those are the main factors, how do you account for the breakdown in the system? Or better, for its recovery?

RSS: Well, you've just distinguished six key factors. What do you think it could be?

DYD: I should use the factors to troubleshoot the system?

RSS: The key factors must be optimally aligned for the system to function optimally.

DYD: And if they're not . . .

RSS: If something is missing or short-circuited or askew, then the performance of the principals in their roles is less than optimal and the outcomes get messed up too—as was manifestly the case with Catholic high school admissions.

DYD: So what was askew?

RSS: You tell me.

DYD: But I can't in fact tell you, can I? I don't have a clue as to what the principals were actually thinking as they made their decisions.

RSS: Excellent. So what does that tell you about what you should do?

DYD: Talk to them?

RSS: Exactly. And what would you want to know?

DYD: Well, they all have their roles and their horizons of concern, but we don't really know how they understand them, do we? Or for that matter, what their primary concerns within that role might be. I imagine it could vary from principal to principal.

RSS: Good. What else?

DYD: We don't know what model or narrative image they're using to guide their thinking about what constitutes an optimal class of first-year high school students. Though it's probably fair to say it's not Paul's letter to the Galatians.

RSS: Probably not.

DYD: So where do we go from here?

RSS: What do you think?

DYD: I don't know.

RSS: Why so?

DYD: Because who gets to say? The principals probably have different notions of their roles, and different understandings of what's significant. They are probably using different models and images of what constitutes an ideal class of students.

RSS: That's true.

DYD: So what do we do with that? You can't just pop their minds open and plug in a broader horizon of concern or an alternative narrative.

RSS: No, the principals have to change their own minds.

DYD: And what does that take?

RSS: You've forgotten to account for the most important factor of all.

DYD: Which is?

RSS: The possibility of self-transcendence.

DYD: You mean the presence of the spirit.

RSS: Yes I do.

DYD: So what are you saying? Regarding the system, I mean.

RSS: You know what I'm saying.

DYD: Okay. It seems to me you're saying that the admissions system is a tangle of roles and horizons and models and narratives—and that when this happens, it constricts the opportunities for self-transcendence in the decision-making of the persons in their roles.

RSS: That's right.

DYD: So the aim is to enhance the probabilities that more self-transcending decisions will be made.

RSS: Yes.

DYD: By releasing the spiritual capacity of the persons in their roles.

RSS: That's right.

DYD: Would you say it's like releasing logs from a logjam?[16]

RSS: That's an interesting way to put it.

DYD: I'm thinking about logjams from the days of Paul Bunyan, the days before logging trucks. I'm fascinated with that time period.

RSS: Okay. What connection are you making?

DYD: In those days, loggers would set up a logging camp, cut original growth white pine into sixteen-foot logs, and roll them into a river with the expectation of floating them downstream to a sawmill. And in their perfect world, the logs would float smoothly and efficiently downriver to the sawmill to be cut into lumber.

RSS: But in the world of real rivers, there were always too many snags, bends, eddies, and other obstacles, so the logs would get jammed up on the way to the mill.

DYD: So a team of loggers would have to travel downriver with the logs to deal with the trouble spots. They were called log drivers in that particular role, and they'd be out on the log flow with their pikes to free the logs and prevent the formation of a jam.

RSS: Good. So when you think about those log drivers out there on the logs, carrying out their role, what do you imagine them doing?

DYD: I imagine them falling into the river. I imagine that it's very tricky to keep your balance—rolling logs beneath your feet, using your pike as a balance bar, moving from log to log to log—and very harrowing when you tumble into the water.

RSS: Big trouble. No doubt about it. But let's say our log drivers have mastered the degree of difficulty involved. What do you imagine then?

DYD: I imagine them using their pikes to push logs free from snags, to pull them out of eddies, to pry loose the logs that are jammed on top of each other.

RSS: In other words, you're imagining the log drivers working to release the capacity of the logs to flow downriver.

DYD: Yes. That's the connection.

RSS: It's a good metaphor. But we're not actually talking about freeing a harvest of logs from the snags and shallows that jam up, are we.

DYD: No. We're talking about freeing a pattern of admissions decisions from the bias and shortsightedness that skews decision-making in the system.

RSS: So we're talking about a tangle of roles, horizons, narrative images, and models, not a tangle of white pine logs.

DYD: Right. And we're not talking about using an iron pike to free up the pinch points.

RSS: No, we're talking about employing a targeted form of curiosity to open up possibilities for self-transcendence.[17]

DYD: A targeted form of curiosity?

RSS: You know how things get jammed up in a system.

DYD: It's hard to keep it all straight in my mind.

RSS: Most of us are embedded in our roles. That's how you put it earlier.

DYD: Yes. We drift from role to role and back again—especially when we are familiar with the roles.

RSS: There's efficiency in that, of course. But when we're not mindful of ourselves in our roles, it's difficult to be curious or self-critical about our performance. That's the downside. It's also difficult to wonder about the adequacy of the role itself.

DYD: Which is when things tend to get jammed up.

RSS: Not simply because we may be missing a relevant question or two.

DYD: No?

RSS: When we become forgetful of ourselves in our roles—and we identify ourselves so closely with the tasks and concerns of our roles, we tend to hold on very tightly to the way we do things.

DYD: Sometimes we hold on for dear life.

RSS: Which is what needs to be released.

DYD: Our fusion of person and role?

RSS: Exactly. So in the case of the principals, you target your curiosity on the way they're using their minds to make their admissions decisions. And when you wonder about their performance, they begin to be curious too.

DYD: So you're heightening their mindfulness of their decision-making—their presence to themselves.

RSS: And if you can do that, you've got yourself an interesting conversation.

DYD: An encounter of persons.

RSS: Not a clash of positions.

DYD: Okay. But how exactly do you do that?

RSS: You just use the model as your guide.

DYD: Easy for you to say.

Connect the Dots[1]

DYD: So tell me, Log Driver, what did you actually do to free up the flow of self-transcendence in the high school admissions process?[2]

RSS: The first thing I did was to get out there on the logjam— to have a conversation with each of the principals.

DYD: All seventy-nine of them?

RSS: It was important to speak with them in person.

DYD: That sounds ambitious.

RSS: It was necessary. That's how I think of it. I began by arranging meetings with the principals of the top fifteen Catholic high schools in the city.[3]

DYD: To get your bearings on the situation.

RSS: Exactly. But I was working full time at the Merchandise Mart when I took on my role with the Catholic Interracial Council. And soon after, I began serving on the Chicago School Board. So it took longer to get around to all of them than I would have liked.

DYD: You're thinking you were slow?

RSS: I'm always impatient when there's important work to be done. Still, we made steady progress at CICC—developing the program, placing students, opening minds, establishing relationships with schools. But if I compare my meeting with the principals to the forced march Bill Moyers and I made on Congress in the spring of 1961—then yes, I'd say I was slow.[4]

DYD: What forced march?

RSS: Moyers and I met with every elected official on Capitol Hill in eight weeks. We wanted Congress to authorize and fund Peace Corps as a permanent program of the US government.

DYD: You met with all one hundred Senators? All 435 members of the House?

RSS: Except for one congressman who had recently passed away, yes.

DYD: Five hundred and thirty-four meetings? Surely you had some idea of who was on your side. Didn't you make a rough count of the votes?

RSS: Yes, but it wasn't just a matter of marshaling and counting votes. Senators and members of Congress are not vote-dispensing machines.

DYD: No. They are persons in roles.

RSS: That's the point.

DYD: So your point was to put them in touch with their roles as elected representatives of the American people?

RSS: And to consciously orient them to the horizon of concern that goes with that role, yes. We wanted to do what we could to ensure that when it came time for them to vote on the Peace Corps bill, they would be reaching for their noblest aspirations.

DYD: How did you go after that?

RSS: Moyers and I would engage them in conversations, and we were especially curious about their response to the idea of creating a Peace Corps—their sense of its design and purpose, and the nature of their hopes and concerns for it.

DYD: And what they worried might go awry if they voted to authorize the program?

RSS: Understanding their concern was important to us, yes. But more constructively, we were interested in their aspirations for the program—in what they could imagine achieving if they voted for it.

DYD: Such as?

RSS: Such as giving their constituents a role in advancing world peace that didn't involve picking up a gun; such as enabling Americans of all ages to dedicate two years of their lives helping to advance the dignity, welfare, and security of people living in the developing world.

DYD: Putting American citizens at play in the world in a new way.

RSS: And releasing their spiritual capacity for self-transcendence.

DYD: That was your aspiration for the Peace Corps?

RSS: How else are you going to make friends and build peace across existing barriers of race, creed, language, and national identity?

DYD: So you were hoping that a self-transcending Congress would authorize and fund a program designed to build world peace as a permanent feature of the US government?

RSS: The House voted 288 to 79 in favor of it.

DYD: Which had to be very gratifying.

RSS: Yes.

DYD: But what about the seventy-nine members who voted No? Or all the others who decided not to cast a vote—nearly seventy of them.

RSS: That shows you what a challenge it was, and why it's important to be realistic. Our ability to discern our noblest aspirations is always a matter of context and probability. Deciding to reach for them, to act on them, is another matter altogether. And it's never certain until the decision is actually made. Even then, there's a good chance we might be confused or hasty and get it wrong.

DYD: Even when the spirit is present—calling and inspiring?

RSS: The spirit is always present. You know that.

DYD: Yes, but if the spirit is always present, how do you account for the variability in results?

RSS: We're the source of variability. You've already named six of the key variables.[5]

DYD: Yes. The spirit is not the only factor in the mix. We have instrumental parts to play too. I'm not sure why I have trouble hanging on to that insight.

RSS: It's a stubborn cultural habit. We're all prone to thinking the spirit is some sort of indomitable, irresistible force.

DYD: I guess that's it. If we fail to detect signs of spiritual power or influence having its way with things, we conclude the spirit is not present.

RSS: It's a question of what we're trying to detect. In my view, clerics and theologians have a lot to answer for. Many of our most familiar notions of spirit are rooted in metaphors of power.

DYD: The spirit as lightning bolt, as irresistible command, as mighty deed.

RSS: Our presence to the spirit can feel like that sometimes. But we're closer to the mark when we draw our metaphors from the conscious dimension of our experiencing: a still small voice, an insensible inspiration, a conscious tug to self-transcendence.

DYD: So when we put on our spiritual thinking caps, we don't think about the spirit as a transcendent source of physical force or power.

RSS: No.

DYD: We're thinking instead in terms of a still, small, conscious presence—an inner impetus to self-transcendence.[6]

RSS: A still small presence to the complex, patterned flow of our conscious minds.

DYD: A pattern specified by roles, models and narrative images.

RSS: You seem to be pretty clear about the key terms and their relations.

DYD: It's still a stretch, actually.

RSS: And it's important to stretch a bit further.

DYD: Stretch how?

RSS: To explicitly account for the spirit in light of our need to transcend ourselves. To acknowledge that we are not just persons in roles, but distracted persons in instrumentalized roles—persons responding to difficult, demanding, often demeaning situations who are unaccustomed to paying attention to the spirit and barely mindful of the metaphors, models and narrative images that guide and direct our aspiring and deciding.

DYD: You're talking about accounting for our inner logjams.

RSS: I'm talking about the need to be consciously present to the spirit as an inner log driver. And the need to be mindful of how jammed up we are.[7]

DYD: You seem to approach thinking with the model—thinking with this spiritual thinking cap—as a kind of devotional practice.

RSS: Absolutely. You could think of it as a form of prayer. Forgive us our inability to transcend ourselves as we forgive those who are unable to transcend themselves in their dealing with us.

DYD: Which brings us back to the main question. If we want to identify the locus of the spirit in a logjam of roles and responses—or better yet, if we want to release the capacity for self-transcendence latent within that situation, how would we go about it?

RSS: Slowly, patiently, and humbly. In this case, my role gave me the opportunity to have genuine conversations.

DYD: To foster encounters of persons.

RSS: That's right.

DYD: But conversation can't be the only way.

RSS: No. It's not. But that doesn't make blunt force an option either.

DYD: As you say, there are no extrinsic switches to flip. No external power sources to access.

RSS: Much as we might spontaneously think otherwise.

DYD: Just logjams to release, sails to trim, mustard seeds to nurture.

RSS: That's right.

DYD: I wish it were easier to keep that in mind.

RSS: Fortunately, we're not alone in the struggle.

DYD: Yes. So let's get back to your conversations with the high school principals. How did you approach them?[8]

RSS: Much the same as we approached our conversations on Capitol Hill—though the conversations with the principals were more open-ended.

DYD: Why so?

RSS: We were at a different stage in the process. By the time Moyers and I started to canvass Congress, we'd already been working for several months to design the Peace Corps program and to get it up and running under the president's executive order. We were already recruiting and training our first cadres of Volunteers for service in Ghana and Tanganyika. So by the time the House finally got around to authorizing the program on September 22, 1961, we already had Volunteers in the field.

DYD: Whereas in the case of Catholic high school admissions?

RSS: We were at the very beginning of the process. We knew we had a systemic problem, but we didn't know exactly where things were jamming up, or precisely why. Nor did we know what, if anything, the principals would be willing to do, what the Education Committee at CICC might do to help. We had a lot to learn.

DYD: You had to understand the problem and design the remedy before you could sell it or ask for support.

RSS: We had to talk to the people involved.

DYD: So what did you talk about?

RSS: Each conversation was its own, but the approach was pretty much the same in all of them.

DYD: You were using your model of spiritual realism to think with?

RSS: I don't know how to think any other way.

DYD: Okay. But what did it mean for those conversations?

RSS: It meant that I would begin by introducing myself in my role as head of the Education Committee with the Catholic Inter-racial Council, and I would thank them for participating in our survey of the racial composition of the high schools.

DYD: That was the reason for the meeting? To follow up on the results of your survey?[9]

RSS: That's right. We'd exchange the usual pleasantries, talk about the survey, and then I'd ask for their help in understanding the results—not just the racial segregation in their own school, but in the diocese as a whole.

DYD: So you were explicitly addressing them in their roles as principals?

RSS: I was intentional about it. I didn't need to be explicit.

DYD: No?

RSS: There was no ambiguity about their role, so I didn't need to clarify or confirm it. The main thing was to evoke their presence to themselves as principals. And for that, all I had to do was inquire about their admissions process.

DYD: Because the admissions process falls within the horizon of concern that comes with being a principal?

RSS: Right.

DYD: So you raised the question of race and student admissions and put them consciously in play in their role as principal.

RSS: Yes.

DYD: What did you say?

RSS: I'd say something like: "The survey you submitted indicates that you were unable to admit any Black students to your school this year. I'm hoping you can help me understand why that was the case."

DYD: And?

RSS: And they would usually give me an affirmative nod, or a verbal go-ahead, and I would follow up with something like, "So here's my question: When it comes to making the final decisions about who gets admitted and who doesn't, what gets in the way of admitting Black students to your school? What obstacles do you have to deal with?"

DYD: That's a bold approach.

RSS: Straightforward, yes.

DYD: But as I listened to your question, I found myself taking on the perspective of the principal on the receiving end of your question. I felt a challenge in it.

RSS: A challenge?

DYD: Well, when you asked so directly about what was getting in the way of admitting students who were Black, I felt the urge to defend myself. I felt put on the spot and I wanted to justify the decisions I'd been making. I expect some principals felt that way too. So my question is, did you get much pushback from them?[10]

RSS: Not much, no.

DYD: Really?

RSS: Yes. We'd already agreed about the subject of the conversation when we set up the meeting, so the focus of my questions didn't catch the principals off guard. Besides, I was genuinely curious about the decisions they were making and the obstacles they faced. I wasn't sitting in judgment. They could tell.

DYD: So how did they receive your question? As an invitation to puzzle through their obstacles with you?

RSS: That's a good way to think of it. I wanted to talk about the way they were thinking about the racial aspect of their admissions decisions.

DYD: And hoping that in the process they might deepen their insight into themselves and the decisions they were making.

RSS: That's right.

DYD: Still, I was nonplussed by your question.

RSS: Fair enough. Not many of the principals had been paying much attention to the conscious component of their admissions process. They'd focus on the task, execute it, and move on. So they had to pause and reflect on their performance a bit to find their answers.

DYD: Concretely then, your opening questions centered them in their roles as principals and threw them back on themselves.

RSS: Much as they did for you, yes.

DYD: So where did you take those conversations from there?

RSS: It depended upon the person and the high school, of course, so the specific details of the conversation varied. The ease and flow of the conversation varied too, depending upon the ability of the principal to reflect on their inner conscious experience. But the conversations were all aimed at getting at the conscious component of the admissions process, so they followed a general pattern. I wanted to connect the dots among the key factors in the model.

DYD: So what was the pattern you pursued?

RSS: You know, don't you?

DYD: I'm afraid I don't. My command of the model isn't good enough yet.

RSS: Sure it is. Take it one step at a time. What question would you want to ask?

DYD: If I wanted to get at what's jamming up the release of self-transcendence in the admissions process?

RSS: Think it through. Think with the model.

DYD: Well, if I'm thinking with the model, I'm guided by the notion that the spirit is present to us in our conscious response to the situations we encounter.

RSS: Good.

DYD: And in this case, the situation is the racial disparity—the color barrier—manifest in the admissions decisions of Catholic high school principals.

RSS: See? Not so hard. So what's the first thing you're curious about?

DYD: I guess the first thing I'd like to understand is the principals' conscious response to their situation—their sense of the segregation in their school.

RSS: So what would your opening question be?

DYD: I'm not sure I'd start out with a question. I'd want to let the principal know where I'm coming from, what my focus is.

RSS: To set their focus too.

DYD: Right. So I might say something like: "The survey indicates that you haven't admitted any Black students to your school."

RSS: And now that they're focusing on that fact . . .

DYD: I'd want to inquire about their response to it. So I might say something like, "I'm curious about your take on the racial make-up of your student body—what your sense of its significance might be, for you, for the students, for the community."

RSS: So you're inquiring about the principal's valuing—about their felt response to being the principal in charge of admissions in a segregated school?

DYD: Well, I'm wondering whether they're dismayed or sanguine . . . whatever it might be.

RSS: And you were thinking *my* approach was bold?

DYD: Point taken. The model certainly gets straight to the point, doesn't it.

RSS: It fosters a straightforward encounter with the person— the person in their role.

DYD: Which can be off-putting.

RSS: I suppose, but it needn't be. We all appreciate it when somebody is genuinely curious about us. It heightens our presence to ourselves. So let's assume what is very likely to be the case, that the principal you're speaking to is just as interested in reflecting on their felt response to the situation as you are in learning about it.

DYD: Okay. What then?

RSS: No. That's my question for you. What's the dot you want to connect? Where are you hoping your line of questioning will take you? Keep thinking with the model.

DYD: Okay. If the principle can identify their felt response to their admissions situation, I'm hoping we could talk about what they are discerning in their admissions situation—how it squares with their aspirations for it.

RSS: What gaps they might be registering?

DYD: Yes. And what decisions they've been making—or wishing they could make—to fulfill those aspirations or close those gaps.

RSS: Which would bring you around to where I started—to reflecting on the obstacles that are getting in their way.

DYD: So we can go at it either way and cover the same ground.

RSS: That's right. If you're thinking with the model, the general aim and pattern of the conversation will be largely the same—though the content will be different.

DYD: Okay. So here's another question. I take it that no matter which way we approach it—whether we wonder about the obstacles to their decision-making or their felt sense of the admissions situation itself—we're still only focusing on the part the principal is playing? Not the part played by the spirit?

RSS: Yes. Either way, the questions get at the conscious component of the principals' role in the admissions process.

DYD: Which leaves us with the spiritual component. How did you raise the question of the spirit?

RSS: I can't say that I did—not explicitly, anyway. If a principal raised the issue, we'd certainly talk about it. But otherwise, I'd let it go.

DYD: Really?

RSS: Do you think I needed to make a point of it? The spirit is playing its part. We can count on that.

DYD: So you focused on enhancing the principals' conscious presence to themselves.

RSS: Do you know why?

DYD: Yes. The more mindful we are—the more explicitly

present to ourselves we become—whether in our roles, our responses to situations, or our aspirations for them, the more likely we are to be open and present to the spirit.

RSS: That's it. The more explicitly present to ourselves we become, the more likely we are to check our tendency to become hasty, uncritical, rash.

DYD: Because the spirit is present to us.

RSS: Because we become open to the still, small voice consciously inspiring, calling, tugging us toward self-transcendence.

DYD: I understand. I just worry that it's too subtle, too nuanced.

RSS: Weren't you the one saying it was bold and direct?

DYD: It's the model that's complex. And thinking with it seems so subtle, so nuanced.

RSS: Too subtle to be true? Too nuanced to guide effective changes in Catholic high school admissions?

DYD: It's ironic, I know. Relying on the spirit the way you do—and the way the model does—makes it feel less certain, less sure of the outcome.[11]

RSS: Compared to what? Paying off the admissions committee? Condemning a principal for the racial bias in their admissions process? Threatening to slice their tires or whack them on the side of the head if they don't change their ways?

DYD: Those approaches are definitely noisier.

RSS: And that's what you get when you take it upon yourself to compel conscious change—a lot of noise, a lot of pain, a lot of misdirected energy.

DYD: You sound so certain about this. I don't know that it's a real choice for most people.

RSS: I'm quite certain.

DYD: Still, most people don't think about it the way you do.

RSS: Meaning?

DYD: Meaning most people don't think about change in terms of releasing self-transcendence. They think in terms of maximizing leverage, of compelling behavior.

RSS: True enough. If you don't think it, you can't think with it either.

DYD: Maybe that's my concern. Even if you can think it, the model is still a challenge. The key factors are subtle, and it's not that easy to identify them—or to link them—in our conscious experience, especially given all the mental noise that clutters our everyday lives.

RSS: Yes. But once you've pinned them down, they become easier and easier to identify, to account for, to think with.

DYD: Practice make perfect.

RSS: But it's not all about practice. Remember, the spirit is always present to you too—tugging, correcting, lifting, loving. So try not to focus on the degree of difficulty involved, or how much practice it takes. It's not all on you. Just strive to be curious, to be open.

DYD: To stretch myself.

RSS: Yes. To risk uncertainty, to risk getting it wrong—to risk being open.

DYD: All right. Walk me through one of your conversations with the principals—one you regard as particularly fruitful.

RSS: All of my conversations with the principals were fruitful. But I'd say my conversation with Sister Mary-Frances was particularly memorable. She was a Sister of Mercy and the Principal of St. Patrick's Academy, a high school for about six hundred girls run by her Order in a predominantly German and Irish neighborhood on the far north side, in Des Plaines.[12]

DYD: I take it Sister Mary-Frances was open to talking about herself in her role?

RSS: She was very interested in connecting those dots. She was also attuned to the racial dynamics in the Church, especially the way they affected the educational opportunities available to young Black women in the city. I learned a lot from her.

DYD: So how did she respond to your opening gambit?

RSS: With alacrity, I must say. She wanted me to understand that even though all the girls at St. Patrick's Academy were White, and most of them of either Irish or German descent, she wasn't in the habit of denying or turning away applications from young Black women. She wasn't getting any of those applications. That was the sticking point for her. That's what she wanted me to understand.

DYD: You're sure she wasn't a bit defensive?

RSS: If that's how it sounds, then I've misrepresented her. She was emphatic, not defensive.

DYD: Emphatic about what?

RSS: Emphatic about the institutional constraint she was experiencing in her role as principal.

DYD: So it wasn't so much her own performance that was concerning her. It was the hand she was being dealt.

RSS: That's a good way to put it, though having a poor hand will limit your ability to play, no matter how good you may be.

DYD: And that's what she found troubling?

RSS: More than troubling. She said it vexed her worse than anything.

DYD: Worse than anything? Really?

RSS: You find that hard to imagine?

DYD: Well, I'm struck by the intensity of it. St. Patrick's Academy was in Des Plaines, wasn't it?

RSS: Yes.

DYD: And there weren't any young Black women in Des Plaines to apply to St. Patrick's, were there?

RSS: Not in those days, no. That's what Sister Mary-Frances was saying.

DYD: That's what I thought. So realistically then, and I mean no disrespect by this, but wouldn't it be fair to say that Sister Mary-Frances had a somewhat inflated sense of her role?

RSS: Inflated? In what sense?

DYD: Inflated in the sense that her aspirations for her role seem to reach beyond its horizon of concern.

RSS: Overreach how?

DYD: Well, if there are no young Black women in Des Plaines to be admitted or educated at St. Patrick's, doesn't her vexation at the applicant pool take her beyond the practical horizon of her concern as the principal of St. Patrick's Academy?

RSS: You're thinking she's being unrealistic?

DYD: Well, I'm wondering about the relationship between reality-testing and self-transcendence—because her aspiring seems to be out of line with the applicant pool she could reasonably expect to receive.

RSS: To which I reply: love isn't blind, no matter what they say. And neither was Sister Mary-Frances.

DYD: Well, if you're saying it's not overreach, how do you account for it?

RSS: Principal wasn't her only role.

DYD: What do you mean?

RSS: I mean that in addition to being the principal of St. Patrick's Academy, Sister Mary-Frances was also a Sister of Mercy.[13]

DYD: Well, St. Patrick's was run by the Sisters of Mercy, wasn't it?

RSS: Yes. But the two roles weren't identical—so their horizons of concern weren't identical either.

DYD: Which means what? That Sister Mary-Frances's aspirations as a Sister of Mercy were broader than the practical reach of her concerns as the principal of St. Patrick's?

RSS: Exactly. As the principal of St. Patrick's, her horizon of concern encompassed the young women enrolled in her school. But as a Sister of Mercy, she was also concerned about young Black women in the city who were educationally underserved. She told me that as a Sister of Mercy, she was concerned for the dignity and self-sufficiency of all women—especially young women disadvantaged by the fact of being poor and female.

DYD: Let alone poor, Black, and female.

RSS: Exactly right. As she put it to me, Sister Mary-Frances felt called to serve young women who were not as privileged educationally as the Lord wanted them to be.

DYD: Would that be the call that led her to join her Order?

RSS: It would.

DYD: So would you also say she was expressly aware of the tension in her roles? Did she talk about it that way?

RSS: During our conversation we certainly did. Her aspirations as a Sister of Mercy cast the more limited horizon of her role at St. Patrick's into stark relief. Into vexing relief.

DYD: So if she hadn't been in both roles, if she hadn't been a Sister of Mercy . . .

RSS: What are you thinking?

DYD: I'm thinking that if she had just been a principal, she would have felt much less vexed in her role at St. Patrick's. She would have been more sanguine. More accommodated to the practical realities of the school and her applicant pool.

RSS: That's probably so. In the absence of a role that explicitly engaged her concerns for educationally underprivileged young women, her aspiration for poor, young, Black women in the city would remain outside the explicit horizon of her conscious concerns.

DYD: Much like you before Lloyd Davis offered you the role with CICC.

RSS: That's true too.

DYD: But as it was, she felt jammed up in her role as principal.

RSS: She was head of a high school run by the Sisters of Mercy, in a role that constrained her from reaching for the highest aspirations of her call to religious life.

DYD: I can see how that would be vexing.

RSS: Worse than anything.

DYD: So let me take stock for a moment. You opened your conversation with Sister Mary-Frances by wondering about the obstacles that were preventing her from admitting Black students into St. Patrick's.

RSS: Right.

DYD: Your question centered her in her role and led her to think about the admissions decisions she'd been making. It brought to mind the applicant pool she'd been dealing with—both the ethnic and racial homogeneity of the pool and the absence of young Black women in it.

RSS: She was emphatic about the constraint that particular admissions pool imposed upon her decision-making.

DYD: And that constraint vexed her. Vexed her, it seems, because the constraint was emblematic of the broader practical constraints she experienced as principal of St. Patrick's—constraints that put her at odds with her highest aspirations as a Sister of Mercy.

RSS: Good.

DYD: Okay, but I can't help noticing that we've changed the subject.

RSS: In what way?

DYD: Well, you started out by focusing on racial segregation in the student body at St. Patrick's, but now we're focusing on the institutional constraints Sister Mary-Frances is experiencing in carrying out her role.

RSS: Something is troubling you about that?

DYD: Well, I'm wondering if we're getting off track.

RSS: Off track?

DYD: It strikes me that we're losing our focus on the problem of segregation in Catholic high school admissions.

RSS: By paying explicit attention to the conscious and spiritual components of the system?

DYD: By focusing on what seem to be the personal, role-related concerns of Sister Mary-Frances rather than the problem of racism in the system, yes.

RSS: Well, I think of it as broadening our focus rather than changing the subject. That's the aim of the conversation in the first place.

DYD: What aim is that?

RSS: The only way sustainable change can happen in a situation like St. Patrick's is if the people involved in the situation are able change the way they are using their minds. They have to know their minds to change them.

DYD: You're talking about the need to foster self-transcendence.

RSS: If the principals in the system change the patterns of their decision-making, the system will change too. That's just the way it works.

DYD: That's an intriguing claim. Yet I keep looking for the magic wand—the power move—that would fix the system for us.

RSS: Yes. When Jesus was in the desert, the Devil tempted him with that too.

DYD: The allure is strong.

RSS: It is.

DYD: But let's get back to your conversation with Sister Mary-Frances. Where did you go next?

RSS: I didn't go anywhere. Not immediately. I wanted to stay where we were. I wanted to commiserate with Sister Mary-Frances—to affirm the bind she was experiencing.

DYD: To let her know you understood?

RSS: To confirm it, yes. But equally, to reflect back to her the vexation she was feeling. I wanted her to hold her conscious presence to herself.

DYD: Because?

RSS: Because conscious self-presence is notoriously fleeting, for one. And two: because that's where the spirit is blowing.

DYD: The spirit was present to her in her vexation.

RSS: Yes. In her vexation she was explicitly aware of being at a pinch point in her reach for self-transcendence.

DYD: And the spirit was present to her in that pinch point.

RSS: The spirit was the precipitant of that pinch point.

DYD: Just by virtue of its presence, calling her. Tugging her.

RSS: Lifting her to transcend the constraints of her role.

DYD: But she's stuck. That's the problem.

RSS: A complex, vexing problem.

DYD: So where do you take the conversation now—to her presence to the spirit?

RSS: Not directly, no.

DYD: Then what?

RSS: You pause. You make room for it. You take a breath together.

DYD: And that's enough?

RSS: It is. For the moment.

DYD: But not for long.

RSS: No. Not for long.

Narrative Image[1]

DYD: I'm struck by Sister Mary-Frances's openness in her conversation with you.

RSS: What's striking you?

DYD: Her willingness to be carried by your line of questioning. To become consciously present to herself, to experience the constriction in her role—and by what you call the pinch of her conscious presence to the spirit.

RSS: She was open.

DYD: Thanks to you.

RSS: It wasn't me.

DYD: But you engaged her in your role with the Catholic Interracial Council and she met you in her role as the principal of St. Patrick's.

RSS: Yes.

DYD: She met your dismay at the segregation of the high schools with her vexation in her role at St. Patrick's.

RSS: It was an encounter of persons.

DYD: Persons in their roles.

RSS: Yes.

DYD: And a singular encounter, it seems to me. If you'd

been in a different role—a teacher at St. Patrick's, for instance, or the parent of a student, or even a member of her Order—the conversation you had with Sister Mary-Frances would not have taken place.

RSS: Not in the same way.

DYD: Not at all, I think. But there you were—the two of you—in your roles—pausing to breathe.

RSS: Right.

DYD: So where did you take the conversation from there?

RSS: Let's work this through together. Where would you have taken the conversation if you'd been in my place?

DYD: I'm not sure.

RSS: Then tell me what you're drawn to in the conversation so far—where your curiosity is leading you.

DYD: Well, I feel for Sister Mary-Frances and the constraint she is experiencing in her role. I'm moved by her vexation. That's the main thing.

RSS: What are you wondering about?

DYD: I'm wondering what I could do to help.

RSS: And what do you want to do with your wondering?

DYD: Assuming I was in your place and in your role with the CICC?

RSS: Sure.

DYD: I think I'd want to talk about how to broaden her application pool—how to make sure she had applications from a racially and ethnically diverse pool of resilient and qualified young women.

RSS: You'd want to fix that for her?

DYD: I'd be tempted, yes.

RSS: What do you find tempting about that?

DYD: On second thought, maybe not.

RSS: No? Why not?

DYD: Because wanting to solve Sister Mary-Frances's admissions problem is probably more about me than it is about her.

RSS: How so?

DYD: I'm frustrated for her. I'm frustrated with her situation. I guess I'm feeling a bit pinched myself, and I just want it fixed.

RSS: You want action. You want results.

DYD: Of course I do.

RSS: But?

DYD: But now that I think about it, I'm not sure adding some brave young women to her applicant pool would do much to free up the constraint Sister Mary-Frances is experiencing in her role.

RSS: Or to reverse the sin of racism in the school system.

DYD: That either.

RSS: So you're aware of feeling frustrated by Sister Mary-Frances's situation. You're tempted to try to fix it for her, but now you're thinking you'd resist that temptation. Where would you want to take the conversation instead?

DYD: That's the problem. I don't really have a second option. In fact, I'm not convinced there is one.

RSS: Really?

DYD: Sister Mary-Frances is a principal in a segregated high school in a segregated school system in a segregated part of Chicago. She feels called to do something about it, but she's stuck in her role, and can't imagine what to do. Neither can I. She's at a dead end. She's vexed about it. And who could blame her?

RSS: But it's not a dead end. It's a logjam. It needs to be released.

DYD: Detonated, maybe.

RSS: That's the temptation, isn't it? Tear it down. Blow it up. Take it over.

DYD: There is a certain satisfaction that comes with imagining that.

RSS: I understand. But even if you could pull that off—and the odds against it are long, I would say—where does that leave you? How would you make things better?

DYD: I don't know. I just know something has to change.

RSS: Right. So tell me. What model of change are you thinking with right now?[2]

DYD: You want me to pay attention to the way I'm thinking about this?

RSS: If you can, yes.

DYD: Well, to be honest, I don't have much of a model of change in mind. Not explicitly anyway. If anything, it feels like I'm channeling a little bit of the big bad wolf.

RSS: You want to huff and puff and blow the house down?

DYD: That sounds cartoonish. But of this I am sure: it's not enough to identify a problem in a system and feel vexed about it. We need action.

RSS: So the question is, what would it take to introduce positive change into a system?

DYD: I know your answer to that. You'd say it takes releasing the spiritual capacity of persons in their roles. Releasing their capacity for self-transcendence.

RSS: See. You're getting this.

DYD: I'm not sure I am. But either way, here's my question. What acts of self-transcendence would we be talking about? What could Sister Mary-Frances do that would make a positive difference in her situation?

RSS: That's the thing. We don't know yet.

DYD: I certainly don't.

RSS: More importantly, neither does Sister Mary-Frances.

DYD: So how can you say we're not at a dead end?

RSS: Because there's an additional factor we need to account for. One we still need to identify.

DYD: Another factor in the model? We've already accounted for her roles, aspirations, and horizons of concern—for the contradiction she feels in her two main roles, for her presence to the spirit.

RSS: Yes. And by paying explicit attention to those factors, she has become consciously present to the constriction in her role. In the process, we've come to understand her too. But what we don't yet know is what's driving the constraint she experiences in her role.

DYD: What do you mean by "driving the constraint she experiences"?

RSS: I'm talking about the factor that carries her response to her situation at St. Patrick's—the factor that makes it difficult for her to imagine or to act in ways that might release her constraint.

DYD: And she isn't aware of it?

RSS: Not directly, I think. She wouldn't be feeling so vexed if she were. She's consciously present to the constriction in her role, of course, but not explicitly aware of the factor that's jamming her up.

DYD: So what's the missing factor?

RSS: It's the narrative image that carries her performance in her role.

DYD: Narrative image?

RSS: Right.

DYD: I remember that we talked about narrative images in connection with Paul's letter to the Galatians.

RSS: Neither Jew nor Greek, slave nor free, male nor female.

DYD: Paul commended it to the church leaders in Galatia, and I remember you transposing it to "neither White nor Black."

RSS: Yes. If I had my way, "neither White nor Black" would carry the conscious performance of every person in every role connected to the high schools.

DYD: Principal, student, teacher, parent, superintendent . . .

RSS: All of them.

DYD: So there's a link between a narrative image and the performance of a person in their role.

RSS: There is.

DYD: And you're saying that if we want to understand what's constraining Sister Mary-Frances in her role, we need to pay attention to the narrative image that's carrying her performance?

RSS: I'm also saying it's more important for Sister Mary-Frances to grasp that relationship herself than it is for us to understand it.

DYD: Because grasping it would enhance the likelihood of her self-transcendence?

RSS: That's right.

DYD: I can't say I understand that.

RSS: What don't you understand?

DYD: I don't understand the connection you're making, for one thing. But more basically, I'm puzzled by the term "narrative image." The example from Paul sounds more like a slogan or a statement of purpose to me. Not a narrative.

RSS: Actually, slogans are a specialized form of narrative image. Statements of purpose can be too.

DYD: I'm not following you.

RSS: Then let me give you a different example. The opening sentence of the Peace Corps Act is at one and the same time a statement of purpose and a narrative image. Our purpose, we said, was "to promote world peace and friendship through a Peace Corps."[3]

DYD: Okay, "purpose" I understand. But the narrative aspect? "Promoting world peace and friendship" sounds more like a mission statement than a narrative.

RSS: The wording is rather formal, I admit. I tend to think of it as "making friends and building peace." But either way, we're not talking about a full-blown storyline, if that's what's getting in your way.

DYD: What are we talking about? When I think of a narrative, I think of a plot line. A linked sequence of events.

RSS: That's right. But we're talking about a narrative *image*, not a narrative per se.

DYD: "Making friends and building peace" is a narrative image?

RSS: That's what I've been saying.

DYD: You're saying it's the *image* of a narrative? As in the way images grasp the whole?

RSS: As the saying goes, a picture is worth a thousand words.

RSS: Okay. But if "making friends and building peace" is the image, then what counts as the narrative?

RSS: That's a good question. "Making friends and building peace" is an image of the narrative *arc* that Peace Corps Volunteers perform as they fulfill their roles.

DYD: The narrative arc they perform?

RSS: There's a narrative arc to our conscious performance in any role. It's not just Peace Corps Volunteers.

DYD: Okay. I know what it means to make a friend. I know something of what it means to build peace. I understand that the horizon of concern of a Peace Corps Volunteer would include both. But I don't really understand what narrative arc you are talking about.

RSS: It's not as mysterious as it seems. I trust you remember our discussion of the link between a particular situation and our conscious response to it?

DYD: Yes.

RSS: All that's new here is to note that our conscious responses to those situations take the form of a narrative arc.

DYD: A narrative arc guided and directed by a narrative image?

RSS: That's it.

DYD: An arc it would probably take a thousand words to describe?

RSS: Yes.

DYD: Would it follow then to say that the spirit is present to our performance of that arc?

RSS: It would.

DYD: As carried by a narrative image?

RSS: Yes, but let's take first things first. And the first thing would be for you to pin down the relationship between narrative images and the narrative arc of your conscious performance.

DYD: You mean pin it down in my own experience.

RSS: That's right.

DYD: So what do you suggest?

RSS: I suggest that you imagine yourself in the role of a Peace Corps Volunteer and bring to mind a situation you'd be likely to encounter in your service placement.

DYD: You want me to role-play a Peace Corps Volunteer?

RSS: Whatever situation comes up for you will work. It doesn't matter what it is.

DYD: Except that I don't exactly know how to fill in that blank. Coming to bat as a baseball player was easy for me, but I'm not as experienced in the ways of Peace Corps. Do you mind helping me out with an example?

RSS: There are so many situations to choose from. But let's go with a particularly dramatic one. It's one of my favorites.

DYD: What is it?

RSS: Try to imagine yourself in the role of a Peace Corps Volunteer serving in the Dominican Republic in April 1965.[4]

DYD: What situation would I be responding to?

RSS: On April 25th, Peace Corps Volunteers in Santo Domingo woke up to the sounds of civil war. It was announced on their radios, and played out in the sound of sniper fire and low-flying military aircraft outside their windows.

DYD: What was going on?

RSS: Junior officers in the Dominican military had launched a coup—a *golpe*, they called it. They were aiming to overthrow the military triumvirate led by Donald Reid Cabral, who some eighteen months earlier had removed and exiled the democratically elected President Juan Bosch—the man, incidentally, who had invited Peace Corps into the country.

DYD: What did the military triumvirate have against Bosch?

RSS: They accused him of being a communist.

DYD: Was it true?

RSS: There was no evidence of it being true. Bosch said no. I believed him. So did the junior officers, who called themselves Constitutionalists by the way, not rebels—and who declared themselves dedicated to restoring democracy in the Dominican Republic. They called upon the people to take to the streets, to take their country back, and for President Bosch to return from exile in Puerto Rico.

DYD: And the forces loyal to the Triumvirate resisted this effort?

RSS: Indeed they did.

DYD: So it was a dramatic situation. Dangerous.

RSS: It was dire. The violence was real. The American Embassy was urging American citizens to evacuate the island. President Johnson was worried about Soviet influence from Cuba and ordered in the Marines—25,000 of them. That was more troops than we had in Viet Nam at the time.

DYD: And the Peace Corps Volunteers?

RSS: They remained in their service placements.

DYD: Really? Doing what?

RSS: Performing their roles. Responding as best they could to the needs of the situation and to the community members they had committed to serve.

DYD: Responding how?

RSS: In many ways. But we had a number of Peace Corps nurses serving in the hospital in Santo Domingo, and their response is emblematic of the others. These nurses stayed in the hospital, working to keep it running even though most of the host country medical staff fled the city at the outbreak of violence. Other Peace Corps Volunteers rallied to help them, braving street fighting and snipers to join in the work at the hospital. Together, they took care of the wounded, conducted triage, assisted in surgery, dealt with power blackouts, cared for the dead.

DYD: It's hard to imagine.

RSS: It wasn't for them. But yes, they were impressive. Tad Szulc, the foreign correspondent who reported on the civil war for the *New York Times*, dedicated his book *Dominican Diary* to those Volunteers.[5]

DYD: But I'm not sure what to make of it all. When you asked me to imagine myself in the position of these Volunteers, what did you mean?

RSS: Let me make the situation more concrete for you. Every Volunteer serving in the Dominican Republic had a very important decision to make. I'd like you to try wrestling with that same decision.

DYD: What decision?

RSS: In my role as Peace Corps Director, it fell to me to ask this question of every Volunteer serving in the Dominican Republic: Do you want to remain in your service placement and continue to work in the community, or do you want to be evacuated to the United States?

DYD: You gave the Volunteers a choice in this?

RSS: As opposed to what? Making the decision for them? They'd made their own decision to join the Peace Corps, and given the extremity of the circumstances, they needed to make their own decision to stay or to leave.

DYD: A big decision.

RSS: For everyone, yes. But the Volunteers knew when they signed up that they might face significant physical risk.

DYD: Life and death risk?

RSS: That too. As part of the intake process, we required every Volunteer to submit their dental records to us.

DYD: So that you could identify their bodies?

RSS: If necessary, yes. In every way we knew how, we impressed upon the Volunteers that going overseas to make friends and build peace would be the toughest job they'd ever love.

DYD: Tough on all three levels I presume? Sensory, conscious, and spiritual?

RSS: That's exactly right. And for most Volunteers, the sensory level was not the toughest. So it was their choice to stay, and their choice to leave. I can tell you that I had no intention of sending them home and shuttering the program.

DYD: So you were at odds with the State Department on that point.

RSS: Yes, but the State Department has its own roles and purposes and we had ours. If we were going to effectively promote world peace and friendship, we needed to be free to make our own decisions.

DYD: That sounds worthy of a conversation in itself.

RSS: It is. We fought hard for the independence of Peace Corps as an organization. So in the end, it was my decision to make, not the State Department.[6]

DYD: And you invited the Volunteers to participate in your decision-making process.

RSS: I did.

RSS: And the nurses and other Volunteers who helped in the hospital evidently decided to stay.

RSS: They did.

DYD: What about the group as a whole?

RSS: Yes. But the point is for you to imagine making that decision for yourself.

DYD: Understood. But tell me what they decided anyway.

RSS: I just did. Of the 108 Peace Corps Volunteers serving in the Dominican Republic at the outbreak of the revolution, all but two decided to stay.

DYD: All but two?

RSS: And those two had just completed their full terms of service.

DYD: So virtually everyone decided to stay?

RSS: And among those who did, many decided to extend their terms of service until the uprising got sorted out.

DYD: Talk about self-transcendence.

RSS: We should. Yes. But for now, just imagine yourself in the role of a Peace Corps Volunteer in the Dominican Republic caught up in the April '65 revolution. You've been notified by Peace Corps staff that you have a decision to make. Are you going to remain in your service placement, or leave the country?

DYD: It's not a simple decision, is it? There's a lot to process.

RSS: Yes. And the thing to note is that your processing takes the form of a narrative arc.

DYD: By which you mean it involves a linked sequence of events?

RSS: Conscious events, yes.

DYD: So what's the sequence?

RSS: Let's take it one step at a time. I think you'll find it's more familiar than you think.

DYD: So what's the first step?

RSS: Step one is to tell me your felt response to my question.

DYD: This is familiar territory.

RSS: It should be.

DYD: Okay. So the question is: Do I want to stay in my service placement, or would I rather evacuate to safety? And what comes up for me in response is a rather strong ambivalence.

RSS: You're feeling more than one thing.

DYD: I'm feeling contradictory things, yes.

RSS: So let's go with the one that's most prominent for you right now.

DYD: Well, I'm definitely feeling relieved that you've given me the opportunity to leave.

RSS: Relieved about what?

DYD: The obvious, I think. The sniper fire terrifies me. I'm not sleeping well. I'm traumatized from working triage in the hospital. I don't want my family to be worried about me any longer.

RSS: You want to be safe, to be free of danger.

DYD: I do.

RSS: You're imagining yourself in a situation in which all the practical threats and difficulties posed by the fighting are no longer in play.

DYD: Yes. I feel safe. I can sleep. I'm not worried about getting shot, or who's been shot, or putting a tourniquet on someone's shattered leg. Someone I may well know from the neighborhood.

RSS: These are aspirations of yours.

DYD: Yes.

RSS: So pay attention for a moment to your felt sense of relief.

DYD: You mean, become consciously present to it?

RSS: That's it, yes. Now notice that your felt sense of relief is more than just a feeling. It's an act of discernment.

DYD: Discernment of what?

RSS: That's a question you can answer. Tell me what you—in your relief—are discerning, recognizing, figuring out.

DYD: Well. I suppose my relief is my recognition of the new possibility that your offer to evacuate has opened up for me. My relief is also discerning that this new possibility is a good thing for me.

RSS: And the possibility is?

DYD: Escaping the threat of physical danger and the trauma that comes with it.

RSS: There's a certain story line opening up in light of your response, wouldn't you say?

DYD: Is that the narrative arc? A felt response to a situation that discerns imaginative possibilities for the future?

RSS: It's the opening scene, yes. What comes next?

DYD: Well, I've discerned and affirmed the possibility of becoming physically safe. But I haven't made a decision about that yet—or taken action. We don't know how the story comes out.

RSS: Very good. Decision and action complete the narrative arc.

DYD: And you say there's a narrative image carrying that arc?

RSS: Consciousness is always carried.

DYD: So what's carrying the narrative arc of my relief?

RSS: You tell me. What's the guiding focus of your relief?

DYD: My guiding focus? I'm certainly relieved at the prospect of being physically safe—of getting to safety. I suppose that's the focus.

RSS: Very good.

DYD: Are you saying "physical safety" is the narrative image?

RSS: That's what it sounds like to me.

DYD: But "physical safety" doesn't capture the whole story.

RSS: Your narrative arc tells the story. Your narrative image guides and directs the way you tell it.

DYD: So I should be paying attention to the way that works.

RSS: Can you identify the way "physical safety" carries the arc of your performance?

DYD: You mean the way it shines the light on what I pay attention to?

RSS: And what it leaves in the dark, yes.

DYD: Well, it brings up the lights on how I hope things turn out, what I could do to make that happen, and what would count as success if I did.

RSS: So how are you imagining things would play out, if the story unfolds that way?

DYD: I'm sketchy on the details, but I can imagine gathering with other Volunteers at a meeting point, boarding a plane or ship, arriving in the U.S . . . being greeted by friends and family, that kind of thing.

RSS: You're imagining the kind of scene Eyewitness News would pick up if they were at the embassy covering the evacuation of Peace Corps Volunteers.

DYD: Yes. That's how I imagine the narrative playing out for me.

RSS: And how does that register with you?

DYD: As I said, I feel ambivalent about it.

RSS: You're of two minds?

DYD: It just feels wrong.

RSS: Evacuating does?

DYD: Yes.

RSS: "Wrong" is a rather elemental response, wouldn't you say?

DYD: I certainly would.

RSS: So let's tease this out. What's wrong with leaving? With being safe?

DYD: Not to put too fine a point on it, deciding to get on that plane would mean abandoning my friends at the very time peace is breaking down. That's what's wrong with it.

RSS: You're talking about your role.

DYD: I'm talking about my performance in my role—about the decisions I make, the actions I take.

RSS: And if you decide to get on that plane?

DYD: Getting on that plane would take me outside the horizon of what I care about as a Peace Corps Volunteer. I'd be abandoning my role.

RSS: Given the circumstances, no one would blame you, you know. I wouldn't have blamed any Volunteer who chose to evacuate.

DYD: But that's not the point, is it?

RSS: No? What is the point?

DYD: I'd blame myself.

RSS: For what?

DYD: I just told you.

RSS: I want to make sure I understand.

DYD: For deciding to abandon my role, abandon my friends, leave them in the lurch.

RSS: You're talking about a very different course of action, a very different narrative arc.

DYD: Presumably with a different narrative image.

RSS: Yes. Are you consciously present to it?

DYD: I'm aware of feeling resolute.

RSS: Resolved?

DYD: Yes.

RSS: What image is carrying your sense of feeling resolved?

DYD: I keep coming back to my image of the Volunteers working in the hospital.

RSS: How so?

DYD: They show me what it means to make friends and build peace as a Peace Corps Volunteer.

RSS: And you're feeling drawn to do the same.

DYD: It casts my concern for physical safety into serious question.

RSS: So you're not just evaluating choices and options, you're evaluating narrative images.[7]

DYD: It's a question of who I want to be. Who I want to become.

RSS: And you're feeling resolute about that.

DYD: Yes.

RSS: How do you imagine this turning out?

DYD: In practical terms? I don't know.

RSS: Does that matter?

DYD: It does. But it's not the most important thing.

RSS: Be it done to me?

DYD: Something like that.

RSS: Exactly like that.

DYD: So you think the spirit is present to me in this response?

RSS: I think you're consciously present to the spirit.

PRACTICAL
IDEALISM

Chicago: On Releasing the Spiritual Power of the People[1]

RSS: So you think you'd have decided to stay in the Dominican Republic?

DYD: Amazed as I am to say it, I felt tugged to stay. It's surprising.

RSS: Those experiences are always amazing. But they're only truly surprising if you're not accounting for the part played by the spirit.

DYD: Yes. But in my case, it was only a role-play.

RSS: What do you mean "only"?

DYD: I mean I wasn't actually in Santo Domingo.

RSS: You mean physically?

DYD: Yes.

RSS: So you're thinking the deciding factor here is the sensory component of the situation?

DYD: I'm thinking that's rather relevant. Don't you? In my role-play experience, there was no actual sniper fire, no shattered limb to bind, no plane waiting to evacuate me.

RSS: Certainly that's relevant, especially when physical safety is a potentially driving factor in decision-making.

DYD: But you're saying there are other factors to consider?

RSS: You know there are. Do you remember the point of the exercise?

DYD: The point was to account for the conscious and spiritual components of the Volunteers' performance.

RSS: More specifically, the point was for you to become consciously present to the narrative image carrying the Volunteers' performance.[2]

DYD: I did feel tugged.

RSS: You felt tugged to transcend your desire for personal safety.

DYD: To make friends and build peace.

RSS: The spirit was present to you. You were consciously present to the spirit.

DYD: Okay. But here's my question. Can we feel truly called to an option we don't really have?

RSS: You doubt that?

DYD: There's something unlikely about it, isn't there? Something contradictory?

RSS: Only if you think of it as a question to be resolved using logic. But it's not. The best way to tackle your question is to test it in your own experience.

DYD: And how would I do that?

RSS: Ask yourself: have you ever felt the urge to pursue your highest aspirations—but at the same time, couldn't concretely imagine the way forward? Couldn't imagine yourself in the proper role?

DYD: Have I ever aspired to be a person I couldn't imagine becoming? Have I ever felt tugged to do something—to contribute something—without knowing how to proceed?

RSS: Well?

DYD: The answer is yes.

RSS: Those experiences are poignant, aren't they?

DYD: To say the least. In my experience, they're distressing. There's a heightened sense of a personal gap—of the need for help.

RSS: Just ask Sister Mary-Frances.[3]

DYD: That's where we left her, isn't it.

RSS: Feeling pinched in her role? Tugged to transcendence? Yes.

DYD: Vexed at not knowing what she could do to improve things.

RSS: Right.

DYD: And you were hoping she might become present to the narrative image constraining her performance.

RSS: And present to her capacity for self-transcendence, yes.

DYD So that's another thing. Were you presuming she'd be familiar with the model—or the relationship of the key factors?[4]

RSS: Not at all, since she didn't really need to be.

DYD: No?

RSS: It helps, of course. But the factors and their relations are operative within us whether we are explicitly aware of them or not—whether we can name them or not.

DYD: Role, horizon of concern, narrative image, conscious arc, presence to the spirit. Do you ever worry that making these connections is just too complex to grasp?

RSS: We are made for this level of complexity. It's who we are. It's how we operate. Why else would we find it so fascinating?

DYD: But you can't be saying it's simple.

RSS: I'm saying it's natural. We do it whether we realize it or not.

DYD: But doing it well? Doing it mindfully?

RSS: Yes. That's trickier.

DYD: So tricky that most of the time we're not explicitly mindful of being conscious at all. We don't think about the narrative image carrying our performance. Most of the time we just react to our circumstances.

RSS: So it's a good thing the spirit is present to us, calling to us. Regardless.

DYD: And when we *are* present?

RSS: You know the answer. When we *are* present, we're more likely to adjust our performance in light of that awareness. Just like you did in the role-play.

DYD: Adjust our performance in the direction of self-transcendence.

RSS: That's right.

DYD: Do you ever worry that this sounds too good to be true?

RSS: Of course not. The fact that it's true doesn't make it any easier.

DYD: Okay. Let's go back to Sister Mary-Frances. What did you do to draw her attention to the narrative image carrying her performance?

RSS: I was as direct as I could be. I asked her for any images or associations that came to mind in connection with her sense of being constricted in her role at St. Patrick's.[5]

DYD: And?

RSS: She asked me to clarify the question.

DYD: No surprise there.

RSS: No. But after she reflected for a moment, she asked me whether I was familiar with the cluster of Catholic churches in Back of the Yards.

DYD: Back of the Yards?

RSS: It's the neighborhood on the south side, just west of the old Union Stockyards.

DYD: I know the neighborhood. I'm just surprised by the image. It seems a bit random, doesn't it?

RSS: How so?

DYD: I would have expected her to come up with an image closer to home—St. Patrick's maybe, or Des Plaines. An image more directly related to her vexation.

RSS: There's a lesson in that.

DYD: Be curious? Don't presume?

RSS: Exactly.

DYD: Okay. What cluster of churches was she talking about?

RSS: Beginning in the early 1870s, the bishops in Chicago approved the formation of seven ethnically distinct Catholic parishes in Back of the Yards. Over a period of fifty years, they approved the construction of seven Catholic churches—all within a half-mile of each other.

DYD: And by ethnically distinct, you mean . . . ?

RSS: German, Irish, Bohemian, French, Slovak, Lithuanian, and Polish.

DYD: That's quite a cluster.

RSS: It is.

DYD: So what connection was Sister Mary-Frances making

between that cluster of churches and the constriction she was experiencing in her role?

RSS: It turns out she was more focused on the decision-making connected to the cluster of churches than she was on the churches themselves.

DYD: I'm not sure what connection you mean. I picture Back of the Yards as a crowded, growing, urban, turn-of-the-century neighborhood inhabited by communities of ethnically diverse Catholics.

RSS: That's right.

DYD: I can imagine community members making all kinds of decisions—practical, personal, social, economic—where to live, where to work, and who to invite for dinner.

RSS: Good. What about the religious decisions they were making?

DYD: I suppose that cluster would have oriented their religious decision-making. The options they considered.

RSS: It would have served as a narrative image for them, yes.

DYD: Catholics of various ethnic stripes would have headed to Mass on Sunday—to Confession on Saturday—but they would have attended their own ethnic churches. And during the week, they would have sent their children to their own ethnic schools.

RSS: The immigrant communities would have gone their own ways religiously, and probably wouldn't have thought twice about it.

DYD: Is that what Sister Mary-Frances was concerned about?

RSS: Not exactly. Sister Mary-Frances was more focused on the decisions being made by the bishops than she was the people living in Back of the Yards.

DYD: You mean the decision-making that clustered the churches and schools in the first place?

RSS: Yes.

DYD: I know next to nothing about those decisions.

RSS: Then let's get some context. I'm sure you know that for many decades the Chicago stockyards were the largest and busiest in the world?

DYD: I know that in 1916 Carl Sandberg wrote a poem that valorized Chicago as the "hog butcher for the world."[6]

RSS: Yes. Sandberg gave voice to a narrative image that was drawing thousands and thousands of immigrants to Back of the Yards every year. But here's the thing. In addition to their desire to earn a living and support their families, these immigrants brought with them the desire to have their own churches and schools.

DYD: And that's what brought the bishops into play.

RSS: Right. Given the horizon of concern that came with their roles, they had some important decisions to make concerning the religious needs of the Catholic communities immigrating to Chicago.

DYD: How did they respond to those developments?

RSS: As it happened, they followed a rather straightforward script. Once a bishop determined that a particular community of immigrants was large enough and economically strong enough to support a church and school, he would greenlight their request for a parish and take it upon himself to recruit priests to lead the parish and nuns to run the school.

DYD: And the communities would take responsibility for raising the money needed to design and build their churches and schools?

RSS: That's how it worked. Still does. In those days, getting a new church built was a process that took years. Decades, in some cases.

DYD: So various communities of Catholic immigrants were clustering in Back of the Yards in their search for work, and the bishops decided to cluster their churches and schools too?

RSS: Basically.

DYD: Was this pattern of decision-making confined to Back of the Yards?

RSS: No. The bishops created ethnically distinct parishes all over the city during this period—south side, west side, north side—though the pattern was particularly concentrated in Back of the Yards.

DYD: I can understand why Sister Mary-Frances picked up on the image—though I'm not clear what she found so vexing. To the bishops, I imagine it seemed the obvious thing to do. A community wants to create a parish. You'd want to help them.

RSS: Yes.

DYD: So the bishops executed a series of decisions that was clearly pragmatic, if not terribly strategic.

RSS: Or terribly prophetic, I might add.

DYD: Okay. So what connection was Sister Mary-Frances making?

RSS: As she put it to me, church leaders in the habit of creating ethnically distinct churches and schools had no trouble racially segregating them later on.

DYD: Later on?

RSS: Black and Mexican immigrants began to arrive in Chicago in large numbers only around 1915. This new wave coincided with the appointment of George Cardinal Mundelein as Archbishop of Chicago. He led the Church for the next twenty-five years, before passing away in 1940.[7]

DYD: I gather then, that Sister Mary-Frances's vexation was linked to Cardinal Mundelein's decision-making in particular?

RSS: The consequences of it, yes—for herself, for young Black women, and for race relations in the Church, Catholic high schools, and the city.

DYD: Would you say Sister Mary-Frances was in some way keyed into the narrative image carrying Cardinal Mundelein's performance in his role?

RSS: Sister Mary-Frances was astute. Her vexation was astute.

DYD: Well, I haven't a clue as to what his narrative image would be.

RSS: None at all? In the Peace Corps example, you made all the relevant connections.

DYD: Yes, but in that case you told me what the narrative image was, and we worked out the connections to the other factors from there. Besides, when you gave me a role in the role-play you focused my attention on the data of my own consciousness. I had a lot to work with.

RSS: And in this case?

DYD: In this case, we're focused on the conscious performance of Cardinal Mundelein and the other Bishops.

RSS: And you don't have direct access to that data.

DYD: It's even more complicated than that, isn't it? What we're really talking about is the connection between Cardinal Mundelein's performance in his role and the constriction Sister Mary-Frances experienced in hers.

RSS: To be fair, we're talking about the constriction Cardinal Mundelein was experiencing too.

DYD: There's an awful lot going on.

RSS: There always is. But you know how to think with the model. You know the key factors.

DYD: I know how to relate them. But in this case, so many of the factors are unknown.

RSS: Where are you stuck?

DYD: At the beginning, I'd say. In particular, I have no idea what narrative image is carrying Cardinal Mundelein's performance.

RSS: You think it's unknowable?

DYD: You don't?

RSS: It's an unknown, not a mystery. You solve for unknown factors by pinning down their relationship to the factors you already know.

DYD: What are you saying? That if I can correlate the narrative image with the other factors in the model, I can extrapolate it from what I already know?

RSS: Exactly.

DYD: But any extrapolation would have to be in the form of an hypothesis, wouldn't it?

RSS: Because you could get it wrong? Because you might have to adjust or revise your proposal? Because you'll have to answer all the relevant questions, and account for all relevant data of sense, consciousness, and spiritual experiencing?

DYD: Yes. That.

RSS: It's an empirical question, so there's no way around it. What's your hypothesis?

DYD: I don't know.

RSS: You mean you're not certain.

DYD: I mean I can say at least this much. Whatever narrative image was carrying the performance of Cardinal Mundelein and the bishops, it wasn't the narrative image Paul was commending to the church leaders in Galatia.

RSS: And what evidence do you have for that?

DYD: You pointed it out. Paul was hoping for a conscious performance different from the one he was getting from the church leaders in Galatia. I'd say that performance was different from the bishops' performance in Back of the Yards too.

RSS: And that performance was?

DYD: Again. It's what you said earlier. Paul was urging the church leaders in Galatia to create a particular kind of church community. He wanted them to take the lead in overcoming the divisions that had emerged within the community.

RSS: Go on.

DYD: Evidently, economic and social differences were dividing the Galatian community. Some community members were Jewish rather than Greek, slave rather than free, female rather than male. The community was apparently structuring itself in terms of those divisions and Paul wanted the church leaders to lead the community beyond them.

RSS: And the bishops?

DYD: The bishops? Given their decision-making in Back of

the Yards, it's clear they did not share Paul's concern to lead the Church beyond the key divisions in the community. Not the divisions rooted in ethnic and racial differences, anyway.

RSS: You mean the bishops didn't make much of an effort to establish multi-ethnic, multi-racial churches and schools.

DYD: On the contrary, they used ethnic and racial differences as their organizing principle for growing the Church.

RSS: Okay. It wasn't Paul's approach. What was it then? What narrative image do you think was at work here?

DYD: What's my hypothesis?

RSS: Yes. What's your hypothesis?

DYD: I have to say what comes to mind is the image of a holding company.

RSS: A holding company?

DYD: A holding company for a set of ethnically distinct Catholic parishes.

RSS: And what role do the bishops perform in your holding company?

DYD: Operators in chief, responsible for policy and oversight. Like the managers of any holding company, they would recruit and hire the priests and nuns needed to fill administrative and leadership and roles in the churches and schools held by the diocese.

RSS: It's not very catchy.

DYD: But that's not the question, is it?

RSS: No. It's not.

DYD: The question is, does the hypothesis account for the conscious performance of the bishops in their roles? Does it account for the relevant performance factors?

RSS: And what factors would you say your notion of a holding company accounts for?

DYD: The main ones—the aspirations the bishops were seeking to realize for the Church, and the decisions they ultimately made to realize them.

RSS: Okay. As far as that accounting goes, we know that for over fifty years the bishops of Chicago created parishes and schools for German Catholics, Irish Catholics, Bohemian Catholics, French Catholics, Slovak Catholics, Lithuanian Catholics, and Polish Catholics.

DYD: And that was just in Back of the Yards.

RSS: Right. They also created parishes for English Catholics, Italian Catholics, Dutch Catholics, Black Catholics, Mexican Catholics, and others.

DYD: Based on that evidence, it's plausible that the bishops' performance was carried by the image of creating a holding company for a set of ethnically distinct churches and schools.

RSS: Would you care to guess what Sister Mary-Frances offered as her hypothesis?

DYD: What was it? I wouldn't want to guess. But I'm certainly curious.

RSS: "Separate but equal."[8]

DYD: Seriously?

RSS: That surprises you?

DYD: It's a bit over the top, don't you think?

RSS: It seems you do.

DYD: I suppose "separate but equal" might make some sense if I take the words literally.

RSS: You mean, it's conceivable the bishops were aiming to create a diocese of ethnically separate but otherwise equal Catholic churches and schools?

DYD: It just doesn't sit right. You know better than I do that "separate but equal" is a racially loaded phrase. It was central to the Supreme Court decision that legalized racial segregation in the United States. It legitimated Jim Crow.

RSS: Yes. I'm very familiar with *Plessy v. Ferguson*. In 1896, the Supreme Court ruled that a person's right to equal protection under the law—a right guaranteed to all Americans by the 14th Amendment—would not be violated by the act of creating racially segregated facilities and services, provided those facilities and services were equal.

DYD: But "separate but equal" was always a hoax. Black and White schools were never equal. Black and White social services were never equal. Black and White justice was never equal under the law.

RSS: True. And that's what the Supreme Court unanimously ruled in *Brown v. Board of Education*.[9]

DYD: But that was fifty years later.

RSS: Yes, 1954—early days in my work with the Catholic Interracial Council and my conversations with Sister Mary-Frances and the other principals. Chief Justice Warren ruled that "separate but equal" was nothing more than a cover story for a pernicious narrative image.

DYD: The notion that people with white skin are superior to people whose skin color is different.

RSS: Justice Warren was particularly concerned with the constricting effect this narrative image was having on young children of color.

DYD: He said that in his ruling?

RSS: Words explicitly to that effect, yes.

DYD: And Sister Mary-Frances knew all this?

RSS: Of course she did.

DYD: She knew "separate but equal" opened the door to a massive infusion of racial bias into local laws, policies, and public practices.

RSS: And according to her hypothesis, into the Catholic high school system as well.

DYD: But it's an hypothesis, isn't it? We still have to ask: "Is it so?"

RSS: Is what so? Is it so that the bishops' decision-making opened the Catholic high schools to the sin of racism?

DYD: No. I think that's clear enough. Is it so that "separate but equal" was actually the narrative image carrying the bishops' performance.

RSS: You think "holding company" might be more apt?

DYD: Frankly, I do. But again, I don't know for sure. That's the point.

RSS: And you're wondering how to sort this out?

DYD: I'm just trying to think with the model.

RSS: So let's stick with that. Take Cardinal Mundelein as your example. How would you think about him?

DYD: How would I use the model to think about his performance?

RSS: Right. How would you correlate all the key factors?

DYD: All of them? I'd begin by thinking about Cardinal Mundelein as a person in a role. I'd think of him next as a conscious person—as using his mind to respond to the concerns he was addressing in his role.

RSS: So in this case, let's focus on his response to the new wave of Black and Brown immigrants in Chicago.

DYD: Okay. Third then, I'd think of his conscious response to this situation as unfolding in a sequence of conscious acts—in a narrative arc, we called it.

RSS: What conscious acts in particular?

DYD: Well, I'd begin with his felt response to the situation—the gaps he discerned, the opportunities he imagined, the options he considered, and ultimately the decisions he made to address the gaps and develop the opportunities.

RSS: Yes.

DYD: Fourth, of course, I'd also be thinking that his conscious performance was carried by a narrative image of some sort. I'd be curious about that correlation.

RSS: And what about the spirit?

DYD: Yes, the spirit would have been present to Cardinal Mundelein's conscious performance—to the narrative arc of his response—consciously tugging and calling him to transcend himself. That would be the fifth point. Sixth, Cardinal Mundelein would have been to one degree or another consciously present to all this—to himself in his role, to the narrative image carrying the narrative arc of his performance, and to the spirit's presence to his response.

RSS: You've come a long way, haven't you?

DYD: It seems that I have, thanks to you.

RSS: You did the work. You pinned down the key factors in the data of your consciousness.

DYD: Okay, but thanks to you I'm now clear that if I want to understand Cardinal Mundelein's performance—whether his performance was making things better, making things worse, or generating some mix of the two—I'd have to account for the key factors and their relations.

RSS: So let's do that.

DYD: Do what?

RSS: You know. Let's think through Cardinal Mundelein's response to the new wave of immigration in Chicago and see where the relevant questions take us.

DYD: Do we know enough about Cardinal Mundelein to do that?

RSS: I'm not an historian, but I know what was going on with the Church during that period.

DYD: So what are you suggesting?

RSS: I'm suggesting that we could each take a part. I'd take on the role of Cardinal Mundelein.

DYD: And I'd use the model to ask the relevant questions?[10]

RSS: Why not?

DYD: Well, the main difficulty is that we don't have direct access to the data of Cardinal Mundelein's consciousness—or his presence to the spirit.

RSS: That's true. We'd have to scour his letters, sermons, and essays for insight to that information. But we already know the main decisions he made in responding to the arrival of the new immigrants. So let's get a sense of how the factors come together and see what we can extrapolate about Cardinal Mundelein's performance.

DYD: Leaving open what we don't know, or what we can't say for sure.

RSS: There's no way around that, but let's do this.

DYD: Okay then, your Eminence, I appreciate your willingness to take my questions. I know you are busy, and that your role as Archbishop engages you in a wide range of concerns.

RSS: It's a complex role, yes.

DYD: So let me concentrate on just one aspect of your concerns. I'm particularly interested in how you responded to the new wave of Black and Brown immigrants that began to arrive in Chicago about the time you were appointed Archbishop.

RSS: You're talking about 1915. That new wave of immigrants was a good thing for the war effort, but it also presented a major challenge to the city and to the Church. Those challenges became thornier as time went on. What are you wondering about?

DYD: Many things, really. But let me ask first about the situation itself. As you think back on that new influx of immigrants, what would you say was the main catalyst for it?

RSS: I'd have to say it was the Great War. First of all, the fighting in Europe shut off the regular flow of immigrants from across the Atlantic. Second, that gave rise to a variety of efforts here in Chicago to recruit workers from different areas, notably Texas and the American south. In addition, there was a prominent ad campaign by *The Chicago Defender* urging Black people in the rural south to move north to Chicago, where the opportunities were better.

DYD: What you're saying suggests that prior to World War I, the immigrant community in Chicago would have been ethnically quite diverse, but racially much less so. Would that be a fair assessment?

RSS: That's fair. The Mexican workers from Texas were new to Chicago. Most of them were Catholic, of course—but there couldn't have been more than a thousand or two in the city at that point.

DYD: Where did they tend to settle?

RSS: For the most part, they moved into a formerly German neighborhood on the near west side, just south of the Loop. Black residents had begun to move there too. It was rapidly becoming racially mixed.

DYD: What about the Black community at the time?

RSS: In comparison, the Black community was already quite established—though only a small percentage of that community was Catholic. The number of Black residents in Chicago had been growing steadily for several decades, doubling roughly every ten years. By the time I was appointed Archbishop, there was a lively, self-contained community of approximately 100,000 people crowded around a six or seven block commercial stretch of South State Street. The commercial area began at 31st Street, and the residential area stretched east to Lake Michigan and as far south as Hyde Park.

DYD: You're talking about Bronzeville?

RSS: That's what it came to be called, yes. The area was widely referred to as the Black Belt at the time. But as the Black community grew and expanded to majority status over the next ten years or so, they gave the community a more appropriate name.

DYD: If as you say, only a small percentage of the Bronzeville community was Catholic, what religious affiliations did the others tend to have?

RSS: Many were affiliated with Baptist or African Methodist Episcopal Churches—others with storefront Pentecostal or holiness churches. Olivet Baptist Church had a large and growing congregation. Quinn Chapel, an old AME Church, was prominent too. There were also quite a few individuals who were unchurched.

DYD: What about Catholic churches?

RSS: There was one only one Black Catholic Church in the area. St. Monica's. In fact, it was the only Black Catholic Church in the entire city—but it was small and struggling, and had been for some twenty years.

DYD: I was under the impression there were quite a few Catholic churches on the south side—in Back of the Yards, for instance.

RSS: That's true. And not just in Back of the Yards. But those churches were in other neighborhoods and dedicated to serving other south side communities. In fact, one of my first acts as the new Archbishop was to consecrate Corpus Christi, a new church on the south side. It was a beautiful limestone church built by an Irish community in a parish originally established by Archbishop Feehan in 1901.

DYD: So they'd been working to build their church for a while. If my math is correct, they'd been working to fund and build it for around fifteen years?

RSS: That's right. And as you might expect, they were very proud of it.

DYD: St. Monica's was fairly close by?

RSS: About twenty minutes away by foot. So yes.

DYD: And how was Corpus Christi doing?

RSS: At the time? The parish was robust. The headcount at Sunday Mass was routinely around two thousand.

DYD: What did you make of that contrast? Corpus Christi is going strong. St. Monica's is struggling.

RSS: The influx of new people was an opportunity, wasn't it?

DYD: An opportunity for what?

RSS: An opportunity to grow St. Monica's.

DYD: So you were aiming for growth. How did you approach that?

RSS: The main problem was a lack of leadership.

DYD: On whose part?

RSS: There's a story there. In the beginning, St. Monica's had fine leadership and a strong start in the Diocese. Archbishop Feehan established the parish in 1887—about thirty years before my time—by placing a strong bet on the small Black community that had been worshipping in the basement of Old St. Mary's Church, downtown.

DYD: What bet was that?

RSS: There couldn't have been more than eight hundred Black Catholics in the city as a whole, and only a small percentage of them were attending Old St. Mary's. But as I understand the story, representatives from some twenty families approached the archbishop and asked him to establish a parish for them on the south side where they lived.

DYD: Twenty families? That would be, what? Sixty adults at most?

RSS: Maybe fewer. It wasn't a large number. But the arch-bishop was extremely supportive of the idea. So he reached out to a young Black priest named Augustus Tolton and recruited him to lead the parish. I think Father Tolton's availability was a main reason Archbishop Feehan agreed to establish the parish.

DYD: I believe I've heard of Father Tolton. He was born into slavery in Missouri, wasn't he? Theologically trained in Rome? Became the first Black Catholic priest ordained in North America?

RSS: That's right. Father Tolton was the first Black man ordained to the priesthood in North America—and at the time, he was the only one.

DYD: And his leadership abilities?

RSS: Exemplary. He was young, charismatic, and proved to be an excellent fundraiser. He completed phase one of St. Monica's capital campaign in just seven years, while growing the parish to over fifty families. He was completely dedicated to the Black Catholic community in Chicago and to providing that community with their own church home.

DYD: So St. Monica's got off to a promising start.

RSS: It did. And in 1894, in a large public ceremony covered by *The Chicago Tribune* and with a number of priests from local parishes concelebrating the Liturgy, Archbishop Feehan dedicated the first phase of St. Monica's building plan. It was an impressive Romanesque building located on South Dearborn at 36th Street. The second phase was already underway. It called for the construction of the formal nave and the church towers. The goal was to have that completed by the millennium.

DYD: But something went wrong?

RSS: Tragically, Father Tolton died three years later. He was just forty-three years old, and the parish never recovered from the loss. The Church building was never completed, pledge support declined, and ultimately Archbishop Quigley, my predecessor, attached St. Monica's to St. Elizabeth's as a mission church.

DYD: St. Elizabeth's?

RSS: Yes, a strong Irish parish with a beautiful church facility just five blocks south of St. Monica's on Wabash.

DYD: And that's where things stood when you were appointed archbishop?

RSS: The arrangement between the two parishes was well intended, but it wasn't terribly fruitful.

DYD: And you saw an opportunity to improve the situation?

RSS: I did.

DYD: So tell me, how were you thinking about that? What were you going for?

RSS: I'd say my chief aim was to renew the leadership at St. Monica's and to restore the parish to its former status.

DYD: Your aim was to replace Farther Tolton's leadership, complete the construction of the church, and renew St. Monica's as a parish?

RSS: Right.

DYD: So how did that plan line up with your broader plans for the Church on the south side?

RSS: I'm not sure what you're asking me.

DYD: I'm still thinking about the immigration question. You indicated earlier that the new waves of immigrants were causing some upheaval.

RSS: Yes, the predominantly Irish community already in place on the south side found the growth of the Black community to be disturbing. The racial animus was significant.

DYD: So the problem you faced was multifaceted. There was the problem of racial tension and hostility on the one hand. Beyond that, the people immigrating from the rural south would have faced serious social and economic hardships—housing shortages, inadequate employment, not to mention massive cultural disruptions. How did you address those problems?

RSS: Means and ends, means and ends. That's what you have to keep in mind.

DYD: I'm not sure what you're getting at.

RSS: I was extremely concerned about the racial tensions in the community and the hardships faced by the immigrants and their families. But you have to remember two things. First, I was archbishop of the Catholic Church in Chicago—not the mayor or the governor. And second, the Church has always met the needs of its people through the local parish.

DYD: You're referring to the limits to what you could and couldn't do in your role?

RSS: That's right. I was in charge of the Church, not public policy and law enforcement. My concern was to strengthen St. Monica's—to recruit religious leaders committed to serving the religious and material needs of the immigrant community.

DYD: So you wanted to strengthen the institutional capacity of the Church in Bronzeville.

RSS: And not just Bronzeville; I was concerned about the whole diocese.

DYD: Understood. But how did you decide to handle the leadership question at St. Monica's?

RSS: The Church was such a minor presence in the immigrant community, and the energy at St. Monica's was disappointingly low. So it was clear I needed to shake things up, to take strong action.

DYD: What did you do?

RSS: I contacted the Provincial of the Society of the Divine Word, and I invited the Divine Word Missionaries to take on the task of operating St. Monica's and ministering to the community.

DYD: The Divine Word Missionaries? I'm not too familiar with that order. What prompted you to reach out to them?

RSS: First of all, I knew they were in the process of establishing a province in North America, so the timing was good. Second, they were a comparatively new and energetic religious order. The Society of the Divine Word had been established in the Netherlands only about forty years earlier. And last but not least, they were committed to serving communities of color and indigenous peoples around the world.

DYD: That was their charism?

RSS: It fit the profile of St. Monica's quite nicely, don't you think? Besides, they had developed a good track record by that point. The Society had been operating a successful mission in Togo, West Africa, for nearly twenty-five years.

DYD: In Africa?

RSS: Yes.

DYD: Your plan for St. Monica's was to invite the Divine Word Missionaries to establish themselves on the south side of Chicago and evangelize the larger Black community in Bronzeville?

RSS: And it worked! Father Eckhart—he was the first of the Divine Word fathers to serve the community—baptized thousands of souls in the Bronzeville community. Not all of them at St. Monica's, as things turned out, but I knew I could count on the dedication of the Divine Word Missionaries to the people in Bronzeville. Their dedication was crucial to the growth and strength of the Church in the ensuing decades. It still is.

DYD: Well, you obviously shook things up. But what about the roads you didn't take? What were you thinking about the leadership capacity of St. Elizabeth's? Or Corpus Christi for that matter? Weren't they serious options for you?

RSS: In what sense?

DYD: I don't know. In Corpus Christi you had a robust Catholic community just twenty minutes away. What connections between the two communities were possible? And St. Elizabeth's was already formally committed to St. Monica's. Why go to Togo?

RSS: Because I can't imagine how Corpus Christi could have provided the necessary leadership. St. Monica's and Corpus Christi were different parishes with different issues and different needs. And St. Elizabeth's had already demonstrated the deficiency of its capacity to steward St. Monica's. The need for a new direction was evident.

DYD: That seems . . . I don't know. How did it seem to you?

RSS: It was what it was.

DYD: And what would you say it was?

RSS: All right. That's enough of this. It was profoundly disturbing. That's what it was.

DYD: Welcome back, Sarge.

RSS: It was time for me to shift out of my role.

DYD: Evidently. So what did you find disturbing about the archbishop's line of thinking?

RSS: Didn't you notice? The narrative image carrying Cardinal Mundelein's handling of St. Monica's was terribly constraining.

DYD: Honestly, I didn't know what to make of the cardinal's decision-making. But what are you saying? That you were consciously present to the narrative image carrying his performance?

RSS: I became aware of it, yes.

DYD: Are you suggesting Cardinal Mundelein was explicitly aware of it too?

RSS: I wouldn't say so, no. The cardinal strongly embraced his role. That's certain. But I don't have the impression he was terribly curious or reflective about his performance.

DYD: Whereas you were?

RSS: Not initially. When I first took on the role, I was focused on the decisions Cardinal Mundelein was making. But your questions heightened my awareness to myself in that role, and to the way I was using my mind to make those decisions.

DYD: And that led you to notice the narrative image carrying your performance?

RSS: It threw me back on myself, yes.

DYD: And you became aware of being constrained?

RSS: And disturbed.

DYD: Help me understand that.

RSS: Didn't you notice the pattern in Cardinal Mundelein's answers to the questions you asked about his decision-making?

DYD: The pattern in his decision-making? I can't say I picked up on that—though I did notice he drew some pretty strict lines between St. Monica's and Corpus Christi, and between the Black community immigrating to the south side and the Irish residents already there.

RSS: Right. He wasn't much for seeking commonalities.

DYD: He tended to focus on differences.

RSS: Differences rooted in sensory-based particulars.

DYD: Sensory-based particulars?

RSS: You know. Differences based on a person's skin color; on where they live; on the church they attend; on the devotional acts they perform.

DYD: Differences based on who, what, when, and where?

RSS: Exactly.

DYD: Okay, but what are you getting at? What's wrong with making distinctions like those?

RSS: There's nothing wrong with it. Up to a point.

DYD: Up to what point?

RSS: Up to the point it becomes irrelevant or inappropriate to use sensory-based particulars to distinguish individuals or identify groups.

DYD: And that's what Cardinal Mundelein was doing? Pushing those distinctions beyond the point of relevance?

RSS: He was.

DYD: And you found that to be constraining?

RSS: Disturbingly so.

DYD: Because?

RSS: I think you know the answer to that question.

DYD: Well, knowing you, I'd say you found it disturbing to make decisions based on sensory particulars, because that's not where we encounter each other as persons.

RSS: It's not where we encounter each other in the spirit either.

DYD: Okay. But this is a strong critique of Cardinal Mundelein's performance. Are you saying it emerged within your performance of the role?

RSS: Yes. When I was in Cardinal Mundelein's role and your questions heightened my awareness of my decision-making, I became consciously present to the constraint in my performance.

DYD: How would you characterize that performance?

RSS: It seemed to me that in my performance as Cardinal Mundelein, I was just moving the pieces around.

DYD: Pieces—not persons?

RSS: That's it. Parishes, Church properties, leaders, religious orders—pieces identified by their sensory particulars.

DYD: The Diocese was a game board? You were playing chess?

RSS: More like the game of Risk.

DYD: That's the narrative image that came to you?

RSS: It's the image that was in my mind, yes.

DYD: But Risk wasn't available in the cardinal's day. It was created in the 1950s, during the Cold War.

RSS: Fair enough. I'm obviously not Cardinal Mundelein, and I can't be sure what image was in his mind. But whatever it was, the narrative image carrying his conscious performance would have been functionally the same. The cardinal was trying to hedge risk, exploit opportunities, and change things up.

DYD: By moving the pieces around.

RSS: In an effort to manage—to improve—a volatile immigration situation that he understood to be rooted in a clash of sensory-based differences, yes.

DYD: A performance you experienced as constraining.

RSS: Once your questions directed my focus beyond the sensory-based particulars of the situation, I began to attend to its other components. I became mindful of it as a tangle of roles, aspirations, decisions, actions, and narrative images.

DYD: As logjam, not a game board.

RSS: Right.

DYD: And you couldn't sustain the role.

RSS: I couldn't sustain the positions Cardinal Mundelein was taking in his role. If he'd faced into the questions you asked me, I don't think he could have sustained those positions either. Not in good conscience, anyway.

DYD: So you broke out of the role.

RSS: That's the thing. There's a terrible cost to the Church, to Church members, to the community at large, and to the wider world when leaders like Cardinal Mundelein fail to account for the conscious and spiritual components of the situations they face.

DYD: Everybody pays. That's what you recognized.

RSS: But not just on the level of sensory particulars, we pay on the level of consciousness and spirit too.

DYD: Can you clarify that?

RSS: You're familiar with the Red Summer of 1919, aren't you?[11]

DYD: The Red Summer? I've heard of it, though I'm not

terribly familiar with the details. I know that right after World War I, there was a string of violent clashes between White and Black people in a number of US cities. I don't remember them all, but I remember the Tulsa massacre was the most egregious and notorious.

RSS: They were all egregious.

DYD: Yes.

RSS: In Chicago, it was late July 1919, when Black and White residents on the south side clashed for five days of horrific violence. That was two years before Tulsa and four years after Cardinal Mundelein's installation. Thirty Black residents died—seven shot by the police, the rest singled out and killed by gangs of young men in their teens and twenties.

DYD: What gangs?

RSS: They were called "athletic clubs"—and they were mostly Irish, mostly Catholic too, focused on personal fitness, ethnic identity, and group solidarity. These gangs marauded through the Bronzeville area, hunting and chasing down Black people—threatening them, injuring them, murdering them.

DYD: Was the community able to defend itself?

RSS: Eighteen White people were killed, and many others injured—a considerable number by sniper fire.

DYD: Sniper fire?

RSS: Yes. Black veterans recently returned from World War I set up snipers' nests in the 34th Street Y and other strategic locations. When the gang members, armed with their hammers, bats, and handguns, took their cars and trucks down State Street in search of Black residents, the snipers opened fire on them.

DYD: They had rifles?

RSS: Rifles they brought home with them from the War. They knew how to use them too. Overall, five hundred people were injured badly enough to go to the hospital—two hundred White people and more than three hundred Black people.

DYD: What finally put a stop to the violence?

RSS: After five days, Mayor Thompson finally asked the governor to deploy the National Guard, and they suppressed it. A heavy rain helped, and the archdiocese ordered local parishes to say Mass five times a day in an effort to keep their people off the streets.

DYD: But Chicago was never the same.

RSS: The south side never was, no.

DYD: And you're thinking Cardinal Mundelein had something to do with all this? I can't imagine he was in favor of the violence, or the mob behavior of the gangs.

RSS: Of course not. But let's think about that. Do you recall the incident that led to the outbreak of the violence?

DYD: You mean the drowning of the teenage boy?

RSS: Yes. His name was Eugene Williams. He was seventeen years old, and his death was not an accidental drowning. It was second-degree murder. I don't know the age or the name of Eugene's assailant. He was never charged.

DYD: He was throwing rocks at Eugene, wasn't he?

RSS: That's right. It was very hot that day. Eugene and three friends were swimming in Lake Michigan—jumping off a raft they had pulled together from boards and barrels they found along the shore. They weren't very good swimmers, but they knew that if they stayed near the raft they'd be safe. Unfortunately, their raft drifted close to the 29th Street Beach—a beach that local White residents claimed for their own. Black residents were expected to swim at the 25th Street beach. Mostly, they did.

DYD: But not that day.

RSS: No. That day a group of Black residents decided to occupy a portion of the 29th Street beach.

DYD: Occupy it?

RSS: You know. Swim. Spread out their blankets. Have picnics.

DYD: But things got testy.

RSS: Very much so. And a man—a young Irishman, I presume—took up a defensive position on the jetty and decided to repel the invaders who were approaching on their homemade raft.

DYD: He hit Eugene in the head with a rock.

RSS: Knocked him out. Eugene slipped under the water and his friends weren't strong enough swimmers to save him. They splashed ashore as quickly as they could and ran to get the lifeguard—the Black lifeguard stationed at the 25th Street beach. A crowd of bathers accompanied them back to 29th Street, where it took thirty minutes to recover Eugene's body.

DYD: That started the melee?

RSS: Not immediately. The boys identified the rock thrower. I presume there were corroborating witnesses too. But as it happened, the policeman on site—a certain Officer Callahan—refused to take the man into custody. Instead, Officer Callahan arrested a Black man whom he evidently thought was complaining too stridently about the way he was performing his role.

DYD: Katie bar the door . . .

RSS: Too late. The reaction of the people on the beach was immediate and their conscious responses were contagious. Any genuine images of justice and civic order flew out of their minds, and both sides moved to take the law into their own hands. By dawn the next day, seventeen people had been killed and over two hundred wounded.

DYD: Horrible. What narrative imagery was carrying that behavior?

RSS: I'm sure your sense is as good as mine. But let's concentrate on the man on the jetty, the one repulsing the invaders by sea.

DYD: He wasn't exactly making friends and building peace, was he.

RSS: No, he wasn't. But let's focus on the narrative arc of his performance. What do you think he knew about those boys?

DYD: About Eugene and his friends? Not much, I imagine— only that they were Black, and that the raft was approaching his sense of the color line on the beach.

RSS: And given that response to the situation, what do you think he was concerned about?

DYD: Extrapolating from his decision to throw rocks? He was obviously concerned about what he saw as their encroachment on the beach, though I don't know what his precise intention might have been. To turn them away, to scare them, to punish their transgression?

RSS: Which raises the question: What role do you think he was filling?

DYD: Well, he was defending the barrier. Perhaps he understood himself to be fulfilling his role as a member of an Irish gang?

RSS: That seems likely to me. In any case, he was focused on the sensory particulars of the situation, wasn't he? Not the conscious component.

DYD: He certainly wasn't wondering about the boys' hopes and fears—or their intentions, or how they made the raft, or what they wanted to be when they grew up.

RSS: If he had been, throwing rocks would not have been his primary option.

DYD: No. He'd have asked the boys what they were up to.

RSS: Instead, his curiosity was constricted by a horizon of concern defined by his focus on sensory particulars of the situation.

DYD: Okay. So, what about the spirit?

RSS: What about it?

DYD: The spirit is always blowing, right? Always tugging us— always calling us to transcend ourselves?

RSS: Yes.

DYD: Well, there's precious little evidence of self-transcendence in this situation. Not on the part of the man on the jetty, not on Officer Callahan's part either.

RSS: I'm sure there were acts of self-transcendence in the melee.

DYD: Maybe there were. But they certainly weren't predominant.

RSS: No. But what are you thinking? That the spirit should have reached into the young man's consciousness, grabbed him figuratively by the scruff of his decision-making, and hauled him toward self-transcendence?

DYD: Well . . .

RSS: We've talked about this. The spirit doesn't work that way.

DYD: I know. The spirit doesn't enter directly into the flow of our conscious operations.

RSS: That's the thing. Divine consciousness transcends the flow of human consciousness.

DYD: That seems like such an abstract thing to say. The situation is concrete.

RSS: Is it abstract? Tell me, when you're writing with a pen, do you experience your mind entering directly into the flow of ink you use to write out your thoughts?

DYD: Of course I don't.

RSS: And you never will—because as a point of fact, human consciousness transcends the physical flow of ink from a pen.

DYD: Okay. Point taken.

RSS: But what the spirit can do—what it does do, what it does without fail—is to consciously call us, invite us, tug us—to elevate the flow of our conscious performance.

DYD: But those invitations aren't exactly direct, are they?

RSS: What do you mean?

DYD: We may be called—we may be tugged—but our response to that call is mediated by our conscious performance in the situation, isn't it?

RSS: Yes.

DYD: So there's always a carrier involved—a carrier of our performance—of whatever self-transcendence we might manage.

RSS: Be it done to me according to thy word.

DYD: Right. And that carrier will be more or less up to the

task. In the case of the stone thrower on the jetty, it seems fair to say that he hadn't been praying the rosary nearly enough.

RSS: Right.

DYD: If he'd had the slightest inclination to make friends and build peace—the slightest inkling there's neither Black nor White

. . .

RSS: Then yes, whether he was explicitly aware of it or not, those narrative images would have positioned him to be just that much more open to the presence of the spirit.

DYD: Just that much more open to questioning his assumption that the boys were invaders.

RSS: To thinking twice about his inclination to repel them with rocks.

DYD: Right.

RSS: Think about that. If we assume the man was faithfully engaged in his role as a member of an Irish gang—if we recognize he perceived a threat in the breaching of the racial barrier at the beach—then any second thoughts he might have had, any critical questions he might have entertained about his performance, would have represented a powerful act of self-transcendence on his part.

DYD: And would have made a powerful difference in the situation too.

RSS: If he could have acted on it.

DYD: Without the rock throwing, there'd be no second-degree murder.

RSS: And without a body to recover, there'd be no arrest and no melee.

DYD: No melee and no Red Summer.

RSS: Very high stakes.

DYD: But that's the point, isn't it? The stakes are so high, but our conscious presence to the spirit is so subtle, so small, so contingent, so precarious.

RSS: It can be, yes.

DYD: Don't you find yourself wishing the spirit would just grab us by the scruff sometimes?

RSS: No. I can't say that I do.

DYD: Really? Don't you wish the man on the jetty had just dropped the rock?

RSS: Of course I do. But you seem to be thinking the spirit has something to answer for. I figure the spirit is doing its part. I'm more focused on the young man's experience as a Catholic in Chicago.

DYD: Meaning?

RSS: Meaning the wind doesn't fill a sail that isn't there. The young man's experience in the Church evidently didn't give him the inner resources and conscious awareness he needed to second-guess his inclination to throw those rocks.

DYD: Evidently other experiences were more influential.

RSS: That's right.

DYD: And you hold Cardinal Mundelein accountable for that?

RSS: Cardinal Mundelein and his predecessors, yes. Not for throwing the rock, of course. The young man is responsible for that. But Cardinal Mundelein was the leader of the Church in Chicago. He was the exemplar of what it means to live a genuinely Catholic life. And to that degree, he was responsible for the aspirations, narrative imagery, and decision-making of all the faithful in Chicago.

DYD: Like Paul in Galatia.

RSS: At a minimum, you'd have thought the violence, death and destruction of the Red Summer would have been a wake-up call—would have given the cardinal all the evidence he needed to shake things up, to change the conversation about race and immigration in the diocese.

DYD: But that's not how it played out?

RSS: The violence stopped, but that didn't mean the conflict between the two communities was over. For one thing, the flow of immigrants from the rural south didn't slow down. In fact, the Black population in the Bronzeville community doubled in the years immediately following the Red Summer. For another, the Irish gangs may have failed to drive the new immigrants out of Bronzeville, but that didn't mean the Irish Catholic community had to stick around to deal constructively with the changes in their neighborhood. Instead, they fled.

DYD: And Cardinal Mundelein didn't take this on? He didn't try to minimize the suspicion and mistrust between the two communities—to heal the racial enmity?

RSS: You know he had to be concerned about it. And it may be that he was trying to manage the situation. But to make any real progress he would have had to address the conscious and spiritual components of the situation.

DYD: And there's no clear evidence he did.

RSS: Not that I know of.

DYD: So, what did he do?

RSS: He doubled down on his previous strategy.

DYD: He kept moving the pieces around?

RSS: It's not clear he could imagine anything else. For example, the number of Irish parishioners attending St. Elizabeth's hollowed out rapidly in the aftermath of the Red Summer, and the cardinal responded by closing St. Monica's and turning St. Elizabeth's over to the Divine Word Missionaries.

DYD: He made St. Elizabeth's the Black Catholic Church in Chicago?

RSS: Yes, he did. It was a beautiful facility, one of the loveliest in the diocese.

DYD: The Black community must have been pleased.

RSS: They were proud of the church building, yes. And Cardinal Mundelein replicated the move a few years later when he decided to turn Corpus Christi over to the Franciscans.

DYD: Corpus Christi?

RSS: By that time, attendance at Sunday Mass had dwindled to less than one hundred.

DYD: So he changed directions and recruited the Franciscans to minister to the Black community?

RSS: He did. Though there was some resistance early on from the original parishioners that held up the transfer for a year or so.

DYD: But he was still thinking in terms of ethnically and racially distinct parishes?

RSS: Schools too.

DYD: What did he do with the schools?

RSS: Just what you might expect. After the transfer, he moved the Sisters of Mercy out of the school at St. Elizabeth's and installed the Sisters of the Blessed Sacrament, an order associated with the Divine Word Missionaries.

DYD: Where did he move the Sisters of Mercy?

RSS: Cardinal Mundelein built Mercy High School, a large new girls' high school where he consolidated the White students who were still at St. Elizabeth's with the girls' high schools from five other south side parishes.

DYD: So it was still on the south side.

RSS: About five miles due south on 81st Street.

DYD: He must have been thinking that the geographic boundaries of the new migration would stabilize.

RSS: Perhaps he had some data on his side. There were over seven hundred students in Mercy High when it first opened and that grew in short order to twelve hundred. But Cardinal Mundelein couldn't anticipate either the economic devastation the Great Depression would visit on the Black business along State Street or the size of the second wave of immigration precipitated by World War II. There wasn't nearly enough housing in the Bronzeville area, and most of what existed was miserable. Those factors completely overwhelmed the vitality of the community and much of the south side.

DYD: Do you think the Church would have been better positioned to address those material difficulties if the Cardinal had been able to think in terms of consciousness and spirit?

RSS: Most certainly. At the same time, we can't discount all the good things that resulted from Cardinal Mundelein's moves. There are lots of stories.

DYD: The spirit is always blowing?

RSS: St. Elizabeth's and Corpus Christi were full. Their schools were educating the children. The needs of individual parishioners were being served. And to tell you a story of my own, the Franciscans at Corpus Christi materially and spiritually nurtured and supported Lloyd Davis, my friend and collaborator at the Catholic Interracial Council.

DYD: But none of those demonstrably good things put the Church at the forefront of racial healing in the city, did they.

RSS: Institutionally? No. Decisions to move the Church in that direction were evidently beyond the horizon of Cardinal Mundelein's concern.

DYD: Which vexed Sister Mary-Frances too.

RSS: Yes, though her vexation was more particular.

DYD: Particular how?

RSS: In 1928, four years after he opened Mercy High School, a project to widen Western Avenue gave Cardinal Mundelein the opportunity to rebuild St. Malachy's Church, an Irish parish established by Archbishop Feehan on the near west side. The racial mix of the area was changing, so as part of the church-building process, Cardinal Mundelein asked the Divine Word Missionaries at St. Elizabeth's to open up a mission to Black Catholics within St. Malachy's parish.

DYD: A mission within a parish?

RSS: That's right. And at the same time, he decided to move the girls' school connected to that parish to Des Plaines.

DYD: What school was that?

RSS: St. Patrick's School.

DYD: Our St. Patrick's?

RSS: The very same. The Sisters of Mercy had built the school in 1883, across the street from the original St. Malachy's church building. And in 1928, they re-established the school in Des Plaines, restructuring it as a girls' high school within a year or so.

DYD: And Sister Mary-Frances knew this bit of history?

RSS: Of course she did. How do you think I learned about it?

DYD: Okay. So let's keep the focus on you—meaning, let's fast forward some twenty-five years to the 1950s. Cardinal Stritch has been installed as Archbishop of Chicago. You're now in your role with the Catholic Interracial Council, and you're contemplating the pieces on the game board Cardinal Mundelein has set up for you.

RSS: We needed to change the game.

DYD: Yes. So how did you go about that?

RSS: You know, don't you?

DYD: Well, I know it's not by mandates, or by moving the pieces around.

RSS: And it's not without attending explicitly to the conscious and spiritual components of the situation.

DYD: Okay. The situation you were addressing is an admissions system that year after year kept on generating a racially segregated Catholic high school system.

RSS: Yes. We needed to actualize—and to institutionalize—a different pattern of decision-making.

DYD: Easier said than done.

RSS: Not easy no, but not unrealistic either, as long as you keep your focus on opportunities for self-transcendence for the people with roles in the system.

DYD: That's how you break the logjam.

RSS: It's how you release the spiritual power of people.

DYD: So you began with the principals. You asked Sister Mary-Frances and the others what was getting in their way and what it would take to for them to admit students of color to their schools?

RSS: And as Sister Mary-Frances made clear, the major obstacle for those willing to consider the decision was the absence of students to admit.

DYD: You mean, Black students with the ability, resiliency, and willingness to attend a Catholic high school in which the vast majority of students were White.

RSS: Yes. Like the principals, they would have to be willing to be forerunners—game changers. And like the principals, we asked them what would get in the way of making such a decision, and what would it take for them to say yes.

DYD: That was your talent search.

RSS: Right. So apart from the question of tuition—which was an easy problem, comparatively speaking—the biggest obstacle was their concern that they would be completely isolated and alone. They recognized that attending a White school could lead them to be disrespected, vilified, even attacked.

DYD: But they needed to have some hope in the possibility of making friends and overcoming the obstacles posed by differences in skin color.

RSS: But this is the thing. You can't mandate friendship and you can't guarantee it—and they knew it. You can only set up the possibility of its emergence.

DYD: You can create roles for students in which making friends across racial lines is a common concern.

RSS: Very good.

DYD: So you arranged for the principals to create school clubs in which the student's role was to meet to discuss their experiences of race and racial justice in their lives, the school, and the city.

RSS: And then we brought those clubs together on a citywide basis for Study Days.

DYD: And the logjam began to shift.

RSS: It certainly felt like it.

DYD: Neither White nor Black. Just opportunities for friendship.

RSS: Yes.

DYD: A high aspiration.

RSS: A practical one.

DYD: No wonder you wanted to get back to Chicago once you'd finished working on the president's campaign.

RSS: Indeed I did.

DYD: Which brings us back to your phone call with President Kennedy.

RSS: I guess it does.

Peace Corps:
Blessed Are the Peacemakers[1]

DYD: You said you wanted to get back to your work with the Catholic Interracial Council once the inauguration was over.

RSS: Yes. By the time I left CICC to join Jack's presidential campaign, we had thirty-one high schools engaged in the program.

DYD: That's quite a contrast to what was happening elsewhere in the country in response to *Brown II* . . .

RSS: Right. In 1954 the Supreme Court ordered school districts across the country to integrate schools "with all deliberate speed." The results were predictably mixed.

DYD: Yes. I imagine the notion of acting with "all deliberate speed" could encompass all manner of aspirations and deliberations.

RSS: Yes. Governor Faubus, the governor of Arkansas, thought the speed of integration in Little Rock was much too reckless— so he shut down the city's nine high schools rather than allowing local officials to continue implementing their integration plan at Central High.

DYD: Comparatively speaking then . . .

RSS: Yes. We were doing pretty well with the Catholic high schools in Chicago.

DYD: That's my question. Given the headway you were making, what did you find so alluring about your opportunity with Peace Corps?

RSS: The spirit was blowing in my response to that situation too, you know.

DYD: Yes, but concretely. What led you to say yes? What did you discern in the president's offer to lead the task force?

RSS: As you can imagine, my initial response was quite elemental. Deeper understanding of what I was being called to only came later. But during my phone call with the president himself, I was consciously present to a call to take on a new kind of challenge.

DYD: The challenge of building peace in a world divided by the Cold War?

RSS: That wasn't new. We were already building peace in Chicago, a city divided by racial difference.

DYD: Okay. I'll stop guessing. Tell me what was new about this challenge.

RSS: It was more a call to take on a new kind of role than to solve a new kind of problem.

DYD: New how?

RSS: Metaphorically, I felt called to be a boat builder rather than a log driver.

DYD: A boat builder?

RSS: Let me put it this way. In Chicago I felt called to release the spiritual capacity of the Catholic high school admissions system.

DYD: Yes.

RSS: In my phone call with Jack, I felt called to design and build a vessel worthy of capturing the aspirations of the American people already released by the spirit.

DYD: You're talking about designing sails that would capture the winds of the spirit?[2]

RSS: I am.

DYD: And the president's request for you to build this boat came without plans or blueprints.

RSS: He trusted me to work out the details, yes.

DYD: Which had to be daunting.

RSS: There's always a cloud of unknowing at the heart of a call. So yes, it was daunting for me.

DYD: And in the face of feeling daunted? What then?

RSS: You try to stay open. You try to maintain your inner balance. You allow room for discovery. Besides, I wasn't without resources.

DYD: You had your experience in Chicago. You had a model to think with.

RSS: I had the backing of the president. And I was present to Mary.

DYD: The spirit was blowing. You were open to it.

RSS: That's the thing. I wasn't alone in this. A lot of people were opening up to those winds.

DYD: So you're saying there was a public, political dimension to this?

RSS: You mean a manifestation of the spirit in history? Of course there was.

DYD: What makes you say that?

RSS: Think about the way the Peace Corps idea caught on in the final weeks of the campaign—the enthusiasm of the Michigan students; Jack's profound response to them.[3]

DYD: Things did come together rather quickly.

RSS: Rather quickly? It was like a case of spontaneous combustion. And between the election and the inauguration, the flames burned even higher and brighter.

DYD: You're talking about the Gallup Poll results? The offers you received from would-be volunteers for a program that didn't even exist?

RSS: Seventy percent of the American people responded positively to the idea of a Peace Corps; thousands offered to get personally involved with it. That's what I'm talking about.

DYD: So you discern the tug of the spirit in those poll numbers and letters of inquiry?

RSS: More concretely, I discern signs of transcendence in those numbers.

DYD: That's quite a claim.

RSS: You think so? There's nothing particularly extraordinary about it, is there?

DYD: Well. I don't know any historians who tell the tale of the Peace Corps' origins as a story of the American people responding to the tug of the spirit.[4]

RSS: Then I'd say those historians are overlooking a critical component of Peace Corps' origins.

DYD: And I'd say you're thinking with the model right now.

RSS: I don't know why I would think any other way.

DYD: Perhaps I don't either, not anymore. But this much I do know: when you claim the spirit is a key factor in the origins of the Peace Corps, you're making an empirical claim—and empirical claims stand or fall on the relevant evidence.

RSS: Right. So let's consider the evidence.

DYD: Excellent. Where should we begin?

RSS: With the historians. Do you know any historian who disputes the claim that the Peace Corps idea was catching fire at the end of the campaign?

DYD: I don't know anybody who uses your metaphor to characterize that development. But it's generally agreed that Senator Kennedy's commitment to the idea of a Peace Corps took shape with surprising speed. In the final three weeks of the campaign, he shifts from posing a rhetorical challenge to a crowd of students at the University of Michigan to making a campaign pledge to the American people in a foreign policy address at Cow Palace in San Francisco.

RSS: And how do the historians account for this surprising shift in Jack's commitment to the idea?

DYD: For the most part, they wonder where he got the idea for the Peace Corps in the first place.

RSS: The idea or the name?

DYD: That's a good question. I'm not sure the distinction is very carefully drawn.

RSS: At the time, there was a lot of discussion about the creation of an international youth corps—but the program ideas varied, and the names varied too.

DYD: Can we assume Senator Kennedy was familiar with all this?

RSS: There's no reason not to. Two weeks before the Michigan event, Lyndon Johnson, Jack's running mate, delivered a speech to the students at the University of Nebraska in which he sounded out their willingness to serve in what he called "Volunteers for Peace and Humanity." A month earlier, Jack's campaign had also commissioned Samuel Hayes, a professor in economic development at Michigan, to write a white paper on the idea of an international youth service. Then, of course, there was Hubert Humphrey, the senator from Minnesota. He was the first to link the idea of an international service corps with the label "Peace Corps." He'd introduced legislation in the Senate several times—including earlier that year—though it never got to the floor for a vote.[5]

DYD: So there's lots of evidence to suggest that the president was familiar with the idea and perhaps intrigued by it.

RSS: Yes, but that's not really the point, is it?

DYD: Not the full point, no.

RSS: This way of thinking about the history of Peace Corps origins is more focused on an Eyewitness News account—who was saying what about the program and when—than it is on the narrative arc of Jack's decision-making, or what role the spirit might have played in it.

DYD: True.

RSS: Do the historians say anything different about the Michigan students?

DYD: They credit the Michigan students with a major role in the creation of the Peace Corps. During that same three-week period, their involvement builds from wanting to catch a glimpse of Senator Kennedy at an impromptu campaign stop—to aspiring to live abroad and build peace in the developing world—to mobilizing a multi-campus appeal to the senator to make that happen.

RSS: But no historians talk about the role of the spirit in that progression of aspirations.

DYD: Only you, I expect.

RSS: Well, the claim is clear. The spirit is at play in the decision-making of both Senator Kennedy and the Michigan students.

DYD: Then let's see if I can use the model to pin down the role of the spirit in these aspects of the Peace Corps origin story.

RSS: Go to it!

DYD: Easier said than done. Thinking with the model isn't all that spontaneous for me yet—not like playing baseball anyway. But I know that, in broad strokes, it involves differentiating the sensory, conscious, and spiritual components of the decisions made by Senator Kennedy and the Michigan students.

RSS: Very good.

DYD: Very complex, you mean.

RSS: As an historical account? Yes. It's complex. There are a lot of key factors to specify and correlate. But as an act of discernment? I'd say it's fairly straightforward.

DYD: Well. Let's start by differentiating the sensory component of the encounter between Senator Kennedy and the students in Ann Arbor. That took place on October 13th, didn't it? The same evening as the senator's third televised debate with Vice President Nixon?[6]

RSS: Not quite. By the time Jack met up with the students, it was actually 2 a.m. the next morning—so he didn't meet with the students until the 14th. But the sequence is right. Jack left the

ABC Studios in New York after the debate with Nixon and caught a flight to Ann Arbor to get a few hours of sleep. He was scheduled to jump on a train later that morning for a whistle stop tour across the state of Michigan.

DYD: Were you with him at that point in the campaign?

RSS: I was heading up the Civil Rights division of the campaign and making a last push with Businessmen for Kennedy. So no. But I've paid careful attention to these events.

DYD: Well, in terms of sensory evidence, it's clear from photographs and firsthand accounts that when the senator arrived on campus that night, he found a large crowd of students waiting for him in the rain.

RSS: Yes, it was an unplanned event, and Jack spoke extemporaneously to the students.

DYD: There's an audio recording of his remarks, so there's no disputing what the senator said that night.

RSS: You're familiar with it?

DYD: I've listened to the recording. It's short. He spoke for less than three minutes.

RSS: I find his remarks to be memorable.

DYD: The student response to them was certainly profound.

RSS: So let's focus on their response.

DYD: Now we're differentiating the sensory and conscious components of the event.

RSS: Exactly. Can you imagine yourself as one of the students participating in the event?

DYD: You mean role-play the event?

RSS: That's what I mean.

DYD: Well, as one of the students, I can imagine myself at the union with the others. It's cold and damp. We've been waiting for hours.[7]

RSS: A typical fall night in Michigan.

DYD: Typical for the weather, but less ordinary for the campus. The dean's office has extended the 10 p.m. student curfew twice already. We're worried they might cancel the event entirely if the senator doesn't arrive soon.

RSS: So there's a certain frisson in the air.

DYD: And it's getting late! I've got an essay due tomorrow for history class, so I really hope I can catch a glimpse of the Senator before I have to call it a night myself.

RSS: In which case you'll be happy to know that the senator's motorcade has just arrived.

DYD: I am.

RSS: The senator is out of the car now and finding a place on the Union steps. He greets you. He says he's come to your campus tonight "as a graduate of the University of Michigan of the East . . . Harvard University."

DYD: There he is. I can see him.

RSS: So tell me: what's going on for you?

DYD: What's my felt response to the senator's arrival?

RSS: Exactly.

DYD: I'm relieved the wait is over. I also recognize the senator is pandering to us when he makes his Michigan-Harvard quip. But I like it. We all do. Smiles all around.

RSS: You're charmed?

DYD: I wouldn't say I'm charmed, but the senator definitely has my attention. I'm interested in what he's going to say.

RSS: What he says is that there are serious problems pressing on the country, and that this is the most important election since 1934.

DYD: Well, that sounds like abstract campaign rhetoric to me. I don't find it terribly interesting.

RSS: Maybe Jack senses that himself, because he abruptly pivots and poses a quite specific challenge to you and the other students.

DYD: What's the challenge?

RSS: He says: "How many of you who are going to be doctors . . . are willing to spend your days in Ghana? . . . Technicians and engineers . . . how many of you are willing to work in the Foreign Service and spend your lives traveling around the world?"

DYD: What kind of question is that?

RSS: It surprises you?

DYD: I'd say I'm more puzzled than anything.[8]

RSS: Why puzzled?

DYD: Am I willing to spend my days in Ghana? It's a totally new thought for me. The question is out of the blue, and I'm not sure what to make of it. Am I supposed to take him seriously?

RSS: Is Jack serious? As he puts it: "On your willingness to contribute part of your life to this country, I think will depend on the answer whether a free society can compete."

DYD: That's what he thinks?

RSS: And he wants you to think it too. "Unless you comprehend the nature of what is being asked of you, this country can't possibly move through the next ten years in a period of relative strength."

DYD: Okay. He's serious—apparently very serious. He's saying the nation will be weakened—unable to compete globally—unless students like me are willing to spend part of our lives in places like Ghana.

RSS: Right.

DYD: It's a wild thought, isn't it? It's not at all clear to me how this could be so.

RSS: So where does that wildness take you?

DYD: It throws me back on myself.

RSS: Does it?

DYD: I find myself asking a string of internal questions. "Am I willing to serve in Ghana?" I'm not sure that I am, but if I were, what would I be doing in Ghana? And what difference could it possibly make?

RSS: Very good. Jack's question has put you in play.

DYD: He's asking me to be of service—not as a soldier, not in the military—but in some alternative way.

RSS: Yes.

DYD: Would he be asking for my service if he couldn't imagine that I might be able to provide it? Would he be seeking my service if he couldn't imagine me contributing in some meaningful, sub-stantial way to the advance of peace and freedom in post-colonial Africa?

RSS: No. He can imagine it and he's inviting you to imagine it too. What would be meaningful to you?

DYD: Helping to advance peace and freedom.

RSS: Good.

DYD: So by raising the possibility, he invites me to imagine myself as a person who might be able to serve in that way.

RSS: Right.

DYD: It feels like a stretch.

RSS: It is a stretch.

DYD: He's inviting me to try on a new narrative image.

RSS: Yes he is!

DYD: It's the image of being a person in service to humanity, committed to advancing peace and freedom.

RSS: So how does that image sit with you?

DYD: It's intriguing, I must say. And I find it strangely uplifting. Though I'm also dubious.

RSS: Dubious about what?

DYD: My ability to make this leap.

RSS: What leap?

DYD: Going from being a student in pursuit of a degree at the University of Michigan to doing who knows what in Ghana.

RSS: You're talking about two very different roles, with two very different horizons of concern.

DYD: So different that I have no idea what spending my days in Ghana would entail.

RSS: The role Jack is asking you to play isn't clear.

DYD: Not at all.

RSS: Yet you find yourself drawn to the possibility of filling it anyway?

DYD: Oddly, I do.

RSS: Maybe it's not so odd. As he says: "This university is not maintained by its alumni, or by the state, merely to help its graduates have an economic advantage in the life struggle. There is certainly a greater purpose. I'm sure you recognize it!"

DYD: He's hoping I'd be open to a purpose greater than my own economic advantage.[9]

RSS: He's challenging you to reach beyond your current horizon as a student, yes.

DYD: He's challenging me to transcend my desire for a degree and a job.

RSS: And?

DYD: As I said, it's a stretch.

RSS: But with that . . . with a wave, a smile, and a thank you he departs, disappearing into the Union. Your three minutes with Senator Kennedy are up.

DYD: So the senator appears, asks for my help, and then moves on—leaving me thrown back on myself.

RSS: Not bad for an extemporaneous encounter.

DYD: He's left me feeling oddly anticipant . . .

RSS: Anticipant about?

DYD: The possibility of being a person who could help advance peace and freedom. My, what an audacious aspiration!

RSS: Audacious beyond words.

DYD: But it's totally humbling at the same time.

RSS: Mystifying.

DYD: Bemusing.

RSS: Let me ask you then. This hankering you have, to become a person committed to advancing peace and freedom—would you say it includes a sense of being consciously tugged to say yes?

DYD: Do I have a sense of larger voices calling?

RSS: That's the question.

DYD: Ah . . . this is where the spirit comes in.

RSS: You know the spirit doesn't actually "come in."

DYD: Because the spirit has been present to me all along.

RSS: Present to you while you waited in the rain for the senator; present to you when you decided to come to the rally rather than to write your essay; present to you when the senator issued his challenge; present in this particular moment.

DYD: The spirit filling my sails. You specifically discerned that?

RSS: Once you know what to look for, you develop a sense for it. It's almost palpable sometimes.

DYD: So what did you notice?

RSS: What do you think it was?

DYD: Well, since I don't actually have a sail, I'm not exactly sure.

RSS: Metaphorically, you do. We all have sails.

DYD: Literally though . . .

RSS: Literally then. What do you have?

DYD: Okay. Let me go back to the model. Literally, I have my mind. I have the flow of my conscious operations. And I have whatever happens to be carrying my consciousness at a particular moment.

RSS: Very good. And what was carrying the flow of your mind at that particular moment?

DYD: At that moment? The senator was challenging me to try on a new narrative image. That in turn carried me to think about the possibility of a new role . . . and a new horizon of concern.

RSS: The possibility of becoming a person in service to building peace and advancing freedom.

DYD: Yes.

RSS: *Voilà la voile.*

DYD: That's the sail?

RSS: Okay. Here's what I noticed. As you were declaring your aspiration to serve—as you stretched yourself in that way—it registered to me as a reach for self-transcendence. As the spirit filling your sails.

DYD: I definitely felt the urge to reach beyond myself as a traditional student.

RSS: Yes.

DYD: But I'm not sure I was consciously present to the spirit just then.

RSS: I understand that.

DYD: You're thinking I was?

RSS: Present to the spirit? No doubt about it. Consciously present? That's for you to discern, question, confirm.

DYD: Which is where the model comes in.

RSS: The model is helpful here, yes. But to put it quite simply, you rose to Jack's challenge. I noticed it and found it moving. *Cor ad cor loquitur.*

DYD: Heart speaks to heart?[10]

RSS: Another good metaphor, yes. Tried and true.

DYD: Suggesting what—that your sense of my reach for self-transcendence activated yours?

RSS: My capacity for self-transcendence, yes.

DYD: Your experience of my openness carried yours?

RSS: That's a good way to put it.

DYD: It certainly raises a host of new questions for me.

RSS: Ask away.

DYD: It seems to me that discerning the conscious and spiritual components of my experience of Senator Kennedy's challenge in a role-play would be one thing—and discerning the experience of Michigan students at the rally quite another.

RSS: That sounds more like a doubt to me than a question. Actually though, the process of discerning is not so different.

DYD: So here's my question. How can we legitimately generalize from my conscious experience in a role-play to the conscious experience of students who were actually at the event that took place decades ago?

RSS: Who said anything about generalizing? We were just using the model to track the flow of your consciousness in response to the senator's challenge. You have a mind. And like every other student on the scene that night, you were using it.

DYD: So we're talking about my response as part of a data set.

RSS: That's right. And the relevant question is, how good is the data? You said the senator's challenge introduced you to a narrative image that threw you back on yourself.

DYD: Yes.

RSS: So my question would be: Is it so? Were you paying careful attention to your inner conscious experience when you said you'd been thrown back on yourself—or were you making that up?

DYD: I didn't make it up.

RSS: I didn't think so. But tell me this. In responding to the senator's challenge, did you actually find yourself aspiring—feeling stretched—to take up the challenge of advancing peace and free-dom?

DYD: I did.

RSS: Is there any chance you were being sloppy or untruthful or inattentive in reporting what was going on for you?

DYD: Not to my knowledge. No.

RSS: Perhaps you felt repugnance or derision rather than puz-zled anticipation in response to the senator's challenge?

DYD: Okay, I get the point. I'm less skeptical now that we've verified the quality of my data set. Still, here's the thing. We were engaged in role-play. We weren't physically present at the actual event.

RSS: Yes. But what does that mean? Are you worried we were just making it up as went along? Are you worried your response was untethered to the real thing?

DYD: Well . . .

RSS: It's true. To get at your conscious response to the senator's challenge, we had to imaginatively recreate the sensory details of the event. Are you concerned that our imaginative simulation fell short in some way?

DYD: When you put it that way, no. We had a record of Sen-ator Kennedy's remarks, and we represented the other historical details as accurately as we could.

RSS: Besides that, our primary focus was to understand the conscious response of a student to the senator's challenge. We wanted to differentiate the conscious and the spiritual components of the event, so we focused on the relevant data of consciousness. In this case, it happened to be yours.

DYD: But that's the thing. It was my response, no one else's.

RSS: Of course it was yours. And people obviously differ. Not every student in the crowd that night would have been as openly attentive to their inner experience as you were.

DYD: Well, exactly. For instance, none of the Michigan students would have had you in their ear keeping them focused on the data of their consciousness.

RSS: Except that it wasn't actually necessary to have me in their ear.

DYD: No? It was certainly helpful to me.

RSS: Yes, but here's the thing. You don't need to be explicitly aware you're wrestling with a new narrative image to be thrown back on yourself. And you don't need to be consciously present to the spirit to feel tugged to self-transcendence—or to say yes to it.

DYD: Okay. But this much is clear. If you hadn't used the model to formulate your questions about my response to the senator's challenge, that experience would have been much more elemental and undifferentiated for me than it was.

RSS: Probably so. The model definitely helped you think about what was going on for you, and it helped us both to understand it. But as I said, the model isn't everything. The students who attended Jack's rally had minds; they were using them; and the spirit was consciously present to every one of them.

DYD: Meaning?

RSS: Meaning there's no reason to assume they weren't seeking to be as attentive and curious and diligent as you were in grappling with their responses to his challenge.

DYD: But they would have been thinking with different categories, raising different questions.

RSS: They'd have been thinking with something, that's for sure. And chances are they would have remained much more focused on the data of sense than you were. But even so, they would have been working through the same basic conscious experience.

DYD: Meaning, they would have been wrestling with their felt response to the senator's challenge.

RSS: Right. They would have discussed it with their friends. They would have wondered together about the possibility of acting on it. And like you, they might have felt some frustration that there was no clear way forward—no clear role to fill.

DYD: If they thought about those things at all.

RSS: Well yes, but the historical record suggests that some of them did, doesn't it?

DYD: True.

RSS: So let's review the evidence from that group of students.

DYD: What evidence do you have in mind?

RSS: Judith and Alan Guskin left us a significant data set.

DYD: The Guskins. They led the student mobilization effort at Michigan.

RSS: Right. They launched the pledge drive for student signatures that prompted Jack to propose the creation of the Peace Corps in his Cow Palace speech.

DYD: Okay, we know some of the actions they took—some decisions they made. Eyewitness News would have picked them up if they'd been on the scene. But if we want to understand the conscious and spiritual components of their response to Senator Kennedy, we need more data.

RSS: And for that data, we can turn to the letter they wrote to the Editor of *The Michigan Daily* following Jack's visit.[11]

DYD: That letter would enable us to differentiate the conscious and spiritual components of their response to Senator Kennedy?

RSS: Yes. You were using your mind when you were responding to my questions in the role-play. Judith and Alan were using their minds when they were writing their letter.

DYD: Let me see if I've got it. You're thinking the letter they wrote to *The Michigan Daily* is on the order of my verbal responses to your questions.

RSS: To the degree it reveals how they were using their minds, yes.

DYD: Okay. So let's find out. Do we have a copy of the letter?

RSS: It's even shorter than Jack's remarks to the students that night. It's only a few sentences long.

DYD: Did they write it that night?

RSS: No, it took them a few days. They composed the letter on October 18th—four days after Jack's visit.

DYD: Do we know what prompted their decision?

RSS: The broader context, yes. On the 18th they decided to attend another campaign event for Senator Kennedy, this time featuring Congressman Chester Bowles.

DYD: The senator's candidacy was obviously on their minds.

RSS: And on the minds of other students too. In the Q & A afterward, a fellow student raised the question of Senator Kennedy's challenge and asked the congressman what he thought about it. Bowles affirmed the idea and validated the contribution the students could make to world peace.

DYD: His affirmation would have made it more real for them.

RSS: Something definitely clicked, because right after the Bowles event, Judith and Alan drafted their letter to the editor on a napkin, in a restaurant near the campus, and three days later, on October 21st, *The Michigan Daily* ran their letter on the front page.

DYD: So exactly one week after the senator's visit to campus, the letter is published. It should tell us about the conscious and spiritual components of the Guskins' response.

RSS: Yes. Let's take it sentence by sentence. Tell me what you notice:

Representative Chester Bowles and Senator Kennedy in their speeches to the students of the University of Michigan both emphasized that disarmament and peace lie to a very great extent in our hands and requested our participation throughout the world as necessary for the realization of these goals.

DYD: What do I notice?

RSS: Right. Think with the model.

DYD: You want me to pin down the key terms?

RSS: Yes. What do you notice first about the way they're using their minds?

DYD: Well, the main thing I notice is that Judith and Alan have picked up the mantle of Senator Kennedy's challenge. It strikes me that they've internalized the narrative image that Senator Kennedy was testing on the Michigan students when he asked for their service.

RSS: What makes you say that?

DYD: Well, I was wondering about the narrative image carrying the Guskins' performance, so the question I asked was: Who are the Guskins imagining themselves to be as they sit down to write their letter?

RSS: And?

DYD: And they're thinking of themselves as persons with the capacity to advance peace and freedom around the world. As they put it, "disarmament and peace lie to a very great extent in our hands."

RSS: Yes. That's it. They find themselves reflected by it in Bowles and Kennedy's remarks.

DYD: They're certainly more confident in their embrace of that narrative image than I was in the role-play.

RSS: You were intrigued. They're bold. Their aspirations open out beyond the horizon of a traditional college student.

DYD: I can imagine wanting to write a term paper on "disarmament and peace" for a public policy or a conflict resolution class. But that's clearly not what's going on here.

RSS: Let's see what's going on.

In reply to this urgent request we both hereby state that we would devote a number of years to work in countries where our help is needed either through the United Nations or through the United States Foreign Service.

DYD: They've decided to commit, and they're using the letter to formally announce their decision. That's the main thing I notice here.

RSS: Yes. Jack wondered who might be willing to spend a number of years in service to Ghana and post-colonial Africa. Here's his answer.

DYD: They don't mention the Peace Corps.

RSS: No. But then neither did Jack. He referenced the Foreign Service and so do they. His first public use of the term is still a week away, in his Cow Palace speech, when he announces his decision to create the Peace Corps.

DYD: In any case, Judith and Alan don't seem overly concerned about the institutional context for their commitment. It could be the Foreign Service. It could be the United Nations. Whatever is best.

RSS: Right. To me, the point here is that their sails are full.

DYD: This is the spiritual component.

RSS: Yes.

DYD: There are signs of self-transcendence in the Guskins' decision-making.

RSS: Go on.

DYD: They say they are willing to serve "as necessary," "where their help is needed"—and in whatever institutional set-up is appropriate.

RSS: They're not focusing on their personal concerns or preferences.

DYD: No.

RSS: Beyond that, the wording they use—their expression of willingness to serve "as necessary," "where their help is needed"—reflects an openness that reminds me of Mary.

DYD: "Be it done to me according to thy word"?

RSS: Yes.

DYD: Okay. But how much can you actually make of that?

RSS: I'm not trying to make anything of it. When self-transcendence is manifest, you can expect to find signs of the spirit. So I'm just saying the spirit is at play here. Devotion to Mary is where I go with it.

DYD: You're saying there's a spiritual component to the letter, but not a specifically religious one.

RSS: That's how I read it, yes.

DYD: Where do the Guskins go with it?

We would also like to request that all students who feel that they would like to help the cause of world peace by direct participation send a letter to this paper and/or our address. These letters will be forwarded to Kennedy and Bowles as an answer of the students of the University of Michigan to their plea for help.

DYD: So, they're introducing an action component to the letter.

RSS: Several of them, actually. But let's not skip over the conscious component of those action steps.

DYD: What are you noticing?

RSS: Notice the way the Guskins are focusing their attention. What they're concerned about.

DYD: They're appealing to "all students who feel that they would like to help the cause of world peace."

RSS: And they want to solicit letters of commitment from them.

DYD: We're getting at their role and horizon of concern, aren't we?

RSS: We are.

DYD: They've taken on the role of student organizers.

RSS: And where do you think they got this role?

DYD: I assume they came up with it in response to the Bowles event. Maybe they just recognized a job that needed to be done—a gap that needed to be filled—and decided to step forward.

RSS: That's often how these things happen.

DYD: But it's a big step forward. You think they were called to take it, don't you.

RSS: The spirit is an active principle of aspiration and commitment. So yes.

DYD: Whether they were explicitly aware of it or not?

RSS: You know we can't answer that question for them.

DYD: Yes. But I'm struck by the Guskins' expectation that they are not alone in their response to the senator's challenge—that other students would be willing to make the same commitment they have.

RSS: But notice the difference. Those other students are not responding directly to the senator's challenge. Not the way the Guskins are.

DYD: They're responding to the Guskins' letter, aren't they.

RSS: Not to the senator's presence. Right.

DYD: Those other students are responding to the startling news that disarmament and world peace lies to a great extent in their hands.

RSS: And to the equally startling invitation to join with the Guskins in committing to serve abroad.

DYD: But the pattern's the same, isn't it? The students respond to the Guskins' letter and its offer of a new narrative image. The spirit is present to their response. A still, small, indomitable voice.

RSS: Yes.

DYD: But I think it's significant the Guskins have given their readers something to do—a decision to make.

RSS: Oh?

DYD: That's what I was missing in the role-play. My sails may have been full at the time. It seemed to you that they were. But I had no sense of my bearings.

RSS: Your role wasn't clear.

DYD: The role of being a Peace Corps Volunteer in post-colonial Africa? Hardly.

RSS: That wasn't a possibility at that point, was it?

DYD: Clarity about the role of a Peace Corps Volunteer? No. That answer wouldn't be available for another four months or so—not until you got together with the Task Force.

RSS: The Guskins are clear about their role.

DYD: Yes. But their concern is to make real the possibility of becoming a Peace Corps Volunteer, and their role is student organizer.

RSS: Right.

DYD: It's one thing to feel moved to transcend yourself. It's another thing to really put yourself on the line.

RSS: To follow through on your aspirations.

DYD: To actually be self-transcending.

RSS: For that, you need a role and a task to carry out.

DYD: If you can't decide, you can't commit. And you can't commit if you don't have something to do.

RSS: It's all in the committing.

DYD: The Guskins were making that possible.

RSS: Let's see what their next move was.

If it is at all possible, we would like students to start asking others in their classes, dorms, sororities, fraternities, houses, etc. to send letters expressing their desire to work toward these goals. We also request that those who have friends at other universities write to them to start similar action on their campuses.

RSS: The Guskins received eight hundred commitment letters in the first week and over one thousand by the time they presented their list of commitments to Jack at the Toledo airport just two days after his Cow Palace speech.

DYD: I take it this is what you mean by spontaneous combustion.

RSS: A sequence of progressive and cumulative decisions grounded in self-transcendence, open to the spirit.[12]

DYD: Operative at the origin of the Peace Corps.

RSS: Operative at the origins of all good things. And yes, evident in the boat we built, the sails we rigged, the commitment and self-transcendence inspires.

DYD: A towering task—making friends and building peace.

RSS: Towering? Yes. Impossible? Clearly not.

DYD: Once you know the model.

RSS: Yes. But now you do.

DYD: Thank you, Sarge.

RSS: My pleasure, my friend. Anytime.

NOTES

Conversation 1

[1] The call

I had a conversation with Sarge in the summer of 1996 in his offices at Special Olympics International in Washington, DC. I asked him about the day that President Kennedy called to invite him to head up the Peace Corps task force. In broad outline, our conversation unfolded something like it does here in the book. I asked Sarge about his reluctance in taking the call, and I asked him why he changed his mind. I was surprised when he told me about his sense of presence to Mary, and we went on to talk about the role of Mary and the Apostle Thomas in his spiritual life.

[2] Sarge was familiar with Lonergan

Shriver was philosophically and theologically educated and was familiar with the work of Bernard Lonergan. He and I discussed Lonergan on a number of occasions. Lonergan's philosophy is an empirical study of the structure of human consciousness and his principal works are *Insight: A Study of Human Understanding*, and *Method in Theology*. The specific reference to the benefit of having a head stocked with questions is from "Bernard Lonergan, The Ongoing Genesis of Methods," in *Collected Works of Bernard Lonergan*, Volume 16, *A Third Collection*.

[3] The first day of Shriver's formal involvement with Peace Corps

The events surrounding Kennedy's first public mention of a "Peace Corps" in the months leading up to the November 1960 election are detailed by Shriver's biographer, Scott Stossel, in *Sarge*, pp. 169–72. In chapters 13–22, Stossel provides an historically detailed account of Shriver's work developing, launching, leading, and overseeing Peace Corps. For Stossel's account of the phone call from President Kennedy, see *Sarge*, pp. 193–5. Other sources on Shriver's role in the design and development of Peace Corps include Hoffman, *All You Need is Love;* Meisner, *When the World Calls;* Redmon, *Come As You Are;* and Rice, *The Bold Experiment.*

[4] Kennedy's hesitations about Peace Corps

The account of Kennedy's hesitations about Peace Corps and his conversations with Rostow and Millikan is provided by Stossel in *Sarge*, pp. 193–4.

[5] Shriver's reluctance to lead Peace Corps

For details related to Shriver's reluctance to lead Peace Corps and his thoughts about possibly running for office as governor or senator, see Stossel, *Sarge*, pp. 136–8, 185–6, 193–5.

[6] The Chicago years

Scott Stossel provides considerable background information on Shriver's work in Chicago with Joseph P. Kennedy and the Merchandise Mart in *Sarge*, chapters 5–8.

[7] Shriver's anti-racism work while President of the Board of Education in Chicago

Shriver's speeches from his Chicago years provide detail to his understanding of the problem of racism and racial segregation. Four of these speeches focus entirely on the problem of racism (SSPI 1956.04.25 Racial Harmony; SSPI 1957.11.18 Saints Church; SSPI 1958.10.26 Hoey Award; SSPI 1959.02.03 Your Brother). Five others deal with racism as part of the broader range of challenges to education in Chicago (SSPI 1957.03.14 Dunbar, pp. 1–2; SSPI 1957.03.30 Career Conference, p. 6; SSPI 1958.02.06 Problems, p. 1; SSPI 1958.02.11 Christians and Jews, pp. 5–7; SSPI 1958.10.07 Everyone, pp. 7–8). In other speeches he includes the fight against racial and religious discrimination as part of his campaign for peace and unity-amidst-diversity on both domestic and international fronts (SSPI 1957.07.09 Education Future, p. 6; SSPI 1957.09.03 Champaign, p. 7; SSPI 1958.02.07 Schoolmasters, pp. 7–8).

Scott Stossel provides an account of Shriver's involvement in public education in Chicago and in the anti-racism activities of the Catholic Interracial Council of Chicago (CICC) in *Sarge*, pp. 119–29. Early influences on Shriver with respect to his battle against racism are noted by Stossel in *Sarge*, pp. 13, 19. Shriver details his own anti-segregation and anti-racism efforts in his speeches (SSPI 1956.04.25 Racial Harmony, pp. 3-4; SSPI 1957.11.18 Saints Church, pp. 6-7; SSPI 1958.10.26 Hoey Award, pp. 3–4; SSPI 1959.02.03 Your Brother, pp. 4–7).

[8] Sarge's public life as a vocation

When Shriver speaks about "feeling called" to a role in Peace Corps, there is no doubt he is referring to a spiritual calling. Reading through the speeches from Shriver's early public life in Chicago (1955–59), what becomes clear is how spiritual values shaped the way he understood his work in public life and how he invited others into this vision. His background was traditionally Catholic, and he makes frequent references to traditional Catholic values (SSPI 1957.03.09 Public Relations, p. 4; see also SSPI 1956.11.19 School Boards, p. 5; SSPI 1957.04.17 Leadership, p. 4; SSPI 1957.10.13 Rutledge, p. 3).

He understands politics as a mission of service and recognizes the role of spiritual values in shaping the "hearts" of citizens towards service to others (SSPI 1955.02.09 Kenwood, p. 1; SSPI 1956.06.16 Veterans, pp. 2–3; SSPI 1957.04.17 Leadership, p. 4; SSPI 1958.04.27 Men Money, pp. 6–7; SSPI 1963.01.15 Religion and Race, p. 2). He appeals to the theological virtue of charity as a transformation of the heart and mind that results from accepting the divine gift of love (SSPI 1956.04.25 Racial Harmony, p. 1; SSPI 1957.11.18 Saints Church, pp. 2, 3, 9; SSPI 1957.09.03 Champaign, p. 7; SSPI 1957.07.09 Education Future, p. 6; SSPI 1957.03.21 Ancient Mystery, p. 2; SSPI 1957.03.30 Career Conference, p. 6; SSPI 1958.02.11 Christians and Jews, p. 7; SSPI 1958.10.07 Everyone, p. 7; SSPI 1959.02.03 Your Brother, p. 8; SSPI 1957.03.04 Livingston, p. 7; SSPI 1957.03.14 Citizenship, p. 5).

Shriver's biographer, Scott Stossel, refers to the way he understood his public life as a "vocation" (Stossel, *Sarge*, pp. 80, 231, 673–6). Shriver speaks of his own role in public life as a form of "stewardship," a public trust handed to him that he also hands on to others (SSPI 1956.01.16 Finance Committee, p. 5; SSPI 1956.02.28 Junior Association, p. 5; SSPI 1956.03.06 Women's Aid, p. 4). And he never ceases to understand citizenship as a rigorous discipline of service to others that needs to be nourished by spiritual traditions, institutions, and practices (SSPI 1957.06.09 Education America, p. 4; SSPI 1957.10.13 Rutledge, p. 4). For a detailed analysis of Shriver's spirituality and how it shaped his work in politics, see Price and Melchin, *Spiritualizing Politics*.

[9] Mary in Sarge's spirituality

Notable in Shriver's spiritual life was the place of Mary, Mother of Jesus. As in many Catholic families, the rosary played a prominent role in Shriver's early devotional life. He prayed the "Hail Mary" frequently while saying the rosary, and his devotion to Mary clearly continued through his adult life. On two occasions, the first from the Peace Corps years and the second two decades later, his speeches highlight his appreciation for Mary's role in the cosmic drama of divine blessing which framed his understanding of political life (SSPI 1964.04.19 Dedication, pp. 1–2.; SSPI 1982.07.01 Dedication). The 1982 Dedication is notable because the manuscript on file is written in Shriver's own hand and it seems to be his own personal effort to place the threat of nuclear war within a spiritual vision of Mary's mediation of divine blessing to women and men on all sides of global conflict.

[10] Spiritual experience and Peace Corps

To my knowledge, no other history of Peace Corps focuses on the influence of Shriver's spirituality. The texts I have surveyed include: Hoffman, *All You Need is Love*; Liston, *Sargent Shriver: A Candid Portrait*; Meisler, *When the World Calls*; Redmon, *Come as You Are*; Rice, *The Bold Experiment*; Schwartz, *What You Can Do for Your Country*; Stossel, *Sarge*.

[11] A Catholic faith that was neither uncritical nor doctrinaire

While Shriver's Catholic faith was traditional, it was neither uncritical nor doctrinaire. His actions in public life focused on nurturing and bolstering a pluralist commitment to democracy, liberty, cultural and religious diversity, and social justice. Notable among these was his concern for cultural and religious diversity. References to diversity arise frequently in his speeches (SSPI 1957.07.09 Education Future, pp. 4–5; SSPI 1957.09.03 Champaign, pp. 5–8; SSPI 1958.02.07 Schoolmasters, pp. 5–6; SSPI 1958.02.11 Christians and Jews, p. 6; SSPI 1958.10.07 Everyone, pp. 4–5). Stossel recounts Shriver's early encounter with cultural diversity when he participated in Donald Watt's "Experiment in International Living" during his high school years (Stossel, *Sarge*, pp. 29–30; see also his account of similar experiences a few years later, pp. 47–51).

[12] An "evidence-based" thinker

When Shriver speaks of himself as an "evidence-based thinker," he is speaking about his empirical approach to correlating his personal experience as a public servant and practicing Catholic and his profound philosophical and theological education. He was an avid reader and he gave a great deal of thought to his authors' ideas (see Stossel, *Sarge*, pp. 20, 27, 183, 627–8, 641). The Personalist philosopher who influenced Shriver significantly was Jacques Maritain (see McCarthy, "Shriver: The Lightweight Label," pp. 9–10; and Stossel,

Sarge, p. 628). Shriver refers frequently to Maritain in his speeches (SSPI 1957.10.28 Teachers Union, p. 8; SSPI 1963.01.15 Religion and Race, p. 6; SSPI 1967.04.17 Yale, p. 1; SSPI 1972.10.11 Brave Ones, p. 3; SSPI 1981.09.22 Job Corps, p. 3; SSPI 2002.09.17 Washington and Lee, p. 3; SSPI 2002.11.16 Knights, p. 3; Shriver, *Point of the Lance*, 201). At times in his speeches he attributes a quotation to "a great man." For example, in SSPI 1958.02.11 Christians and Jews, p. 7, the text cited is from Maritain, *Ransoming the Time*, p. 136, reprinted in *Christianity, Democracy, and the American Ideal*, p. 98.

[13] Cultural and linguistic difference

In his speeches, Shriver developed a way of speaking about a normative thrust in human interiority that provides a spiritual and ethical unity-amidst-diversity. He recognized people's diversity but he also recognized the practical, conscious fact that they were able to transcend differences to achieve understanding across cultures, religions, and traditions. In this connection, in his speeches from the Chicago years, Shriver refers often to the transformation of the "hearts" of citizens and the importance of this transformation for political life in a democracy. On numerous occasions he speaks of the need for women and men with ". . . a heart dedicated to the enlightenment of man's mind and the inspiration of his soul." See, e.g., SSPI 1957.04.17 Leadership, p. 4; SSPI 1958.04.27 Men Money, p. 7; see also SSPI 1955.02.09 Kenwood, p. 1; SSPI 1956.06.16 Veterans, p. 2; SSPI 1958.10.07 Everyone, p. 4. Democracy is a high calling for citizens, and for democracies to function, citizens rise to this calling by engaging in rigorous forms of service to others in need.

Shriver's reference to "hearts" reveals his creativity in navigating a difficult challenge that arose in Catholic theology during the Chicago and Peace Corps years. It was a challenge that Lonergan refers to as the transition from classicism to historical consciousness (see, Lonergan, *A Second Collection*, pp. 3–10). While many Catholic theologians sought to affirm diversity and historical change, they did so by rejecting the traditional Catholic natural law framework for affirming universal human values, notably spiritual values. Shriver was influenced by his intellectual mentor, Jacques Maritain, in retaining this framework. But his novel achievement was to interpret this not in metaphysical terms, but in terms of human interiority.

[14] Doubting Thomas

Sarge and I spoke several times about his interest in the Apostle Thomas and the role he played in his devotions. In John's Gospel 20:24, Thomas is identified as Didymus.

[15] "It would be easier to fire a relative than a friend"

See Stossel, *Sarge*, p. 193, for details related to Kennedy's phone conversation telling Shriver: "it would be easier to fire a relative than a friend."

Conversation 2

[1] "Differentiating spirit" and explaining things

The word "differentiating" in the conversation's title refers to Didymus's concern to gain an empirical, explanatory understanding of spiritual experiencing. This was a concern shared by Shriver, who sought not only to put ideas and convictions into practice, but also to think things through and to explain what he was trying to do, so that he could learn from others and improve his performance.

Jacques Maritain's pursuit of precision in philosophical and theological explanation undoubtedly influenced Shriver in this regard. References to Maritain in Shriver's speeches are documented in the notes to Conversation 1. Reading through Shriver's speeches of the 1950s, it is not difficult to discern a resonance with core ideas of Maritain's Christian humanism as it is expressed in the volume of selected readings, *The Social and Political Philosophy of Jacques Maritain*, particularly pp. 155–70. Colman McCarthy recounts a meeting in which Shriver took out this book and began reading pages aloud to him (McCarthy, "Shriver: The Lightweight Label," p. 10). The chapter on Christian humanism was published initially in *The Range of Reason*, pp. 185–99; and the chapter on natural law was published initially in *Man and the State*, pp. 84–94.

As previously noted, Shriver was also familiar with Bernard Lonergan. Lonergan's work draws heavily on Aquinas and Aristotle: two figures whose thinking influenced both Maritain and Shriver. During his years at Yale, Shriver joined the St. Thomas More Society and took it upon himself to read systematically through the works of Thomas Aquinas (Stossel, *Sarge*, pp. 32, 36–7). In January 1937, when he took over as chair of the editorial board of the *Yale Daily News*, he declared that the upcoming year's publications would be guided by five principles: they would be Christian, Democratist, Aristotelian, American, and Optimistic (Stossel, *Sarge*, pp. 36–37).

Lonergan's philosophy is empirically grounded by a phenomenological study of the structure of human consciousness. His principal works are *Insight* and *Method in Theology*. Other significant works include: *Understanding and Being, Method in Theology, Phenomenology and Logic, Philosophical and Theological Papers 1958–1964*, and *Philosophical and Theological Papers 1965–1980*.

On several occasions, Sarge expressed enthusiasm for my interest in drawing on Lonergan to help explain his ideas and his work. Thus, from time to time, ideas proper to Lonergan are introduced into the conversation by Didymus. As was often the case in his public life, so too in this dialog, Sarge exercised originality and leadership by listening and seeking to understand, not just by speaking and acting. This trait is illustrated by Stossel in *Sarge*, chapters 14 and 18: "Shriver's Socratic Seminar" and "Shriverizing," pp. 209–17, 246–58.

[2] A spiritual call

While Shriver's spiritual formation was traditionally Catholic, it was never purely "otherworldly." Thus, it is not surprising that Shriver would speak about "discerning a spiritual call" in his public life in politics. In fact, for Shriver the call to the service of others was central to his spiritual practice, which in turn framed his understanding of his own involvement in politics and citizenship. See SSPI 1955.02.09 Kenwood, p. 1; SSPI 1956.06.16 Veterans, pp. 2–3; SSPI 1957.04.17 Leadership, p. 4; SSPI 1958.04.27 Men Money, pp. 6–7; SSPI 1963.01.15 Religion and Race, p. 2; SSPI 1958.01.21 Big Sisters, pp. 1–2; SSPI 1958.02.07 Schoolmasters, p. 7; SSPI 1959.06.04 Procopius, p. 7. Shriver situated politics and political service within a cosmic drama whose stakes were world peace and the future of civilization (SSPI 1956.04.25 Racial Harmony, pp. 4–5; SSPI 1957.03.04 Livingston, p. 7; SSPI 1957.03.14 Citizenship, p. 5; SSPI 1957.07.09 Education Future, pp. 5–6; SSPI 1958.02.11 Christians and Jews, pp. 6–7; SSPI 1958.10.26 Hoey Award, pp. 4–5; SSPI 1959.02.03 Your Brother, pp. 7–8). For a detailed analysis, see Price and Melchin, *Spiritualizing Politics*.

[3] Wind filling your sails

A traditional Catholic theology of nature and grace provides the theological context for Sarge and Didymus's use of the metaphors of "wind and sails" to explore the spiritual component of human experience. Shriver was conversant with these theological ideas due to his familiarity with Thomas Aquinas and Jacques Maritain. Aquinas uses the term "charity" to refer not to something we do, but to something God does. As Aquinas explains it, charity is a theological virtue and a gift of divine grace. And while grace may be divine, we cooperate with grace using abilities that are proper to us as human beings, notably our conscious capacities. Shriver refers to the theological virtue of charity in a number of speeches, notably SSPI 1957.11.18

Saints Church, pp. 2, 3, 9; SSPI 1957.09.03 Champaign, p. 7; SSPI 1957.07.09 Education Future, p. 6; SSPI 1957.03.21 Ancient Mystery, p. 2; SSPI 1957.03.30 Career Conference, p. 6; SSPI 1958.02.11 Christians and Jews, p. 7; SSPI 1958.10.07 Everyone, p. 7; SSPI 1959.02.03 Your Brother, p. 8.

For a brief discussion of the primacy of the theological virtue of charity in Aquinas, see, e.g., Jean Porter, *The Recovery of Virtue*, pp. 168–71. Another avenue of influence on Shriver regarding the theological virtue of charity would likely have been the idea of "social charity" from the Encyclical of Pius XI, *Quadragesimo anno*, of May 15, 1931, particularly pars. 88–90. For a discussion of social charity in a textbook that was influential in American Catholic circles during the years of Shriver's early public life, see Cronin, *Social Principles and Economic Life*, pp. 76–80. Charles Curran refers to the influence of Cronin's text in *American Catholic Social Ethics*, pp. 1–2.

[4] "The spirit is an independent principle of action"

Didymus restates what he takes Sarge to be saying: "the spirit is an independent principle of action." Once again, this reflects a Catholic theology of nature and grace, rooted in Aquinas and Maritain. For instance, when Shriver speaks about "charity" in his speeches, he is using the term in a technical theological sense. He is not thinking of charity as the simple act of helping someone who is in need. Rather, he is referring first and foremost to something that the spirit does in us as "an independent principle of action." Experientially, the conscious effect of charity is to "lift" or "elevate" our capacities to do what previously we would not have been able or inclined to do. For Shriver—as for Aquinas, Maritain, and Lonergan—we become capable of truly helping others in need when we receive and cooperate with the gift of the spirit. For texts by Maritain on charity, see Maritain, *The Social and Political Philosophy of Jacques Maritain*, pp. 3–9, 163–70. For discussions of the role of spiritual practice in cooperating with grace in enabling and liberating moral life, see Maritain, *The Range of Reason*, pp. 108–117, 192–9.

[5] Explanation is not metaphor

Didymus asks for precision and Sarge is happy to oblige. Here, Didymus employs the term "explanation" with a meaning consistent with the notion of explanation developed by Lonergan. For his part, Lonergan makes a fundamental distinction between "description" and "explanation"—or rather, between what we are doing when we are describing something as distinct from what we are doing when we are explaining it. (See Lonergan, *Insight*, pp. 316–18). In describing something, we express our understanding of the object in relation to us, that is, in relation to the way we are experiencing it. Whereas when we explain something, we express our understanding of the object in terms of its relationship to itself, that is, in its own terms. An explanatory account of water understands water to be constituted by two hydrogen molecules and one oxygen molecule—H_2O—whereas a descriptive account of water experiences it as wet, cool, refreshing.

The need for greater precision and for moving beyond the use of metaphors comes to light when we observe metaphors being used in confusing or misleading ways. This is particularly important when it comes to the relationship of religious teaching and spiritual practice. Shriver was acutely aware of this distinction between constructive and misleading forms of spirituality. In his 1963 address to the Religion and Race Conference, Shriver refers to the positive role of spirituality in the abolition of the Slave Trade and the mid-twentieth century campaign against racism (SSPI 1963.01.15 Religion and Race, p. 4). And he contrasts this with the negative problem of "religious laissez-faire," a type of spiritual illness resulting in the failure of religions to mobilize action in service of racial justice and peace (SSPI 1963.01.15 Religion and Race, pp. 2–3).

[6] "It's a type of conscious experiencing"

This reference to conscious experiencing reflects Shriver's familiarity with the philosophy and theology of Pierre Teilhard de Chardin. Teilhard provided Shriver with philosophical and theological resources for situating his role in politics within a wider spiritual drama of cosmic proportion. Stossel speaks of Teilhard as "his favorite theologian" (*Sarge*, pp. 183, 641), and he speaks of the religious and intellectual seriousness with which Shriver read his works (*Sarge*, 627–8). For Teilhard, one of the central categories in the evolutionary process is the emergence of consciousness, and he uses the term, "noosphere" to speak about consciousness operative in the universe. This is the sphere in which events are no longer simply the product of physical or chemical forces. Rather, they are now the products of human consciousness. Technology and the conscious operation of innovation provide the prime examples, but numerous others abound. See, e.g., Teilhard de Chardin, *The Phenomenon of Man*, pp. 200–234. Shriver would also have observed this preoccupation with consciousness in the way Maritain draws on Aquinas to respond to other major figures in contemporary philosophy (see *The Range of Reason*, pp. 3–21, particularly 12–15). For Maritain, the conscious operation of knowing is not simply gaining information, it involves a form of "becoming."

[7] Investigating consciousness empirically

When Shriver says, "It's a simple matter of catching yourself in the act—of becoming explicitly aware you are using your mind," he is referring to an empirical and methodological principle that he draws on frequently throughout these conversations. There is a method and a discipline required for cultivating this focus on one's own conscious mind. Maritain refers to this discipline in *The Range of Reason*, pp. 10–16. But while Maritain speaks of this in metaphysical terms, Shriver makes it concrete and practical. Shriver's genius in public life was not simply his ability to understand complex philosophy and theology, it was his ability to translate complex ideas into real actions and programs that change people's lives for the better. His originality was in producing concrete empirical results. Lonergan's philosophy provides an explanation of Shriver's work that, arguably, is consistent with Shriver's own preoccupation with demonstrable empirical analysis and concrete results. See Lonergan, *Method in Theology*, chap. 1; Morelli, *Self-Possession*, chaps. 2–4; and Byrne, *The Ethics of Discernment*, pp. 31–35. Lonergan's method involves our awareness of our own consciousness. This provides data we can examine, and Lonergan makes the distinction between the data of sense and the data of consciousness (see Lonergan, *Insight*, pp. 95–97, 260–61, 299–300).

[8] Experiencing the spirit

The reference to "the capacity to experience the presence of the spirit" has roots in Aquinas. As usual, Shriver makes it come alive in a concrete, practical context. The idea is developed by Lonergan in *Insight* chaps. 19 and 20 and *Method in Theology*, chap. 4. Instead of using the term "spirit," Lonergan uses the terms "transcendence" and "religious experience."

[9] "Aspiring" and Sarge's spirituality of public life

The language of "aspiring," "hankering," and "hoping" describes Shriver's total mode of engagement in public life. Shriver reveals a great deal about the way he acted and spoke in public life when he states: ". . . I'm consciously aware that my aspiring—my hankering—my hoping—for a particular situation is being tugged to reach beyond my own pleasure and pain—beyond my own advantage and disadvantage—to my highest aspirations for that situation." During the Peace Corps years, even though his speeches reveal a language that appears more secular, he continues to understand his public life as a spiritual calling, a spiritual vocation. This is evident in a number of speeches delivered to religious audiences, notably SSPI 1961.06.04

Notre Dame, pp. 2, 4; SSPI 1961.06.07 DePaul, p. 4; SSPI 1962.06.02 St. Louis, p. 1; SSPI 1963.01.15 Religion and Race, pp. 2–5; SSPI 1963.02.24 Knights of Columbus, pp. 14–15; SSPI 1963.06.12 Fordham, p. 3. Shriver's speeches reveal that he continued to see his public life in Peace Corps as a spiritual vocation, in continuity with the explicit language of his speeches of the Chicago years, rooted in his Catholic tradition, as a commitment of service to others, and as a work of cooperation with the spirit, situated within a cosmic spiritual drama of the unity of the human family. This notion of "calling" or "vocation" as cooperation with the spirit sets the framework for understanding Shriver's language in speaking about spirituality.

[10] Spiritual claims to being called, tugged, elevated

The terms "elevated" and "self-transcending" have roots in the theology of Aquinas. Maritain uses a variety of terms to present the idea of "spiritual elevation" in *The Person and the Common Good*, pp. 31–89. Lonergan explains "self-transcendence" in *Method in Theology*, pp. 99–101. Both ideas have their counterparts to Aquinas's theology of charity and grace.

What distinguishes Shriver's grasp of this theological tradition and its technical use of terms like "charity" is that his understanding of them is not primarily conceptual. It is experiential. It is the experience of being spiritually elevated—of transcending oneself—that grounded Shriver's understanding of these terms. This experiential focus is front and center in Sarge's conversation with Didymus.

Shriver's biographer, Scott Stossel, tells us that Shriver read the work of Thomas Aquinas carefully during his years at Yale (Stossel, *Sarge*, pp. 32, 36–7). And it is not difficult to discern the influence of ideas from Aquinas in his speeches of the 1950s and '60s. Maritain's work, based as it is in Aquinas, explains much of this influence. Yet Shriver's own reading of Aquinas would likely have played a role in shaping his thought and action in directions that seem to go beyond Maritain.

[11] Differentiate

The use of the term "differentiate" draws on an idea that Lonergan discusses in *Method in Theology*, p. 27. The term is also used by Maritain (*The Range of Reason*, p. 5).

[12] The three experiential components

Sarge's penchant for differentiating three experiential "components" of an event—its sensory particulars, the conscious engagement of our mind, and our conscious presence to the spirit—is evident in his speeches from the Chicago years (see Shriver, SSPI 1957.03.14 Citizenship, p. 5; SSPI 1956.04.25 Racial Harmony, p. 1; and SSPI 1957.03.04 Livingston, p. 7). Here, we can observe Shriver using the three components to help Didymus understand how spirituality "works." Traces of this framework are discernible in the work of Maritain (see *The Range of Reason*, pp. 86–87 and in the pages that follow). The difference is that Maritain's analysis is abstract and metaphysical, whereas Shriver's spiritual realism is concrete, empirical, and practical.

Conversation 3

[1] Meditation practices that cultivate mystical states of knowing

As a devout and well-educated Catholic, Shriver was familiar with an array of spiritual disciplines, traditions, and mystical figures. Scott Stossel provides an account of an interview of Shriver by George Will in which Will had an opportunity to explore Shriver's personal theological library (Stossel, *Sarge*, pp. 627–9). It was not only extensive, but the hand-written notations in the books revealed that Shriver had read the books carefully and thought about them.

² Conscious presence to yourself

On the topic of "consciousness" and "conscious presence to yourself," this conversation builds on and develops the discussions from the previous conversation. Later in this conversation, when Shriver returns to his discussion of the conscious component in his model for understanding spirituality, he is drawing on an approach followed by Teilhard de Chardin in *The Phenomenon of Man*. For Teilhard, understanding consciousness is central to his understanding of spirituality in relation to evolution.

Lonergan's philosophy provides a resource for explaining the method of this approach. It is a self-reflective method for attending to one's own operations of consciousness. In ordinary life, our attention focuses on the objects of sensory experience. But, in addition to this focus, we can also become aware of another type of experience that is present to us, the experience of consciousness itself. This happens, for example, when we say to someone: "I have a question I need to ask you." It also happens when we've been trying to understand something and suddenly we shout: "I've got it!" In these examples, our awareness does not focus solely on the objects of sensory experience, it also focuses on our operations of consciousness itself, in this case, our operations of questioning and insight.

Lonergan's principal study of this method for attending to our operations of consciousness is *Insight*. Other significant philosophical works include: *Understanding and Being, Method in Theology, Phenomenology and Logic, Philosophical and Theological Papers 1958–1964*, and *Philosophical and Theological Papers 1965–1980*. Secondary works that provide helpful introductions to Lonergan include: Byrne, *The Ethics of Discernment*; Flanagan, *Quest for Self-Knowledge*; Hefling, *Why Doctrines?*, Mathews, *Lonergan's Quest*; Meynell, *Introduction to the Philosophy of Bernard Lonergan*; and Melchin, *Living with Other People*; Price and Melchin, *Spiritualizing Politics*. For secondary works that situate Lonergan within wider conversations in philosophy, see McCarthy, *The Crisis of Philosophy*; Fitzpatrick, *Philosophical Encounters*; Crysdale, ed., *Lonergan and Feminism*; Meynell, *Redirecting Philosophy*; and Braman, *Meaning and Authenticity*. Lonergan's most explicit discussion of the relevance of this method to the field of education is *Topics in Education*. John Haughey provides an excellent analysis of a theory of human rights that is rooted in this method of cultivating a conscious presence to self. See Haughey, "Responsibility for Human Rights: Contributions from Bernard Lonergan."

[3] The Spiritual Exercises

The Spiritual Exercises were important to Maritain—Shriver's intellectual mentor—and also to Lonergan, both of whom were Jesuits. For a contemporary account of the Spiritual Exercises informed by Lonergan's theological method, see Tad Dunne, *Spiritual Exercises for Today: A Contemporary Presentation of the Classic Spiritual Exercises of Ignatius Loyola*.

[4] Batting practice

In presenting Shriver's extended discussion of baseball, I am drawing on my memory of a conversation we had when we attended a Baltimore Orioles game together in the summer of 1995. Sarge's technical knowledge of the game astonished me at the time, as did the insights he provided about his personal experience as a baseball catcher. The anecdote is telling, not simply for its information about baseball, but for what it reveals about Shriver's discipline and the role of daily practice in cultivating this discipline. Sarge understood the need for discipline, not simply in baseball, but also in spiritual life. Moreover, he was able to draw on his knowledge of one to gain insights into the other. He understood how the discipline of daily practice is necessary to cultivate the skills for subtle discernment when it comes to understanding the relationship of spiritual experiencing to the operations of consciousness. Stossel refers to

Shriver's experience as the starting catcher on the varsity baseball team at Canterbury School in 1931 in *Sarge*, p. 24.

[5] Relevant questions

As Shriver and Didymus delve deeper into the baseball analogy, Shriver raises the topic of "relevant questions." He tells Didymus that the task is to raise the relevant questions, and he reminds him that "Missing a question—asking an irrelevant question—will derail your thinking and your decision-making." Lonergan's method and his philosophy of consciousness are in the background here (see, e.g., Lonergan, *Insight*, pp. 308–24). Shriver is clear that good baseball requires good judgments. Making good judgments requires distinguishing between relevant and irrelevant questions. Lonergan's philosophy explains how and why this makes sense. The method behind the philosophy involves catching ourselves in the act of doing things when we're at our best and focusing on how our consciousness is operating when this occurs.

[6] "Role" and "horizon"

As the dialog unfolds in this conversation, two terms keep popping up: "role" and "horizon." These terms and their precise meanings reflect Shriver's ability to combine a practical, active focus with a profound philosophical education. The first of these terms, "role," reflects his familiarity with a way of understanding human sociality that is rooted in the "common good" philosophical tradition. Jacques Maritain presents key elements of this approach in *The Person and the Common Good*, particularly pp. 47–89. Human sociality is neither an aggregate of individuals nor a collectivity that absorbs or fully determines persons. Rather, it is a structured pattern involving meaning and consciousness. Persons participate meaningfully through the roles they take on. Moreover, while individual persons contribute to this pattern through their meaningful roles, sociality flows back upon persons and is oriented to supporting their elevation towards transcendence.

Lonergan provides further explanation by situating "role" within his analysis of operations of consciousness, the "structure of the human good," and the orientation of human consciousness towards transcendence (see Lonergan, *Method in Theology*, pp. 47–51). The second term, "horizon," is used widely in philosophy but is developed particularly by Lonergan (see, e.g., Lonergan, *Method in Theology*, pp. 99–101; and *Philosophical and Theological Papers 1965–1980*, pp. 10–23). The discussions of "role" and "horizon" in terms of meaning, consciousness, and transcendence signal the importance of understanding consciousness and our operations of consciousness in both practical and spiritual experience. Shriver's familiarity with these resources enabled him to draw on insights from baseball and apply them to spiritual experiencing. It illustrates his practical ability in taking complex ideas from philosophy and theology and making them come alive in real-life practice.

[7] Operating with a model of the game in mind

Shriver tells Didymus, "We use the model to think with—to guide and direct our curiosity." He offers this as a statement of fact. Shriver's ability to think explicitly in terms of "models" reveals his facility for bringing philosophical resources to bear on the role of consciousness in practical action. Shriver had a gift for distinguishing these factors and linking them all together. See Conversation 4 and the related notes for a more extensive discussion of resources.

The focus on "models" reflects his appreciation of the importance of science in relation to both philosophy and theology. Teilhard de Chardin is known for his work relating science, theology, and consciousness. Following an intrinsically empirical path like that traced by Teilhard, Shriver's model helps us to understand the role of consciousness in both baseball and spirituality.

[8] Spirituality and aspiration

Shriver brings the conversation back to the topic of the spirit with his comment, "You know the spirit is always blowing." The focus on baseball, to this point, has been on the role of consciousness and the importance of a method for exploring our operations of consciousness in baseball. Now the conversation turns back to the relevance for spirituality. Lonergan's self-reflective study of human consciousness provides a framework and resource for explaining Shriver's achievements. The method reveals a preoccupation with a horizon that lies beyond ordinary living—a horizon of ultimate, comprehensive, or transcendent concern. This horizon is intrinsically connected to our efforts of reaching for our noblest aspirations when we are acting at our best. Lonergan shows how exploring the unrestricted character of the questioning that grounds empirical science reveals features of this transcendent horizon that can be affirmed by women and men from diverse traditions (see Lonergan, *Insight*, chap. 19; *Method in Theology*, chap. 4; and *Philosophy of God and Theology*). He extends this analysis in a direction that retrieves and transposes core elements from Catholic tradition related to the theological virtue of charity. See Lonergan, *Insight*, chap. 20. This analysis provides grounds for an understanding of the theological virtue of charity and its transformative role in social living that is central to the vision reflected in many of Shriver's speeches. See Price and Melchin, *Spiritualizing Politics*.

[9] All three components are related

For background resources on the threefold model developed by Shriver and Didymus—the sensory component, the conscious component, and the spiritual component—see Conversations 2 and 4 and the related notes. Shriver's speeches from his Chicago years reveal his creativity in drawing on resources from Maritain and taking them out of the arid world of metaphysical abstraction and into the vital world of practical illustration and application.

[10] Special Olympics

For a short presentation of some background material on Shriver and Special Olympics, see Stossel, *Sarge*, pp. 658–72. For a powerful analysis that provides considerable detail on the Shriver family and Special Olympics, see Timothy Shriver, *Fully Alive*.

[11] "Self-transcendence" and "spiritual elevation"

Both Lonergan and Aquinas explore the ideas of "spiritual elevation" and "self-transcendence." "Spiritual elevation" in particular has roots in Aquinas and likely came to Shriver both directly and via Maritain. As noted earlier, Scott Stossel tells us that Shriver read the work of Thomas Aquinas carefully during his years at Yale, and it is not difficult to discern the influence of ideas from Aquinas in Shriver's speeches of the 1950s and '60s (see Stossel, *Sarge*, p. 32). Maritain's work, based as it is in Aquinas, explains much of this influence. The idea of "self-transcendence" reflects Lonergan's effort to transpose Aquinas's intrinsically metaphysical language into the realm of conscious interiority. (See, e.g., Lonergan, *Method in Theology*, pp. 99–111). For further research resources related to the theology of nature and grace behind Shriver's approach, see the notes to Conversation 2. The idea of "transcendence" and its relation to human consciousness is also discussed by Teilhard de Chardin. Teilhard's influence on Shriver is discussed by Stossel, in *Sarge*, pp. 183, 627–8, 641. Teilhard's discussions of consciousness and transcendence are clearly evident in *The Phenomenon of Man*, pp. 200–234.

[12] Self-transcendence in the Peace Corps

For discussions and research resources on the relation of the spirit and the Peace Corps program, see Conversations 6, 7 and 9 and the related notes.

Conversation 4

[1] Using the model of spiritual realism

In Conversations 2 and 3, Shriver and Didymus discuss how models guide and direct our curiosity and thought processes, making it evident that Shriver would agree with Kurt Lewin, who famously remarked that "there is nothing so practical as a good theory." Shriver was familiar with a number of authors who used models. In his Foreword to *The Phenomenon of Man*, Teilhard de Chardin outlines the book's project as an effort to develop a new way of understanding ourselves in the universe. To develop this new way of understanding, he argues, we need to cultivate a new set of "senses" in addition to our five physical senses. He goes on to list these seven "senses" in terms of seven sets of qualities to which we need to attune our consciousness if we are to understand more correctly: spatial immensity, depth, number, proportion, quality or novelty, movement, and organic structural unity. We need this heightened sensitivity or attunement to "illuminate our vision" of humanity's place in the universe (see Teilhard, *The Phenomenon of Man*, pp. 37–8). This approach is an example of what Shriver means when he says that we use models to think with.

[2] Evidence of the model in Shriver's speeches

Evidence of the threefold model proposed by Shriver, ". . . the sensory, conscious, and spiritual components . . ." can be observed in Shriver's speeches from his earliest years of public life in Chicago. As evidenced in the telephone call with President Kennedy, the use of the model helps Shriver differentiate the sensory particulars of the call, the conscious responses of his mind to those particulars, and his conscious presence to the spirit in the process.

Some years before this—in his March 1957 speech—Shriver seeks to evoke the power of the model for his audience of his address to the 16th Annual Vocational Conference in Chicago. The sensory focus of his concern is Chicago and the strife evident in the relations between Whites and Blacks in the city. He goes on to highlight the conscious component of the situation: "We can change Chicago. That's easy. The hard part is to change ourselves—to change ourselves from men and women looking for the easy job with 'the most in it for me' as the popular expression puts it." He then draws the attention of his audience to the spiritual component of the situation and the capacity for self-transcendence that it fosters: "But if like a scientist you will take the raw materials of your mind and your body and process them through the laboratory of humility, prayer and neighborly love . . . the result will be a second explosion heard 'round the world. You will be raised into a life of overwhelming love, great peace, and heroic achievement. And these things no man will ever be able to take from you." (SSPI 1957.03.14 Citizenship, p. 5).

This same threefold model can be observed structuring his analyses in two other speeches to educators from his Chicago years, at DePaul University (SSPI 1956.04.25 Racial Harmony, p. 1, and at the Livingston County Institute (SSPI 1957.03.04 Livingston, p. 7).

[3] The spirit is present to conscious response

In trying to understand and apply the threefold model, Didymus begins by reflecting back on the baseball example from the prior chapter. He gets bogged down as he tries to grasp the link between the spirit and "consciousness." He asks: "You're saying the spirit is simply present to my conscious response?" Shriver answers: "That's what I'm saying." The centrality of "consciousness" as the locus for discerning the operation of the spirit reveals Shriver's experiential and empirical focus. As noted earlier, there is an echo of Teilhard in this emphasis. Teilhard's focus, like Shriver's, is on advancing our understanding of the role of consciousness in explaining humanity, the universe, and the spirit (see Teilhard, *The Phenomenon of Man*, pp. 181–234). Both

Shriver and Teilhard insist that we must gain a properly empirical understanding of our consciousness at play in the events of life if we are to properly understand the spiritual component of our experience. For Shriver, proper understanding requires more than simply quoting sacred texts, or citing authorities, or adhering to traditions, or speculating abstractly, or feeling deeply. It requires the appropriate application of empirical method in examining consciousness itself. Lonergan's work as a methodologist clarifies the significance of Shriver's methodological approach to the conscious component of spiritual experiencing.

[4] Shriver, the spirit, and the pursuit of racial justice in Chicago

I have drawn on four sets of resources to develop this portrait of the spiritual component of Shriver's meeting with Lloyd Davis. The first resource is the framework of spiritual realism discussed by Sarge and Didymus in the previous conversations. I use the threefold differentiation of sense, consciousness, and spirit to think with. A second resource is provided by the speeches Sarge gave during his Chicago years. They provide a great number of particular details from his work with Lloyd Davis and the Catholic Interracial Council in Chicago during the 1950s. Five of the speeches focus entirely on the problem of racism (SSPI 1956.04.25 Racial Harmony; SSPI 1957.11.18 Saints Church; SSPI 1958.08.29 Roots of Racism; SSPI 1958.10.26 Hoey Award; and SSPI 1959.02.03 Your Brother). Five others deal with racism as part of the broader range of challenges to education in Chicago (SSPI 1957.03.14 Dunbar; SSPI 1957.03.30 Career Conference; SSPI 1958.02.06 Problems; SSPI 1958.02.11 Christians and Jews; SSPI 1958.10.07 Everyone). The speeches reveal the central role of Shriver's spirituality in his work for racial equality. They reveal how he understood his public life in Chicago as a spiritual vocation—a mission of service to others. And they reveal how he recognized the role of spiritual values in shaping the "hearts" of citizens towards service to others (SSPI 1955.02.09 Kenwood; SSPI 1956.06.16 Veterans; SSPI 1957.04.17 Leadership; SSPI 1958.04.27 Men Money; SSPI 1963.01.15 Religion and Race). He speaks of racial equality using explicitly religious language, he appeals to the theological virtue of charity, and he situates the entire project within a cosmic drama of divine blessing (SSPI 1956.04.25 Racial Harmony; SSPI 1957.11.18 Saints Church).

A third resource is provided by the histories of Shriver. In *Sarge,* pp. 117–129, Scott Stossel offers details on events, places, and dates related to Lloyd Davis, his meeting with Shriver, and their work together at CICC. In *Sargent Shriver: A Candid Portrait,* pp. 79–89, Walter Liston provides further detail.

The fourth resource is provided by notes and documents gathered from my visit to the CICC archives at the Chicago Historical Society in May 2017. My research assistant, Tyler Ross, gathered copies of materials from the collection in 2015, and my own visit allowed me to immerse myself in documents—newsletters, correspondence, minutes, reports—that helped me gain a feel for the events and times and Shriver's work with the Catholic Interracial Council.

[5] Segregation in Chicago's Catholic high schools

The data on the CCIC projects in seventy-nine Chicago area Catholic high schools come from Shriver's speech at DePaul University, April 25, 1956, "Exploring Future of Racial Harmony—Cultural Level." See SSPI 1956.04.25 Racial Harmony, p. 3.

[6] Sarge's use of scripture

Shriver's biblical quote is from Paul's Epistle to the Galatians 3:28. Notice that Shriver does not quote scripture simply as an authority to bolster his argument. Rather, he cites the quote as an empirical example that helps explain how things actually operate when they are being shaped by the influence of the spirit. What the quote illustrates is how religious resources can draw attention to features of a human situation that might normally escape notice, notably features related to consciousness. In this instance, what arises in consciousness is the discrepancy or "gap" between expectations and actual performance in ourselves and in our own religious communities.

[7] Scripture and aspiration

When Shriver refers to St. Paul's letter to the Galatians, he offers the text as an example of an aspiration intended to help the Galatians "... to be the sort of community they were originally called to become." This is a distinctive way of citing scriptural texts that reflects Shriver's ability to differentiate the sensory, conscious, and spiritual components of a situation. It reveals an approach that focuses on human consciousness as the lynchpin in the relationship between a particular situation and the presence of the spirit to it. As Sarge makes clear, a spiritual call—or any other form of spiritual experiencing—will inevitably be articulated (if it is in fact articulated) in the language of a particular religious institution or cultural tradition. But for Shriver, these expressions of the spirit must be differentiated from the presence of the spirit itself.

In his speeches from the 1950s, Shriver uses the traditional metaphor of "the heart" to refer to the spiritual component of human consciousness. On numerous occasions in his speeches of the Chicago years, Shriver speaks of the need for cultivating women and men who have "... a heart dedicated to the enlightenment of man's mind and the inspiration of his soul." (SSPI 1957.04.17 Leadership, p. 4; SSPI 1958.04.27 Men Money, p. 7; see also SSPI 1955.02.09 Kenwood, p. 1; SSPI 1956.06.16 Veterans, p. 2; SSPI 1958.10.07 Everyone, p. 4). He was clear that for good and for ill, "transformed hearts" do not arise in the absence of communities and traditions that nourish them (see, e.g., SSPI 1956.11.30 Mary McDowell, pp. 4–5). The design and development of institutions and programs that would enhance the probability of cultivating spiritually transformed hearts was central to

Shriver's understanding of the role and place of the spirit in political life. For an analysis of these ideas operative in the words and deeds of Shriver's public life in Chicago, see Melchin and Price, "Religion and Politics in the Early Public Life of Sargent Shriver."

[8] Personalism

When Shriver and Didymus use the language of "transcend[ing] our blind spots and limitations," they are using the language of a philosophy of Personalism that influenced Shriver most directly through the work of Maritain. The basic idea is that I am not simply one single self. Rather, I have multiple ways of being and acting. Some of these are more responsible, more authentic than others. Maritain speaks about our capacity to choose our higher selves, and this means developing, growing, and extending ourselves in the direction of the spiritual. "But if the development occurs in the direction of spiritual personality, man will be orientated towards the generous self of the heroes and saints." (Maritain, *The Person and the Common Good*, p. 44.)

[9] The person and cooperation with the spirit

Shriver reveals the influence of Personalism on his thinking when he says: "We need the spirit to lift us beyond our self-referenced aspirations, and beyond our own group interests and affiliations." More than that, however, he is revealing the influence of Aquinas's theology of operative and co-operative grace. The work of the spirit in our hearts—in filling our sails—is to help us reach for the fullness of our higher selves in a way that on our own, we would not be able to achieve. For Didymus, of course, the point is to push beyond the metaphysics of a statement like this to the inner experience of its reality.

[10] "I became consciously present to the spirit when Lloyd offered me the role with CICC"

Shriver and Didymus develop their analyses by referring to how "roles" within projects and institutions open up ways of thinking and feeling about directions for transformative action. This line of analysis is developed in the previous conversation. The idea of "role" within organizations and institutions that serve "the common good" has roots in the work of Maritain and is developed by Lonergan. See Maritain, *The Social and Political Philosophy of Jacques Maritain*, pp. 82–88; *The Person and the Common Good*, pp. 47–89; and Lonergan, *Method in Theology*, pp. 47–51.

[11] Surprise and transformative experience

Shriver makes a number of interesting statements about the way the spirit works: "Lloyd surprised me, you know. Intrigued me too." ". . . this was a bolt out of the blue." "It threw me back on myself." "It put me in play in a new way." This feature of surprise and novelty, and the way it transforms us by changing our state of consciousness, is central to the way Shriver understands spiritual experience as "transformative experience." This understanding of the spirit as transformative is revealed in the earliest speeches of his public life (see SSPI 1957.03.14 Citizenship, p. 5), it is present as an operative idea in his retrospective reflections two decades after his years with Peace Corps (see SSPI 1986.09.20 Volunteers, pp. 6–7), and it is evident in his speeches of the Peace Corps years (see SSPI 1964.01.28 Secret; SSPI 1963.06.12 Fordham; SSPI 1963.10.11 Commonwealth Club). For an analysis, see Melchin and Price, "Religion and Politics in the Early Public Life of Sargent Shriver."

[12] Service

"Be it done to me according to thy word." Shriver's final reply is, perhaps, the most revealing evidence of how he understood the spirit. The key is not just what he says, but what he does. For Shriver, a marker for discerning the presence of the spirit is the tug to self-transcendence that manifests in a call to "service." For an analysis of this theme of "service" in Shriver's speeches, see Melchin and Price, "Religion and Politics in the Early Public Life of Sargent Shriver."

This theme of service is evident in his speeches on Peace Corps, but it is also evident in his speeches on racism. See Shriver, *Point of the Lance*, pp. 48, 50, 113, 116–21, 137–38, 152, 220–21, 222. The speeches referred to in these texts are: SSPI 1964.01.28 Secret; SSPI 1964.06.10 New York University; SSPI 1964.06.08 Georgetown; SSPI 1963.01.15 Religion and Race; SSPI 1963.02.24 Knights of Columbus; and SSPI 1964.06.02 Providence College. See also Price and Melchin, *Spiritualizing Politics.*

Conversation 5

[1] "Logjam"

Didymus begins by asking Sarge what he did about racial segregation in Catholic high schools when he discovered that ". . . the system was seriously jammed up." The expression "seriously jammed up" and the chapter title, "Logjam," refers to the image of the log driver that is introduced towards the end of this conversation. The image is taken up again in the next conversation. The image provides a way of speaking about the challenge of clearing away blockages to our natural dynamism of self-transcendence as it unfolds in the personal relationships of social systems. Sarge replies by saying: ". . . we worked to release the spiritual capacity of the people involved in the admissions process." While the image of the "logjam" comes from Didymus, it expresses a way of understanding relations between "the person and the common good" that has links to Aquinas and Maritain and would have been familiar to Sarge. The "common good" is achieved as a pattern of cooperation that functions well when persons pursue their social living in accordance with their natural dynamism of self-transcendence. See, e.g., Maritain, *The Person and the Common Good*, pp. 52–55 and 81–82.

[2] Persons and systems

One of the lines of analysis running through this chapter is what Didymus calls Sarge's "intriguing approach to systems change." Shriver's approach to organizations and systems never lost sight of the role of persons as change agents within systems. This focus on persons is evident in Stossel's account of Sarge's "Socratic Seminar" during the Peace Corps years (see Stossel, 209–17). This way of thinking about persons and systems has roots in Maritain's philosophy of "Personalism" with its "common good" approach to relations between persons and social systems. It would also have been evident to Sarge in his own experience, something he tries to impress upon Didymus. See Maritain, *The Social and Political Philosophy of Jacques Maritain*, 82–88; and *The Person and the Common Good*, 47–89. This philosophy, however, is developed by Lonergan, in *Method in Theology*, 47–51. Here readers observe explicit discussions of roles and horizons and how self-transcendence is operative in building and transforming organizational systems. Lonergan uses the term "good of order" to speak about the way that acts of meaning link together to create social schemes that offer roles that can call persons towards self-transcendence. Readers will observe this line of analysis of persons and social systems emerging in the interaction between Sarge and Didymus throughout this conversation.

[3] Systems and spirituality

Didymus makes the observation that "Most people would have trouble imagining how the spirit factors into the workings of a system." In Shriver's account of spirituality and social systems, readers familiar with Maritain will observe features in common with Maritain's account of persons, the common good, and the divine. See, e.g., Maritain, *The Person and the Common Good*, chap. 4, especially pp. 76–82. Shriver was influenced by Maritain, but he was able to use Maritain's complex metaphysical language to illuminate his own personal experience. This was a gift he had. Sarge was profoundly aware that an invitation to self-transcendence arising as transformative opportunities in connection with a new role was a defining mark of the work of the spirit. For Sarge, the act of responding authentically to the spirit's invitation was exemplified by Mary's response to the angel Gabriel (Lk 1:38).

4 Intellectual rigor and realism

Sarge replies: "We should all be able to think rigorously and realistically about this." His commitment to intellectual rigor and realism was notable throughout his public life, and this commitment extended seamlessly into his understanding of spiritual reality. Notable in Sarge's approach is his attention to detail, his commitment to questioning, his concern for evidence, and his focus on concrete experience. Like Jacques Maritain, Shriver held that our drive to know enabled us to come to true and objective understandings of our circumstances, whether our knowing was carried by the natural sciences in the case of the material world, or by our spiritual practice in the case of our conscious presence to the spirit. Maritain's analyses of the "realism" of knowing in science, philosophy, art, and mysticism are provided in *The Range of Reason*, 3–29.

5 Mustard seeds

The mustard seed metaphor is a reference to the Gospel parable of Mk 4:30-32.

6 Racial justice in Chicago high schools

In the notes to Conversation 4, readers will find the research resources used in this chapter's account of Shriver's meeting with Lloyd Davis and his work for racial justice in CCIC and the Catholic high school system during the Chicago years.

7 Self-transcendence

Readers may find the term "self-transcendence" rather esoteric or obscure. As used here, however, the meaning is quite straightforward.

Transcendence refers to the simple matter of "going beyond." When coupled with "self," it refers to the fact that I am never merely a single, fixed self. Rather, I can grow, mature, and develop. I can choose to seize growth opportunities presented in situations, and when I do, I give myself over to the dynamism of transcendence at work within myself. I go beyond my lesser self towards a wiser, more responsible self. See, e.g., Lonergan, *Insight*, pp. 658–9; *Method in Theology*, pp. 104–105.

[8] Being mindful with the model

Didymus poses the question: "Are you asking me to be mindful again?" The reference here is to Shriver's way of speaking about persons and systems that focuses attention, not on outward objects and events, but on the way our consciousness is engaged. The spirit's role is discerned in the way our consciousness shifts to seize opportunities for self-transcendence. Attending to these shifts in consciousness involves a self-reflective way of thinking about how we use our minds. Readers will find resources for Shriver's attention to "consciousness" in relation to spirituality in the notes to Conversations 2 and 3. The centrality of "the conscious component" in Shriver's model for understanding spirituality comes into play again later in this conversation.

[9] Systems, consciousness, and the spirit

Part way through their analysis of the school admissions system, Didymus gets stuck and asks: "What more do I need to know?" Sarge responds by speaking about the "conscious" and "spiritual" components of social systems. Readers will observe, here, Sarge's application of the threefold model developed in earlier chapters and discussed in detail in Conversation 4. The three components are the sensory, the conscious, and the spiritual components. Applying the model involves attending, first, to the sensory particulars of an event; then second, to the conscious engagement of the minds of the persons involved; and third, to their conscious presence to the spirit. For information on the model, see the notes to Conversation 4.

[10] "Individuals who carry out the tasks in the system are conscious people" Once again, Sarge refers to the importance of consciousness in the model. He turns attention to what people are doing when using their minds. For relevant resources and background information see the notes to Conversations 2 and 3.

[11] Roles and new possibilities

Sarge speaks about the way the role offered to him by Lloyd Davis ". . . opened up new possibilities." He says, "It put me in play in a new way." He says the new role ". . . engaged me in different horizons of concern, different states of play, different options and opportunities for engagement and action." His reference here is to the way the spirit operates as "transformative experience." It transforms us by changing our state of consciousness. For relevant resources, see the notes to Conversation 4, notably Melchin and Price, "Religion and Politics in the Early Public Life of Sargent Shriver."

[12] "The sin of racism"

Mid-way through the chapter, Sarge and Didymus begin speaking about how Shriver responded to the challenge presented by the "sin of racism" while working with the Chicago Merchandise Mart. The event referred to is detailed by Stossel in *Sarge*, p. 119.

[13] The method: consciousness and self-awareness

In trying to understand Shriver's way of speaking about the spirit and consciousness, Didymus says: "I'm asking if you would have been consciously present to the spirit if you hadn't been consciously present to yourself." Then, after Sarge responds, he asks: "Indulge me one more time, then. Davis offered you the role, and in response to the offer you became consciously present to yourself. You were aware of asking yourself, 'Will I commit to this?' and in that moment, also present to the spirit calling you to say yes." The key terms in these statements are "consciously present to yourself" and "present to the spirit." In order to gain a proper understanding of spirit and spirituality, the focus needs to be on my own consciousness and not simply on objects and events in the world around me. The spirit's operation is discernible in subtle shifts in consciousness that arise in the midst of events and opportunities presented by events. This is the insight Didymus is gradually gaining. Shriver's own background of spiritual practice gave rise to a highly developed capacity for discerning the spirit's operation in his own consciousness. The theological framework for this way of thinking is present in the works of a number of figures who influenced him, notably Teilhard de Chardin and Jacques Maritain. It is made explicit by Lonergan. Resources for these lines of influence are offered in the notes to Conversations 2 and 3. For a more detailed analysis, see Price and Melchin, *Spiritualizing Politics*, pp. 90–95.

[14] Universality of the model

As Didymus begins understanding Sarge's use of the model, he tells Sarge: "It was one conscious moment in which you differentiated two components—one spiritual, one personal." He follows up by saying: "Mary was carrying your presence to the spirit and modeling your response." Then Sarge tosses out a reference to "my Hindu friends" that reveals the universality of his model. Shriver recognizes that the spirit can be discerned acting in the lives of persons from diverse religious, cultural, or philosophical traditions. Shriver's own background was Catholic, but his words and deeds in public life revealed a way of thinking about spirituality that was attuned to the spirit's operation in diverse traditions. For a detailed analysis of this perspective in Shriver's speeches of the Chicago and Peace Corps years, see Price and Melchin, *Spiritualizing Politics*, chapters two and three.

[15] Six factors of the spiritual realism model

Towards the end of the chapter, Sarge invites Didymus to "Use the model to think it through." In reply, Didymus offers a six-point analysis of the variables or factors in the system. Examining the six points, readers will notice the influence of the threefold model developed in earlier conversations and discussed in detail in Conversation 4. As noted, applying the model involves attending, first, to the sensory particulars of an event, second, to the conscious engagement of the minds of the persons involved, and third, to their conscious presence to the spirit.

[16] Logjam

In the final pages of the conversation, Didymus refers again to the image of the "logjam." For a more detailed discussion of this image and the theological analysis it evokes, see the notes to Conversation 6.

[17] Curiosity, transformation, and conflict

When Sarge speaks about "employing a targeted form of curiosity to open up possibilities for self-transcendence," he is referring to Lonergan's understanding of the role of curiosity and questioning in the process of personal and social transformation. Scholars in the field of conflict have drawn on Lonergan to develop the Insight Approach to Conflict. See Price and Melchin, *Spiritualizing Politics*; Price, "Method in Analyzing Conflict Behavior," "Method in Peacemaking," "Explaining Human Conflict," and "Practical Idealism;" and Melchin and Picard, *Transforming Conflict through Insight*. See also the longer discussion and additional resources provided in the notes to Conversation 6.

Conversation 6

[1] The components of the spiritual realism model

The title of this chapter, "Connect the Dots," refers to Sarge's way of summarizing and clarifying the various components of his Spiritual Realism model in a practical application. Midway through the chapter, he uses this very expression: "I wanted to connect the dots among the key factors in the model."

[2] Log driver

Didymus begins this conversation by calling Sarge "Log Driver." This image of the "log driver" and the "logjam" is introduced in Conversation 5 as a way of speaking about the challenge of clearing away blockages to our natural dynamism of self-transcendence in social systems. While the image of the "logjam" comes from Didymus, it expresses a way of understanding relations between "the person and the common good" that has links to Aquinas and Maritain and would have been familiar to Sarge. The "common good" is achieved as a pattern of cooperation that functions well when persons pursue their social living in accordance with their natural dynamism of transcendence. See, e.g., Maritain, *The Person and the Common Good*, pp. 52–55 and 81–82. This approach finds contemporary expression in Lonergan in his understanding of "the good of order." See, e.g., Lonergan, *Method in Theology*, chapter two, particularly pp. 47–9.

This approach also finds expression in the work of scholars who have drawn on Lonergan to develop the Insight Approach to Conflict. For an analysis of Shriver's work in the Peace Corps and an explanation of his achievements that draws on the Insight Approach to Conflict, see Price and Melchin, *Spiritualizing Politics*, chapters four and five. The Insight Approach understands conflict as arising from blockages created by feelings of threats-to-cares. Conflict is resolved when the blockages are removed and the self-transcending dynamism of authentic curiosity is allowed to flourish.

For resources on the Insight Approach to Conflict, see Alfani, Bartoli and Garofalo, "Seeking Peace through Insights"; Jull, "Aspiring to Change"; D. Melchin, "Insight, Learning, and Dialogue in the Transformation of Religious Conflict"; Melchin and Picard, *Transforming Conflict through Insight*; Melchin and Price, "Religion and Politics in the Early Public Life of Sargent Shriver"; Picard, *Practicing Insight Mediation*, "Learning about Learning"; Picard and Jull, "Learning through Deepening Conversations"; Price, "Method in Analyzing Conflict Behavior," "Method in Peacemaking," "Explaining Human Conflict," "Practical Idealism," "Sargent Shriver, Insight Skills, and Retaliatory Violence"; Price and Bartoli, "Spiritual Values, Sustainable Security, and Conflict Resolution"; Price and Melchin, "Recovering Sargent Shriver's Vision for Poverty Law"; Price and Price, "Insight Policing and the Role of the Civilian in Police Accountability"; M. Price, "Intentional Peace," "The Process and Partnerships behind Insight Policing," "The Practical Value of Linking the Personal and the Social."

[3] Chicago high schools and racial justice

Background resources on Sarge's work with CCIC and Catholic high schools during the Chicago years are provided in the notes to Conversations 4 and 5.

[4] Launching the Peace Corps

Shriver's biographer, Scott Stossel, provides detailed background information on the "forced march" that led to the launch and funding of the Peace Corps in the early months of 1961 in *Sarge*, chapters 13 to 17. Other sources on Shriver's role in the design and development of the Peace Corps include Redmon, *Come As You Are*, and Rice, *The Bold Experiment*.

[5] The six factors of the spiritual realism model

The reference to "six of the key variables" at work in understanding the role of the spirit in social systems is a reference to the framework of six "key factors" that is developed by Sarge and Didymus towards the end of Conversation 5. The six key factors are: (1) the persons in their roles; (2) their horizons of concern; (3) their aspirations to achieve their best; (4) the image or model that carries their aspirations; (5) the spirit's presence to them as the tug or call to live up to their best selves; and (6) the persons' conscious presence to this spiritual tug or call. Readers will note that this sixfold model is an expansion and further differentiation of the threefold model first introduced in Conversations 2 and 3 and explained in Conversation 4. The basic model is offered as a way of understanding the role of the spirit in our lives: (1) the particulars of an event; (2) the conscious engagement of our minds; and (3) our conscious presence to the spirit. See the notes to Conversation 4 for background resources for this model in Shriver's speeches and in the resources that influenced his thought and his work.

[6] A "still, small, conscious presence"

This way of thinking about the spirit as a "still, small, conscious presence" as opposed to a "source of physical force or power" is discussed in the notes to Conversation 5, and resources for this approach are presented in the notes to Conversation 3. The basis of this approach is a method of self-reflection that is present in the works of Augustine and Aquinas and best developed by Lonergan.

[7] "The spirit as inner log driver"

With the return of the image of the "log driver," we come back to the discussion of Shriver's work for racial justice in Catholic high schools during the Chicago years. The basic resources for the narrative of events related to Shriver's meeting with Lloyd Davis and the launch of his work for racial justice in Chicago are presented in the notes to Conversations 4 and 5.

[8] Conversations with Chicago high school principals

In developing this portrait of Sarge's conversations with the Chicago high school principals, I have drawn on research from four sets of sources. During the years of our friendship, our personal conversations provided ample opportunity for insight into his spirituality, how it informed every aspect of his work, and how he talked about it. These insights have been confirmed and developed by the second and third sets of resources, his speeches from these years and the information provided by Sarge's biographer, Scott Stossel. The list of speeches dealing with race-related topics during the Chicago years is provided in the notes to Conversation 4. And the relevant pages from Stossel's book, *Sarge*, are those of chapter 9, pp. 117–129. The fourth resource is provided by my study of one book, two doctoral theses, one master's thesis, a published article, and a collection of websites dedicated to the topic of Catholic religious orders involved in education in Chicago in the early- and mid-twentieth century. The book-length study is Mary Beth Fraser Connolly, *Women of Faith*. The two doctoral theses are Joseph J. McCarthy, "History of Black Catholic Education in Chicago, 1871–1971"; and Alison Mary Kline-Kator, "Mercy Charism and Professional Development." The master's thesis is by Sister Mary Robert Dennis, S.B.S., "St. Elizabeth's Parish and the Negro." The journal article is Suellen Hoy, "Lives on the Color Line." And the various websites are listed in the bibliography as: Illinois High School Glory Days, "Chicago Mercy High School"; Illinois High School Glory Days, "Des Plaines St. Patrick Academy"; "Sisters of Mercy"; "St. Patrick Academy"; "Holy Cross Church"; "St. Joseph's Church"; and "St. Joseph's Parish."

[9] The survey

> At one point in the Sarge-Didymus discussion of Sarge's conversations with the high school principals, Sarge tells Didymus: "I would thank them for participating in our survey of the racial composition of the high schools." I learned of this survey and reviewed many of the relevant documents during my visit to the CICC archives at the Chicago Historical Society in May 2017. The reference to the CCIC archives is also listed in the notes to Conversation 4.

[10] The Insight approach to conflict

> In their discussion about the conversations with the high school principals, Didymus tells Sarge: "But as I listened to your question, I found myself taking on the perspective of the principal on the receiving end of your question. I felt a challenge in it." When invited to clarify, he replies, "I felt the urge to defend myself." What emerges in this exchange is a central ingredient in the Insight Approach to Conflict. The Insight Approach understands conflict as arising from blockages created by feelings of threat. Threat feelings give rise to attack-defend responses which provoke further threat feelings and attack-defend responses in other parties. Threat feelings tend to narrow and focus curiosity onto defense and attack, thus blocking parties' abilities to engage mindfully in understanding each other. Conflict is resolved when the blockages are removed and the self-transcending dynamism of authentic curiosity is allowed to flourish. Sarge tells Didymus that he was "genuinely curious about the decisions they were making and the obstacles they faced. I wasn't sitting in judgment. They could tell." His form of participation in the conversations with the principals models the role that genuine curiosity plays in de-escalating conflict in the Insight Approach. Research resources on the Insight Approach to Conflict are provided in the second note of this conversation.

[11] Certainty and curiosity

As they work with various aspects of the model, Didymus once again pushes Sarge to help him better understand the role of the spirit. He admits the subtlety and complexity of the model and then wonders out loud about the effectiveness of such an approach. "It's ironic, I know. Relying on the spirit the way you do—and the way the model does—makes it feel less certain, less sure of the outcome." Sarge's response is rather dramatic: "Compared to what? Paying off the admissions committee? Condemning a principal for the racial bias in their admissions process? Threatening to slice their tires or whack them on the side of the head if they don't change their ways?" What emerges in this exchange is another central feature of the Insight Approach to Conflict, the focus on the parties' certainty and the role of certainty in exacerbating conflicts. Feelings of threat have the effect of narrowing the focus of parties' minds on attack-defend, and along with this narrowed focus comes a certainty about the other. Conflicts are resolved when genuine curiosity—with its uncertainty about the other—begins taking over as the parties' mode of engagement. For a fuller analysis, see Melchin, Bartoli, and Price, "The Insight Approach to Conflict." See also the other research resources listed in this conversation's second note.

[12] Sister Mary-Frances

As usual, Sarge helps Didymus better understand the model by providing a concrete example, the example of Sister Mary-Frances. I came across the name of Sister Mary-Frances during my visit to the CICC archives at the Chicago Historical Society in May 2017. I have developed a fictional, yet arguably plausible portrait of the character I call Sister Mary-Frances by consulting Mary Beth Fraser Connolly, *Women of Faith*; Alison Mary Kline-Kator, "Mercy Charism and Professional Development"; and the websites listed in the bibliography as Illinois High School Glory Days, "Chicago Mercy High School";

Illinois High School Glory Days, "Des Plaines St. Patrick Academy"; "Sisters of Mercy"; and "St. Patrick Academy." I have drawn on the wealth of information provided in Joseph J. McCarthy, "History of Black Catholic Education in Chicago, 1871–1971" to understand the background context related to racism in Chicago during the years when Sister Mary-Frances was Principal at St. Patrick's in her real life.

[13] The Sisters of Mercy

At one point, Sarge tells Didymus: "But as a Sister of Mercy, she was also concerned about young Black women in the city who were educationally underserved. She told me that as a Sister of Mercy, she was concerned for the dignity and self-sufficiency of all women— especially young women disadvantaged by the fact of being poor and female." In order to understand the sense of mission and purpose that dynamized Sister Mary-Frances as a Sister of Mercy in Chicago in the 1950s, I consulted the following resources: Mary Beth Fraser Connolly, *Women of Faith*, chapters 2–4, particularly pp. 107–114; and Alison Mary Kline-Kator, "Mercy Charism and Professional Development," pp. 2–14.

Conversation 7

[1] Narrative Image

"Narrative image" is a term that comes up frequently at this point in the conversation. This is because it plays a key role in the model that emerges in Sarge's efforts to help Didymus identify the presence of the spirit in significant decisions of public life. As a gifted speaker, Shriver was aware of the power of images and stories in making ideas come alive for his audience. But he was also able to draw on philo- sophical resources for analyzing and explaining how narrative images do their work. One of the likely influences in this regard would have been Aquinas's understanding of poetic knowledge as knowledge through inclination. Maritain offers an account of this aspect of poetic knowledge in *The Range of Reason*, pp. 16–18, 19-21, and 25–26. His point is that, in contrast to knowledge gained through reasoning and argument, there is an aesthetic mode of engagement in which values become present to us in ways that can be emotionally compelling without achieving explicit formulation.

Lonergan formulates the expression "feelings as intentional responses to values" in order to explain how our feelings can point us or direct us towards values even when the objects of these feelings remain unclear or obscure. For an excellent account of Lonergan's analysis of feelings and values, see Patrick Byrne, *The Ethics of Discernment*, chapters 4–8. In this conversation, Sarge helps Didymus get in touch with shifts in his own feeling and valuing, and he invites his friend to notice and understand the role of narrative images in shaping the direction of his valuing. As he engages Didymus in this self-reflective exercise, the focus on narrative images becomes Sarge's way of helping Didymus notice the presence of the spirit in his own deliberation process.

[2] A model of change emphasizing curiosity and openness to uncertainty
At one point, Sarge asks Didymus: "What model of change are you thinking with right now?" After a question for clarification and some initial comments, his friend replies: "If anything, it feels like I'm channeling a little bit of the big bad wolf." Sarge responds by asking: "You want to huff and puff and blow the house down?" Although he does not use the term, Sarge is directing Didymus's attention to the role of "narrative image" in his thinking here. In this case, the narrative image pertains to his expectations about change, the pace of change, how change happens, our agency in forcing or pushing change, and our certainty about what must be done to effect change. The image

recalls Sarge's question to Didymus in the previous chapter: "Compared to what? Paying off the admissions committee? . . . Threatening to slice their tires or whack them on the side of the head if they don't change their ways?" One of the issues here, as in the previous chapter, is explained by the Insight Approach to Conflict. It is the certainty that conflict situations typically evoke in parties when they feel threatened. In contrast to this, Sarge directs his friend towards a different approach, one in which genuine curiosity and openness to uncertainty plays a key role. When asked "What could sister Mary-Frances do that would make a positive difference in her situation?" Sarge replies by affirming a stance of uncertainty that evokes genuine curiosity. "That's the thing. We don't know yet."

[3] The Peace Corps Act

The opening sentence of the Peace Corps Act can be found on the Peace Corps website. See the link in the bibliography under "Peace Corps Act." For a fuller discussion of Sarge's understanding of the Peace Corps and the role of his spirituality in the thoughts and actions that guided his work in designing and directing the Peace Corps, see Price and Melchin, *Spiritualizing Politics*, chapters 3 and 5.

[4] Peace Corps, the Dominican Republic, and Kirby Jones

I have drawn my information on the background situation and the involvement of the Peace Corps Volunteers in the violence in the Dominican Republic in April 1965 from Kirby Jones, *Journal Written by Kirby Jones, Peace Corps Volunteer in Dominican Republic, 1963–65*, pp. 513–608. At one point in the conversation, Sarge invites his friend to imagine himself involved in the situation: "But for now, just imagine yourself in the role of a Peace Corps Volunteer in the Dominican Republic caught up in the April '65 revolution. You've been notified by Peace Corps staff that you have a decision to make. Are you going to remain in your service placement, or leave the country?" In authoring the dialog of this page and the pages that follow, I have been guided by the information provided by Jones in his *Journal*. Moreover, in four speeches delivered between June 1965 and March 1968, Sarge refers to the involvement of the Peace Corps Volunteers in the April 1965 violence in the Dominican Republic. The detail provided in these speeches supports the line of analysis offered in the pages of this chapter. See SSPI 1965.06.12 Western Michigan, p. 3; SSPI 1965.06.13 St. John's, pp. 3–4; SSPI 1968.02.07 Notre Dame, p. 2; SSPI 1968.03.17 Institute, pp. 4–5.

[5] Peace Corps in the Dominican Republic

For another study of the involvement of Peace Corps Volunteers in the violence in the Dominican Republic in April 1965, see Tad Szulc, *Dominican Diary*.

[6] The independence of Peace Corps

For details related to the independence of the Peace Corps from other agencies of the US government, see Stossel, *Sarge*, 218–32.

[7] Evaluating narrative images

In the final pages of the conversation, Sarge tells Didymus: "So you're not just evaluating choices and options, you're evaluating narrative images." His reference here is to the work of Lonergan and the role of the cognitional operation of judgment with respect to feelings, images, and values. Judgments of value are never simply about outward events; they are also constitutive of the persons we are becoming through our decisions and actions. See, e.g., Melchin, *Living with Other People*, chapter three. Of course, Sarge's point here is that, when we are present to the spirit, the person we are becoming in our self-transcending decisions, is often something we do not know at the time. Openness to uncertainty is a feature of the model that Didymus appears to be discovering in this conversation.

Conversation 8

[1] Applying the model: Sarge's work for racial justice in Chicago

As noted in the Introduction to the book, the question that has guided me throughout is this: "Does the model of spiritual realism that Didymus and Sarge elucidate in the course of their conversation ring true to the inner conscious experience of the reader?" This conversation shifts from the development of Sarge's model of spiritual realism to the application of the model to Sarge's civil rights work in Chicago. The conversation between Sarge and Didymus invites readers to follow Didymus in applying the model and discovering the presence of the spirit in his own consciousness. As Sarge makes clear, doing this requires engaging with the details of particular situations and events, and so I have structured the conversation to provide considerably more historical detail than readers observe in previous conversations.

Most of the historical detail is provided by Sarge in the dialog. In attributing this considerable range of historical detail to Sarge, I have been guided by three sets of resources. First, as his biographer establishes in the first twelve chapters of the book, *Sarge*, Shriver was religiously and theologically educated. His education included detailed knowledge of Catholic Church history in America, particularly in those areas where he became involved actively as a public person. Stossel makes it clear that, throughout his life, he got to know Church leaders personally, and he also got to know women and men who worked on the front lines of Church life. This portrait of Sarge is confirmed by the other resources consulted in our study of Sarge. See Price and Melchin, *Spiritualizing Politics*.

Second, historical details on Sarge's work with CICC are provided in his speeches. Between April 1956 and February 1959, Sarge delivered five speeches that focus explicitly on this work: SSPI

1956.04.26 Racial Harmony; SSPI 1957.11.18 Saints Church; SSPI 1958.08.29 Roots of Racism; SSPI 1958.10.26 Hoey Award; and SSPI 1959.02.03 Your Brother. There can be no doubt that his hands-on involvement in these activities resulted in his gaining considerable historical background knowledge related to the challenges addressed by this work.

Third, as in Conversation 6, the framework for the exploration of this historical detail is provided by my portrait of the character I call Sister Mary-Frances. I came across the name of Sister Mary-Frances during my visit to the CICC archives at the Chicago Historical Society in May 2017. Resources for my understanding of her as a Sister of Mercy are provided by Mary Beth Fraser Connolly, *Women of Faith*; Alison Mary Kline-Kator, "Mercy Charism and Professional Development"; Suellen Hoy, "Lives on the Color Line"; Illinois High School Glory Days, "Chicago Mercy High School"; Illinois High School Glory Days, "Des Plaines St. Patrick Academy"; and the web pages listed as "St. Patrick Academy"; and "Sisters of Mercy." I have drawn on Joseph J. McCarthy, "History of Black Catholic Education in Chicago, 1871–1971" for historical details on the background context related to racism in Chicago during the years when Sister Mary-Frances was principal at St. Patrick's in her real life.

[2] Narrative image

For an explanation of the term "narrative image" and a list of resources related to Sarge's use of the term, see the notes to Conversation 7.

[3] Sister Mary-Frances

For background references related to Sister Mary-Frances, see the first note of this conversation.

[4] The model of spiritual realism

When Didymus refers to "the model" and "the key factors," he is referring to the model of Spiritual Realism developed in Conversations 3 to 7. For a concise presentation of the model, see the notes to Conversation 6.

[5] Historical background and Sister Mary-Frances's role at St. Patrick's School

After initial discussions of the Dominican Republic and the model of Spiritual Realism, Sarge and Didymus get down to a detailed examination of the historical background for the challenges faced by Sister Mary-Frances at St. Patrick's School. Sarge begins by speaking about the Catholic Churches in the "Back of the Yards." For a quick sketch of the history of this neighborhood, see James R. Barret, "Back of the Yards." Joseph J. McCarthy provides an account of the ethnic separation of the various Catholic Churches in Chicago and the establishment of seven Catholic parishes in the Back of the Yards in "History of Black Catholic Education in Chicago, 1871–1971," pp. 89–91.

[6] Hog butcher for the world

Sarge makes references to the expression "hog butcher for the world," from the Carl Sandberg poem, in four speeches from his time in Chicago: SSPI 1956.11.19 School Boards, p. 5; SSPI 1957.10.13 Rutledge, p. 4; SSPI 1958.04.27 Men Money, p. 7; and SSPI 1959.06.04 Procopius, p. 7.

[7] George Cardinal Mundelein

For brief introductory portraits of George Cardinal Mundelein, see Joseph J. McCarthy, "History of Black Catholic Education in Chicago, 1871–1971," pp. 19–26; Michael Sean Winters, "'Crossing Parish Boundaries' Sheds Light on Chicago Racial History"; Timothy B. Neary, "Bishop Sheil, the CYO, and Reflections for our Times," pp. 46, 48–52; and the web page listed as "George Mundelein."

[8] "Separate but equal"

In the conversation, Sarge asks Didymus about the narrative image carrying the performance of Cardinal Mundelein in his decisions to create ethnically distinct parishes and schools. After some discussion, Sarge invokes the expression "separate but equal." It is clear from his speeches that Sarge strongly criticized the lines of thought and action evoked by this image. This criticism is expressed most clearly in his February 3, 1959 speech delivered in Delaware. Sarge lists four arguments against racial integration and proceeds to refute them all. See SSPI 1959.02.03 Your Brother, p. 2.

[9] The 1954 Supreme Court decision

Sarge refers to the 1954 Supreme Court decision, *Brown v. Board of Education*. There can be no doubt that Shriver would have been familiar with this ruling. In his November 18, 1957 address to Saints Faith, Hope and Charity Church, Sarge refers to this decision. See SSPI 1957.11.18 Saints Church, p. 4.

[10] Applying the model in a role-play: background resources

When Sarge takes on the role of Cardinal Mundelein to illustrate the application of the model, he provides a considerable amount of historical information. In order to assemble this information, I have consulted a range of resources. On the background history of the Great Migration and its impact on Chicago, see: James Grossman, "Great Migration; Journey to Sanctuary"; "Introduction to the Great Migrations"; National Park Service, "Chicago's Black Metropolis"; Chicago Public Library, "Housing and Race in Chicago"; and the web page listed as "History of African Americans in Chicago." On the impact of Mexican immigrants on Catholic Chicago, see US Catholic, "How Mexican Immigrants Changed Chicago's Parishes." On the Catholic school system in Chicago, see Ellen Skerrett, "Catholic School System." On the Black Belt and Bronzeville neighborhoods in Chicago, see Wallace Best, "Black Belt"; Timothy B. Neary, "Black Belt Catholic Space"; Chicago Detours, "The Incredible History and Cultural Legacy of the Bronzeville Neighborhood"; and Joseph J.

McCarthy, "History of Black Catholic Education in Chicago, 1871–1971," pp. 40–50.

For background information on the specific Catholic Churches of the Bronzeville neighborhood, see Frederick H. Lowe, "Keeping the Faith," (on St. Malachy Church); Rev. Donald Ehr, et al., "Communities of the Word," (on St. Elizabeth and St. Anselm Churches); *Chicago Tribune* 1894, "Augustus Tolton," (on St. Monica Church); and the web pages listed as "St. Malachy Church"; and "Corpus Christi Catholic Church." On the story of St. Monica and St. Elizabeth Parishes, Father Augustus Tolton, the Divine Word Missionaries, and the decisions of Cardinal Mundelein, see Michael Sean Winters, "'Crossing Parish Boundaries' Sheds Light on Chicago Racial History"; Sister Mary Robert Dennis, S.B.S., "St. Elizabeth's Parish and the Negro"; and Joseph J. McCarthy, "History of Black Catholic Education in Chicago, 1871–1971," pp. 68–81.

[11] The Red Summer of 1919

For historical information on the Chicago race riots of 1919, see Associated Press, "Hundreds of Black Americans Were Injured in Chicago's 'Red Summer' of Race Riots"; Associated Press, "Hundreds of Black Americans Were Killed During 'Red Summer.' A Century Later, Still Ignored"; Adam Green, "Opinion: How a Brutal Race Riot Shaped Modern Chicago"; William M. Tuttle, *Race Riot*; and Chicago 1919, "Confronting the Race Riots." For a helpful discussion of religious responses to the riots, see Heath W. Carter, "Making Peace with Jim Crow."

Conversation 9

[1] Applying the model: Peace Corps

This final conversation reconnects with the original question of

Conversation 1 and brings the dialog to a close with Didymus discovering that he can indeed use the model successfully to discern the presence of the spirit. As the conversation unfolds, readers observe that the key to using the model is shifting attention from the objects of sensory experience to the operations of one's own consciousness.

[2] Spirituality in Sarge's speeches

When Didymus asks Sarge, "You're talking about the winds of the spirit?" he answers: "I am." The analysis of this conversation focuses on how Shriver understood the role of the spirit in the events leading up to Kennedy's decision to launch Peace Corps. One of the primary resources for affirming that Shriver did indeed understand the spirit's role in these events is the body of speeches that he delivered during the Peace Corps Years, 1961–64. These speeches provide evidence on how Shriver understood his own role in public life as a spiritual vocation. And they provide indications of how he understood the spirit's role in the events of politics.

As Shriver moved into his role as director of Peace Corps, the language of his speeches became noticeably different from that during the earlier period in Chicago. In many of his speeches, he no longer uses explicitly religious language and he cites no religious sources (see, e.g., Shriver, SSPI 1961.03.24 Youth Forum; see also, e.g., SSPI 1961.06.29 Student Education; SSPI 1961.07.24 Higher Education; SSPI 1961.09.12 Agricultural; SSPI 1961.10.13 Corn Picking; SSPI 1961.10.13 Wisconsin; SSPI 1962.02.09 Student Editors; SSPI 1963.06.09 Springfield). This evidence, however, cannot lead to the conclusion that he no longer understood his public life as a spiritual vocation. In a number of speeches delivered to religious audiences, continuity with the Chicago period can be observed (Shriver, SSPI 1961.06.04 Notre Dame, pp. 2, 4; SSPI 1961.06.07 DePaul, p. 4; SSPI 1962.06.02 St. Louis, p. 1; SSPI 1963.01.15 Religion and Race, pp. 2–5; SSPI 1963.02.24 Knights of Columbus, pp. 14–15; SSPI

1963.06.12 Fordham, p. 3). Shriver continued to see his public life in Peace Corps as a spiritual vocation rooted in his Catholic tradition, as a commitment of service to others, and situated within a cosmic spiritual drama of the unity of the human family.

Sarge was able to mobilize the resources of his traditional Catholicism towards diversity, justice, and peace. He remained committed to cultural and spiritual diversity (Shriver, SSPI 1961.06.04 Notre Dame, pp. 2, 4), he saw his own tradition as a mission of service to women and men of all cultures and religions (Shriver, SSPI 1961.06.07 DePaul, p. 4), and he continued to understand citizenship in democracies as a high calling requiring the mobilization of strong spiritual resources (Shriver, SSPI 1963.01.15 Religion and Race, pp. 2–3, 5). This self-understanding seems to have prevailed throughout Shriver's life, and we can observe evidence of similar features recurring in speeches delivered years later (Shriver, SSPI 1967.10.04 University of California, p. 3; and SSPI 1986.09.20 Volunteers, p. 3).

[3] Early history of Peace Corps

For background historical resources on the early history of the Peace Corps idea and the events of the final weeks of the Kennedy presidential campaign, see Coyne, "Early '60s Analysis of Youth Service"; and the video by Long, "A Passing of the Torch."

[4] Spirituality and Peace Corps

To my knowledge, no other history of the Peace Corps focuses on the influence of Shriver's spirituality. For a list of texts I have surveyed, see the notes to Conversation 1.

[5] Humphrey and Peace Corps

For background information on Hubert Humphrey's efforts to promote an international service corps called "Peace Corps," see Humphrey, *The Education of a Public Man*, pp. 184–5.

[6] The third Kennedy-Nixon debate

For the transcript of the third televised presidential debate between Senator Kennedy and Vice President Nixon, see Commission on Presidential Debates, "The Third Kennedy-Nixon Presidential Debate." For the audio recording of Kennedy's short speech delivered to the university students in Ann Arbor, Michigan, see Kennedy, "University of Michigan, Ann Arbor Speech." See also Peace Corps, "The Founding Moment."

[7] The role-play method

In this, as in prior chapters, Sarge uses the role-play method—a method used commonly in professional skill training—to help Didymus practice using the model of Spiritual Realism. Anyone who has been involved in conflict resolution training (as I have) will know that the personal experiences evoked in the role-play method are quite real. They provide important data for gaining the type of reflexive self-knowledge that is central to the method and model of Spiritual Realism.

[8] The role-play method and attention to operations of consciousness

As Didymus follows Sarge's questioning through the role-play, he is able to shift his attention away from the objects of sensory experience and onto the operations of his own consciousness. He first observes his own operation of questioning when he replies: "I'd say I'm more puzzled than anything." Then he observes the operation of self-questioning when he replies: "It throws me back on myself . . . I find myself asking a string of internal questions. Am I willing to serve in Ghana?"

[9] Discovering the work of the spirit

As Sarge leads Didymus step-by-step through the role-play, he is able to help him discover the operation of the spirit in the call to a "purpose greater than my own economic advantage." Sarge asks him: "This hankering you have to become a person committed to advancing peace and freedom in post-colonial Africa—would you say it includes a sense of being consciously tugged to say yes?" Didymus responds by affirming the presence of the spirit in the call to say yes. [10] The spirit works in our hearts calling us to our noblest aspirations

At one point Sarge offers a simple explanation of what the model of Spiritual Realism illuminates: "The model is helpful here, yes. But to put it quite simply, you rose to Jack's challenge. I noticed it and found it was moving. *Cor ad cor loquitur*." Didymus replies: "Heart speaks to heart?" Central to Shriver's understanding was his conviction that the spirit operates as a force for change that transforms events by working in people's "hearts" (see Shriver, SSPI 1963.01.15 Religion and Race, p. 2). This way of thinking is rooted in the theology of his Catholic tradition, notably the theology of Thomas Aquinas that understands the theological virtue of charity, not as something we do, but as a gift from God that calls us and enables us to reach towards our highest aspirations.

Shriver's understanding of the theology of charity is clear in his speeches of the Chicago years (Shriver, SSPI 1956.04.25 Racial Harmony, p. 1; SSPI 1957.11.18 Saints Church, pp. 2, 3, 9; SSPI 1957.09.03 Champaign, p. 7; SSPI 1957.07.09 Education Future, p. 6; SSPI 1957.03.21 Ancient Mystery, p. 2; SSPI 1957.03.30 Career Conference, p. 6; SSPI 1958.02.11 Christians and Jews, p. 7; SSPI 1958.10.07 Everyone, p. 7; SSPI 1959.02.03 Your Brother, p. 8; SSPI 1957.03.04 Livingston, p. 7; SSPI 1957.03.14 Citizenship, p. 5). The role of charity arises as a dynamizing force in our efforts of service to others.

One author whose name shows up in the speeches of the 1950s and 1960s, when Shriver speaks about charity and public life, is Léon Bloy (see, e.g., Shriver, SSPI 1958.02.11 Christians and Jews, p. 6; SSPI 1966.06.05 Illinois Wesleyan, p. 4; SSPI 1966.10.12 Catholic Charities, p. 3; SSPI 1966.02.12 Xavier Alumni, p. 6). The influence of Bloy on Shriver seems linked to Dorothy Day and her selfless dedication to the poor in the Catholic Worker Movement. Charles Curran makes the link between Bloy and Dorothy Day in *American Catholic Social Ethics*, p. 130. For a portrait of Léon Bloy that explores the links between the supernatural gift of charity and his personal dedication to the poor, see Dubois, *Portrait of Léon Bloy*, pp. 69–79, 96, 100–102.

During the Peace Corps years, Shriver developed a language for communicating these theological ideas to diverse publics in terms that would facilitate understanding. He began using the language of "spirit" and "spirituality" (see Shriver, SSPI 1961.07.24 Higher Education, p. 3; SSPI 1961.10.18 Women, p. 4; SSPI 1962.06.03 Kansas State, p. 4; SSPI 1962.06.26 Women's Clubs, p. 6; SSPI 1963.05.28 Salem, pp. 1, 3; SSPI 1963.06.09 Springfield, p. 3). Instead of using the language of "sin and grace," he spoke of the fact that spiritual traditions themselves can fall prey to corruption and forms of "spiritual flabbiness" that require renewal (Shriver, SSPI 1963.05.28 Salem, p. 1; see also SSPI 1961.10.18 Women, p. 4; SSPI 1963.06.09 Springfield, pp. 1–2; SSPI 1962.06.03 Kansas State, p. 2). Central in this renewal is the role played by charity, and in the Peace Corps years, he began speaking about charity using terms like "compassion" (Shriver, SSPI 1963.01.15 Religion and Race, pp. 1–2; SSPI 1963.06.12 Fordham, p. 3; SSPI 1964.04.19 Dedication, pp. 1–2). Clearly the term "compassion" remained central for Shriver throughout his life, and we see the term reappear again two decades later in a manuscript that reveals both his devotion to Mary, Mother of Jesus, and his way of understanding the Divine gift of charity as compassion (Shriver, SSPI 1982.07.01 Dedication).

[11] The Guskin letter

For the text of the letter by Judith and Alan Guskin, see Guskin and Guskin, "A Letter to *The Michigan Daily*." For accounts of the events surrounding the letter by the Guskins, see Stossel, *Sarge*, pp. 169–72;

Coyne, "Early '60s Analysis of Youth Service"; Long, "A Passing of the Torch"; and Redmon, *Come As You Are*, pp. 12–14.

[12] The design of Peace Corps: harnessing the power of the spirit

At the end of the final conversation, we observe a short back-and-forth between Sarge and Didymus in response to the comment about "spontaneous combustion." Sarge says: "A sequence of progressive and cumulative decisions grounded in self-transcendence and open to the spirit." Didymus replies: "Which is what you tried to set up in the Peace Corps." Shriver affirms: "It's what we achieved, yes."

To say that the Peace Corps was intentionally designed to harness the power of the spirit is to make a bold claim, yet evidence in support of this claim can be found scattered throughout Shriver's speeches. Shriver's speeches provide considerable detail on how he understood the role of service within the Peace Corps and the role spirituality played in the organizational structure it would implement to achieve its goals of service. Central to the Peace Corps was the call to the service of others. For Shriver, the commitment to service could be expected to result in transformative experiences that promote peace in situations of adversity and conflict (Shriver, SSPI 1964.01.28 Secret, p. 3).

A notable example of this transformative process in action is provided by Shriver's 1965 account of the experiences encountered by Peace Corps Volunteers in Panama during the anti-America riots of January 1964. The dramatic upshot of these events was that host country villagers had developed such strong bonds of respect and friendship for the Volunteers that they took them into their homes and sheltered them from marauding bands. The proof, for Shriver, was that the dedication to service within the Peace Corps actually works (Shriver, SSPI 1965.01.25 Poverty Southwest, p. 2).

For other accounts of how the Peace Corps works through service and transformative experiences, see Shriver, SSPI 1963.05.30

Roosevelt, p. 3; SSPI 1963.11.19 YMCA, pp. 2–3; SSPI 1965.12.07 International Living, pp. 2–3; and Shriver, *Point of the Lance*, pp. 202–5. A significant Catholic figure who influenced Shriver was Dorothy Day. Stossel speaks about the influence of Dorothy Day on Shriver during his years at Yale (*Sarge*, p. 44). Like Maritain, Day was influenced by a school of Catholic philosophy called "Personalism." In *American Catholic Social Ethics* (pp. 30–32), Charles Curran traces the influence of Personalism on Dorothy Day and her commitment to the service of the others in the Catholic Worker. It is not difficult to observe similarities between Shriver's and Day's spiritually grounded dedication to the service of others.

For Shriver, one idea, "the most powerful idea of all," was central in his understanding of how the Peace Corps works: ". . . the idea that free and committed men and women can cross, even transcend, boundaries of culture and language, of alien tradition and great-disparities of wealth, of old hostilities and new nationalisms, to meet with other men and women on the common ground of service to human welfare and human dignity" (Shriver, SSPI 1964.01.28 Secret, p. 3). Shriver explicitly structured Peace Corps programs so that Volunteers and international partners would be changed or transformed by this call to service. For a detailed analysis of this influence, see Price and Melchin, *Spiritualizing Politics*.

Central to this were his "few and simple rules": learn the language; commit to personal sacrifice; live within the local customs and traditions; adopt their standard of living; and believe in the power of integrity, humility, and determination (Shriver, SSPI 1963.10.11 Commonwealth Club, p. 4). For Shriver, the intended effect of the Peace Corps was never to proselytize or promote political, economic, or religious objectives (Shriver, SSPI 1964.01.28 Secret, p. 3). Rather, Shriver's aim was for the Peace Corps to be an agency for the "compassion and service" that can ". . . dissolve obstacles of race or belief anywhere in the world. People are hungry for contact, for fellowship, for the breaking down of barriers" (Shriver, SSPI 1963.06.12 Fordham, p. 3). Shriver's language reflects a transposition of the traditional Catholic theological language of charity into the language of spirituality and compassion. The distinguishing mark of this spirituality is the self-transcending call to the service of others in need.

BIBLIOGRAPHY

(All online documents accessed March–June, 2022)

Speeches by Sargent Shriver, Online, Sargent Shriver Peace Institute (SSPI)

SSPI 1955.02.09 Kenwood

"Speech at Kenwood and Murray Schools PTA." Kenwood School, February 9, 1955. http://www.sargentshriver.org/speech-article/speech-at-kenwood-and-murray-schools-pta

SSPI 1956.01.16 Finance Committee

"Speech to Finance Committee, City Council of Chicago." Chicago, IL, January 16, 1956. http://www.sargentshriver.org/speech-article/speech-to-finance-committee-city-council-of-chicago

SSPI 1956.02.28 Junior Association

"Speech to the Junior Association of Commerce and Industry." Chicago, IL, February 28, 1956. http://www.sargentshriver.org/speech-article/speech-to-the-junior-association-of-commerce-and-industry

SSPI 1956.03.06 Women's Aid

"Speech to Chicago Women's Aid." Chicago, IL, March 6, 1956. http://www.sargentshriver.org/speech-article/speech-to-chicago-womens-aid

SSPI 1956.04.25 Racial Harmony

"Exploring Future of Racial Harmony—Cultural Level." DePaul University, April 25, 1956. http://www.sargentshriver.org/speech-article/exploring-future-of-racial-harmony-cultural-level

SSPI 1956.06.16 Veterans

"Address to Illinois Veterans of Foreign Wars." Chicago, IL, June

16, 1956. http://www.sargentshriver.org/speech-article/address-to-illinois-veterans-of-foreign-wars

SSPI 1956.11.19 School Boards

"Address to the Forty-Second Annual Conference of the Illinois Association of School Boards." Chicago, IL, November 19, 1956. http://www.sargentshriver.org/speech-article/address-to-the-forty-second-annual-conference-of-the-illinois-association-of-school-boards

SSPI 1956.11.30 Mary McDowell

"Address to the Mary McDowell Settlement House." Chicago, IL, November 30, 1956. http://www.sargentshriver.org/speech-article/address-to-the-mary-mcdowell-settlement-house

SSPI 1957.03.04 Livingston

"Address before the Livingston County Institute." Pontiac, IL, March 4, 1957. http://www.sargentshriver.org/speech-article/address-before-the-livingston-county-institute

SSPI 1957.03.09 Public Relations

"Public Relations and Public Schools." Bloomington, IL, March 9, 1957. http://www.sargentshriver.org/speech-article/public-relations-and-public-schools

SSPI 1957.03.14 Citizenship

"Citizenship." Grand Ballroom, Sheraton Hotel, Chicago, IL, March 14, 1957. http://www.sargentshriver.org/speech-article/citizenship

SSPI 1957.03.14 Dunbar

"Address to Dunbar Vocational School." Chicago, IL, March 14, 1957. http://www.sargentshriver.org/speech-article/address-to-dunbar-vocational-school

SSPI 1957.03.21 Ancient Mystery

"The Ancient Mystery of Guiltless Suffering." Chicago, IL, March 21, 1957. http://www.sargentshriver.org/speech-article/the-ancient-mystery-of-guiltless-suffering

SSPI 1957.03.30 Career Conference

"Career Conference Speech." Illinois Institute of Technology, March 30, 1957. http://www.sargentshriver.org/speech-article/career-conference-speech

SSPI 1957.04.17 Leadership

"Leadership in Education." Chicago Historical Society, April 17, 1957. http://www.sargentshriver.org/speech-article/leadership-in-education

SSPI 1957.06.09 Education America

"Article Concerning Education in America." Chicago Tribune Magazine, June 9, 1957. http://www.sargentshriver.org/speech-article/article-concerning-education-in-america

SSPI 1957.07.09 Education Future

"Education for the Future—A Cooperative Approach." Northwestern University, July 9, 1957. http://www.sargentshriver.org/speech-article/education-for-the-future-a-cooperative-app.roach

SSPI 1957.09.03 Champaign

"Address to Champaign Community Schools General Staff Meeting." Champaign, IL, September 03, 1957. http://www.sargentshriver.org/speech-article/speech-at-champaign-community-schools-general-staff-meeting

SSPI 1957.10.13 Rutledge

"Dedication of Rutledge Hall, Lincolnwood School." Lincolnwood, IL, October 13, 1957. http://www.sargentshriver.org/speech-article/dedication-of-rutledge-hall-lincolnwood-school

SSPI 1957.10.28 Teachers Union

"Twentieth Anniversary Birthday Greetings to the Chicago Teachers Union." Medinah Temple, October 28, 1957. http://www.sargentshriver.org/speech-article/twentieth-anniversary-birthday-greetings-to-the-chicago-teachers-union

SSPI 1957.11.18 Saints Church

"Remarks About Race to Saints Faith, Hope and Charity Church." Winnetka, IL, November 18, 1957. http://www.sargentshriver.org/speech-article/address-to-saints-faith-hope-and-charity-church

SSPI 1958.01.21 Big Sisters

"Speech to Jewish Big Sisters." Standard Club, January 21, 1958. http://www.sargentshriver.org/speech-article/speech-to-jewish-big-sisters

SSPI 1958.02.06 Problems

"The Problems of Education in Chicago." Standard Club | February 6, 1958. http://www.sargentshriver.org/speech-article/the-problems-of-education-in-chicago

SSPI 1958.02.07 Schoolmasters

"Address to the Illinois Schoolmasters Club Meeting." Illinois State Normal University, February 7, 1958. http://www.sargentshriver.org/speech-article/address-to-the-illinois-schoolmasters-club-meeting

SSPI 1958.02.11 Christians and Jews

"Address to the Annual High School National Conference of Christians and Jews." Kankakee, IL, February 11, 1958. http://www.sargentshriver.org/speech-article/address-to-the-annual-high-school-national-conference-of-christians-and-jews

SSPI 1958.04.27 Men Money

"Men, Money and Missions in the Far East." Rockford, IL, April 27, 1958. http://www.sargentshriver.org/speech-article/men-money-and-missions-in-the-far-east

SSPI 1958.08.29 Roots of Racism

"The Roots of Racism." Chicago, IL, August 29, 1958. http://www.sargentshriver.org/speech-article/the-roots-of-racism

SSPI 1958.10.07 Everyone

"Everyone Wants to Get into the Act." University of Illinois, Urbana, October 7, 1958. http://www.sargentshriver.org/ speech-article/everyone-wants-to-get-into-the-act

SSPI 1958.10.26 Hoey Award

"Presentation of the James J. Hoey Award by New York Catholic Interracial Council." New York University, October 26, 1958. http://www.sargentshriver.org/speech-article/presentation-of-the-james-j-joey-award-by-new-york-catholic-interracial-council

SSPI 1959.02.03 Your Brother

". . . And Your Brother shall Live With You." Delaware, February 3, 1959. http://www.sargentshriver.org/speech-article/and-your-brother-shall-live-with-you

SSPI 1959.06.04 Procopius

"St. Procopius College Commencement Speech." Lisle, IL, June 4, 1959. http://www.sargentshriver.org/speech-article/st-procopius-college-commencement-speech

SSPI 1961.03.24 Youth Forum

"Speech to the *New York Herald Tribune* Youth Forum." New York, March 24, 1961. http://www.sargentshriver.org/speech-article/speech-to-the-new-york-herald-tribune-youth-forum

SSPI 1961.06.04 Notre Dame

"University of Notre Dame Commencement Address." South Bend, IN, June 4, 1961. http://www.sargentshriver.org/speech-article/university-of-notre-dame-commencement-address

SSPI 1961.06.07 DePaul

"DePaul University Commencement Address." Chicago, IL, June 7, 1961. http://www.sargentshriver.org/speech-article/depaul-university-commencent-address

SSPI 1961.06.29 Student Education

"Speech to the Student National Education Association." Atlantic City, NJ, June 29, 1961. http://www.sargentshriver.org/speech-article/speech-to-the-student-national-education-association

SSPI 1961.07.24 Higher Education

"Speech at the Institute of Higher Education, Board of Education, Methodist Church." Nashville, TN, July 24, 1961. http://www.sargentshriver.org/speech-article/speech-at-the-institute-of-higher-education-board-of-education-methodist-church

SSPI 1961.09.12 Agricultural

"Speech Before the National Association of County Agricultural Agents." New York City, September 12, 1961. http://www.sargentshriver.org/speech-article/speech-before-the-national-association-of-county-agricultural-agents

SSPI 1961.10.13 Corn Picking

"Speech at the National Corn Picking Contest." Worthington, MN, October 13, 1961. http://www.sargentshriver.org/speech-article/speech-at-the-national-corn-picking-contest

SSPI 1961.10.13 Wisconsin

"Wisconsin Speech (Draft)." Wisconsin, October 13, 1961. http://www.sargentshriver.org/speech-article/wisconsin-speech-draft

SSPI 1961.10.18 Women

"Women in the Corps." New York City, October 18, 1961. http://www.sargentshriver.org/speech-article/women-in-the-corps

SSPI 1962.02.09 Student Editors

"Statement to the Student Editors of the Conference on International Affairs." New York City, February 9, 1962. http://www.sargentshriver.org/speech-article/statement-to-the-student-editors-of-the-conference-on-international-affairs

SSPI 1962.06.02 St. Louis

"St. Louis University Commencement Speech." Kiel Auditorium,

June 2, 1962. http://www.sargentshriver.org/speech-article/st-lou-is-university-commencement-speech

SSPI 1962.06.03 Kansas State

"Kansas State University Commencement Address." Manhattan, KS, June 3, 1962. http://www.sargentshriver.org/speech-article/kansas-state-university-commencement-address

SSPI 1962.06.26 Women's Clubs

"Address to the 71st Annual Convention of Women's Clubs." Washington, DC, June 26, 1962. http://www.sargentshriver.org/speech-article/address-to-the-71st-annual-convention-of-womens-clubs

SSPI 1963.01.15 Religion and Race

"Speech to the National Conference on Religion and Race." Chicago, IL, January 15, 1963. http://www.sargentshriver.org/speech-article/speech-to-the-national-conference-on-religion-and-race

SSPI 1963.02.24 Knights of Columbus

"Knights of Columbus." Chicago, IL, February 24, 1963. http://www.sargentshriver.org/speech-article/address-to-the-knights-of-columbus-in-1963

SSPI 1963.05.28 Salem

"Address to Salem College." Salem WV, May 28, 1963. http://www.sargentshriver.org/speech-article/address-to-salem-college

SSPI 1963.05.30 Roosevelt

"Speech at Eleanor Roosevelt Memorial Service." Hyde Park, NY, May 30, 1963. http://www.sargentshriver.org/speech-article/speech-at-eleanor-roosevelt-memorial-service

SSPI 1963.06.09 Springfield

"Springfield College Commencement Address." Springfield MA, June 9, 1963. http://www.sargentshriver.org/speech-article/springfield-college-commencement-address

SSPI 1963.06.12 Fordham

"The Meeting of Church and State (Fordham Commencement Address)." New York City, June 12, 1963. http://www.sargent-shriver.org/speech-article/the-meeting-of-church-and-state-fordham-commencement-address

SSPI 1963.10.11 Commonwealth Club

"Speech Before the Commonwealth Club of California." San Francisco, CA, October 11, 1963. http://www.sargentshriver.org/speech-article/speech-before-the-commonwealth-club-of-california

SSPI 1963.11.19 YMCA

"Address at the Annual Dinner of the YMCA of Greater New York." New York City, November 19, 1963. http://www.sargent-shriver.org/speech-article/address-at-the-annual-dinner-of-the-ymca-of-greater-new-york

SSPI 1964.01.28 Secret

"The Secret of Your Greatness." Bangkok, Thailand, January 28, 1964. http://www.sargentshriver.org/speech-article/the-secret-of-your-greatness

SSPI 1964.04.19 Dedication

"Dedication of the Vatican Pavilion at the New York World's Fair." New York City, April 19, 1964. http://www.sargentshriver.org/speeches/address-by-sargent-shriver-opening-of-the-vatican-exhibit

SSPI 1964.06.02 Providence College

"Providence College Commencement." Providence, RI, June 2, 1964. http://www.sargentshriver.org/speech-article/providence-college-commencement

SSPI 1964.06.08 Georgetown

"Georgetown University Commencement." Washington, DC, June 8, 1964. http://www.sargentshriver.org/speech-article/georgetown-university-commencement

SSPI 1964.06.10 New York University

"New York University Commencement." New York City, June 10, 1964. http://www.sargentshriver.org/speech-article/new-york-university-commencement

SSPI 1965.01.25 Poverty Southwest

"Address to the National Conference on Poverty in the Southwest." Tucson, AZ, January 25, 1965. http://www.sargentshriver.org/speech-article/address-to-the-national-conference-on-poverty-in-the-southwest

SSPI 1965.06.12 Western Michigan

"Western Michigan University Commencement Address." Kalamazoo, MI, June 12, 1965. http://www.sargentshriver.org/speech-article/western-michigan-university-commencement-address

SSPI 1965.06.13 St. John's

"Address to St. John's University." Jamaica, NY, June 13, 1965. http://www.sargentshriver.org/speech-article/address-to-st-johns-university

SSPI 1965.12.07 International Living

"Address to the Dinner of the Experiment in International Living." New York City, December 7, 1965. http://www.sargentshriver.org/speech-article/address-to-the-dinner-of-the-experiment-in-international-living

SSPI 1966.02.12 Xavier Alumni

"Address at the Xavier Alumni Association Diamond Jubilee Banquet." New Orleans, LA, February 12, 1966. http://www.sargentshriver.org/speech-article/address-at-the-xavier-alumni-association-diamond-jubilee-banquet

SSPI 1966.06.05 Illinois Wesleyan

"Commencement Address at Illinois Wesleyan University." Bloomington, IL, June 5, 1966. http://www.sargentshriver.org/speech-article/commencement-address-at-illinois-wesleyan-university

SSPI 1966.10.12 Catholic Charities

"Address at the National Conference of Catholic Charities Annual Convention." New Orleans, LA, October 12, 1966. http://www.sargentshriver.org/speech-article/address-at-the-national-conference-of-catholic-charities-annual-convention

SSPI 1967.04.17 Yale

"Address before the 89th Annual Yale Daily News Banquet." New Haven, CT, April 17, 1967. http://www.sargentshriver.org/speech-article/address-before-the-89th-annual-yale-daily-news-banquet

SSPI 1967.10.04 University of California

"Address at the University of California." Berkeley, CA, October 4, 1967. http://www.sargentshriver.org/speech-article/address-at-the-university-of-california

SSPI 1968.02.07 Notre Dame

"Address at a University of Notre Dame Student Assembly." South Bend, IN, February 7, 1968. http://www.sargentshriver.org/speech-article/address-at-a-university-of-notre-dame-student-assembly

SSPI 1968.03.17 Institute

"Remarks at the Institute of North American Studies." Barcelona, Spain, March 17, 1968. http://www.sargentshriver.org/speech-article/remarks-at-the-institute-of-north-american-studies

SSPI 1972.10.11 Brave Ones

"Where Have All the Brave Ones Gone?" October 11, 1972. http://www.sargentshriver.org/speech-article/where-have-all-the-brave-ones-gone

SSPI 1981.09.22 Job Corps

"Address at the National Job Corps Competition Expo Lunch." Washington, DC, September 22, 1981. http://www.sargentshriver.

org/speech-article/address-at-the-national-job-corps-competition-expo-lunch

SSPI 1982.07.01 Dedication

"Dedication for the Catholic Bishops' Pastoral Letter on War and Peace." Washington, DC, July 1, 1982. http://www.sargentshriver.org/speech-article/dedication-for-the-catholic-bishops-pastoral-letter-on-war-and-peace

SSPI 1986.09.20 Volunteers

"Speech at the National Conference of Returned Peace Corps Volunteers and Staff." Washington, DC, September 20, 1986. http://www.sargentshriver.org/speech-article/speech-at-the-national-conference-of-returned-peace-corps-volunteers-and-staff

SSPI 2002.09.17 Washington and Lee

"Speech at Washington and Lee University." Lexington, VA, September 17, 2002. http://www.sargentshriver.org/speech-article/speech-at-washington-and-lee-university

SSPI 2002.11.16 Knights

"Address to the Knights of St. Gregory." Hartford, CT, November 16, 2002. http://www.sargentshriver.org/speech-article/address-to-the-knights-of-st-gregory

Books, Articles, and Other Online Resources

Alfani, Roger, Andrea Bartoli, Mauro Garofalo. "Seeking Peace through Insights: The Community of Sant'Egidio in the Central African Republic." *Theoforum* 50 (no. 2, 2020): 207–21.

Associated Press. "Hundreds of Black Americans Were Injured in Chicago's 'Red Summer' of Race Riots." *USA Today* (July 25, 2019). https://www.usatoday.com/story/news/nation/2019/07/24/chicagos-red-summer-segregation-still-issue-after-race-riots/1812339001/

Associated Press. "Hundreds of Black Americans Were Killed During 'Red Summer.' A Century Later, Still Ignored." *USA Today* (July 24, 2019). https://www.usatoday.com/story/news/nation/2019/07/23/racial-violence-red-summer-1919-witnessed-white-black-murder/1802371001/

Barrett, James R. "Back of the Yards." http://www.encyclopedia.chicagohistory.org/pages/99.html

Best, Wallace. "Black Belt." http://www.encyclopedia.chicagohistory.org/pages/140.html

Braman, Brian. *Meaning and Authenticity*. Toronto: University of Toronto Press, 2008.

Byrne, Patrick. *The Ethics of Discernment.* Toronto: University of Toronto Press, 2016.

Carter, Heath W. "Making Peace with Jim Crow: Religious Leaders and the Chicago Race Riot of 1919." *Journal of Illinois History* 11 (2008): 261–76. https://heathwcarter.files.wordpress.com/2011/07/making-peace-with-jim-crow.pdf

Chicago 1919. "Confronting the Race Riots." https://www.chicago1919.org

Chicago Detours. "The Incredible History and Cultural Legacy of the Bronzeville Neighborhood." https://chicagodetours.com/bronzeville-neighborhood/

Chicago Public Library. "Housing and Race in Chicago." https://www.chipublib.org/housing/

Chicago Tribune 1894. "Augustus Tolton." https://tolton.archchicago.org/about/life-and-times/chicago-tribune-1894

Commission on Presidential Debates. "The Third Kennedy-Nixon Presidential Debate, October 13, 1960, Debate Transcript." https://www.debates.org/voter-education/debate-transcripts/october-13-1960-debate-transcript/

Connolly, Mary Beth Fraser. *Women of Faith: The Chicago Sisters of Mercy and the Evolution of a Religious Community*. New York: Fordham University Press, 2014.

"Corpus Christi Catholic Church." http://www.corpuschristichicago.org/cc_church_history.html

Coyne, John. "Early '60s Analysis of Youth Service." In the Series "To Preserve and Learn—Occasional Essays about the History of the Peace Corps." http://peacecorpswriters.org/pages/2003/0307/prntvrs307/pv307pchist.html

Cronin, John. *Social Principles and Economic Life*. Milwaukee: Bruce Publishing Company, 1959.

Crysdale, Cynthia, ed. *Lonergan and Feminism*. Toronto: University of Toronto Press, 1994.

Curran, Charles. *American Catholic Social Ethics*. Notre Dame: University of Notre Dame Press, 1982.

Dennis, Sister Mary Robert, S.B.S. "St. Elizabeth's Parish and the Negro." MA diss., Loyola University Chicago, 1940. https://ecommons.luc.edu/cgi/viewcontent.cgi?article=1135&context=luc_theses

"Divine Word." http://www.svdvocations.org/about-divine-word/history

Dubois, E. T. *Portrait of Léon Bloy*. London: Sheed and Ward, 1950.

Ehr, Rev. Donald, et al. "Communities of the Word." https://www.svdcuria.org/public/histtrad/docs/2014usc/2014usc07.pdf

Fitzpatrick, Joseph. *Philosophical Encounters: Lonergan and the Analytic Tradition*. Toronto: University of Toronto Press, 2005.

Flanagan, Joseph. *Quest for Self-Knowledge*. Toronto: University of Toronto Press, 1997.

"George Mundelein." https://en.wikipedia.org/wiki/George_Mundelein

Green, Adam. "Opinion: How a Brutal Race Riot Shaped Modern Chicago." *New York Times* (August 3, 2019). https://www.nytimes.com/2019/08/03/opinion/how-a-brutal-race-riot-shaped-modern-chicago.html

Grossman, James. "Great Migration." http://www.encyclopedia.chicagohistory.org/pages/545.html

Guskin, Judith and Alan Guskin. "A Letter to *The Michigan Daily*, October 21, 1960." Reprinted in James Tobin, "JFK at the Union: The Impromptu Campaign Speech that Launched the Peace Corps," 7. https://www.peacecorpsconnect.org/articles/jfk-at-the-union-the-impromptu-campaign-speech-that-launched-the-peace-corps

Haughey, John. "Responsibility for Human Rights: Contributions from Bernard Lonergan." *Theological Studies* 63 (2002): 764–785.

Hefling, Charles, *Why Doctrines?* Cambridge, MA: Cowley Press, 1984.

"History of African Americans in Chicago." https://en.wikipedia.org/wiki/History_of_African_Americans_in_Chicago

Hoffman, Elizabeth Cobbs. *All You Need is Love: The Peace Corps and the Spirit of the 1960s.* Cambridge, MA: Harvard University Press, 1998.

"Holy Cross Church." https://en.wikipedia.org/wiki/Holy_Cross_Church_(Chicago)

Hoy, Suellen. "Lives on the Color Line." *U.S. Catholic Historian* 22 (no. 1, 2004): 67–91. https://www.jstor.org/stable/25154892?seq=1

Humphrey, Hubert H. *The Education of a Public Man: My Life and Politics.* New Edition. Minneapolis: University of Minnesota Press, 1991.

Illinois High School Glory Days. "Chicago Mercy High School." http://leopardfan.tripod.com/id825.html

Illinois High School Glory Days. "Des Plaines St. Patrick Academy." http://www.illinoishsglorydays.com/id821.html

Jones, Kirby. *Journal Written by Kirby Jones, Peace Corps Volunteer in Dominican Republic, 1963-65.* Archived at the John F. Kennedy Presidential Library and Museum.

Journey to Sanctuary, "Introduction to the Great Migrations." https://www.journeytosanctuary.org/new-index

Jull, Marnie. "Aspiring to Change: Insight, Conflict and Change-making." *Theoforum* 50 (no. 2, 2020): 223–40.

Kennedy, John F., President. "University of Michigan, Ann Arbor Speech, October 14, 1960." https://www.youtube.com/watch?v=y-dTaoZ9JSGk

Kline-Kator, Alison Mary. "Mercy Charism and Professional Development." DEd diss., University of Michigan-Dearborn, 2016. https://deepblue.lib.umich.edu/bitstream/handle/2027.42/134058/Kline-Kator%20Final%20Dissertation.pdf?sequence=1&isAllowed=y

Liston, Robert A. *Sargent Shriver: A Candid Portrait.* New York: Farrar, Straus, 1964.

Lonergan, Bernard. *Insight: A Study of Human Understanding.* Eds. Frederick Crowe and Robert Doran. Vol. 3 of *Collected Works of Bernard Lonergan.* Toronto: University of Toronto Press, 1992 [orig. 1957].

______. *Method in Theology.* Eds. Robert Doran and John Dadosky. Vol. 14 of *Collected Works of Bernard Lonergan.* Toronto: University of Toronto Press, 2017 [orig. 1972].

______. *Phenomenology and Logic.* Ed. Philip McShane. Vol. 18 of *Collected Works of Bernard Lonergan.* Toronto: University of Toronto Press, 2001.

______. *Philosophical and Theological Papers 1958-1964.* Eds. Robert Croken, Frederick Crowe, and Robert Doran. Vol. 6 of *Collected Works of Bernard Lonergan.* Toronto: University of Toronto Press, 1996.

______. *Philosophical and Theological Papers 1965–1980.* Eds. Robert Croken and Robert Doran. Vol. 17 of *Collected Works of Bernard Lonergan.* Toronto: University of Toronto Press, 2004.

______. *Philosophy of God, and Theology.* London: Darton, Longman & Todd, 1973. Republished in *Philosophical and Theological Papers*

1965–1980, eds. Robert Croken and Robert Doran, 159–218. Vol. 17 of Collected Works of Bernard Lonergan. Toronto: University of Toronto Press, 2004.

______. *A Second Collection.* Eds. William Ryan and Bernard Tyrrell. Toronto: University of Toronto Press, 1996 [orig. 1974].

______. *Topics in Education.* Ed. Frederick Crowe. Vol. 10 of Collected Works of Bernard Lonergan. Toronto: University of Toronto Press, 1993.

______. *Understanding and Being.* Eds. Frederick Crowe, Robert Doran, Thomas Daly, Elizabeth Morelli, and Mark Morelli. Vol. 5 of Collected Works of Bernard Lonergan. Toronto: University of Toronto Press, 1990 [orig. 1980].

Long, Paul. "A Passing of the Torch." Emmy Award winning video of the formation of the Peace Corps. https://vimeo.com/73799145

Lowe, Frederick H. "Keeping the Faith." https://chicagoreader.com/news-politics/keeping-the-faith-2/

Maritain, Jacques. *Christianity, Democracy, and the American Ideal: A Jacques Maritain Reader.* Ed. James Kelly. Manchester, NH: Sophia Institute Press, 2004.

______. *Man and the State.* Chicago: University of Chicago Press, 1951.

______. *The Person and the Common Good.* Trans. John Fitzgerald. Notre Dame: University of Notre Dame Press, 1985 [orig. 1946].

______. *The Range of Reason.* London: Geoffrey Bles, 1953.

______. *Ransoming the Time.* New York: Charles Scribner's Sons, 1941.

______. *The Social and Political Philosophy of Jacques Maritain.* Eds. Joseph Evans and Leo Ward. Notre Dame: University of Notre Dame Press, 1976.

Mathews, William. *Lonergan's Quest.* Toronto: University of Toronto Press, 2005.

McCarthy, Colman. "Shriver: The Lightweight Label." *The Washington Monthly* 8 (June 1976):

4-10. http://www.unz.org/Pub/WashingtonMonthly-1976jun-00004

McCarthy, Joseph J. "History of Black Catholic Education in Chicago, 1871-1971." PhD diss., Loyola University Chicago, 1973. https://ecommons.luc.edu/cgi/viewcontent.cgi?article=2378&context=luc_diss

McCarthy, Michael. *The Crisis of Philosophy*. Albany: State University of New York Press, 1989.

Meisler, Stanley. *When the World Calls: The Inside Story of the Peace Corps and its First Fifty Years.* Boston: Beacon Press, 2011.

Melchin, Derek. "Insight, Learning, and Dialogue in the Transformation of Religious Conflict: Applications from the Work of Bernard Lonergan." PhD diss., McGill University, 2008.

Melchin, Kenneth. *Living with Other People*. Ottawa: Novalis; Collegeville, MN.: Liturgical Press, 1998.

Melchin, Kenneth, Andrea Bartoli, and James Price. "The Insight Approach to Conflict: Recent Achievements and Future Hopes." In *Practicing Insight Mediation*, by Cheryl Picard, 147–65. Toronto: University of Toronto Press, 2016.

Melchin, Kenneth and Cheryl Picard. *Transforming Conflict through Insight*. Toronto: University of Toronto Press, 2008.

Melchin, Kenneth and James Price. "Religion and Politics in the Early Public Life of Sargent Shriver." *Theoforum* 50 (no. 2, 2020): 337–66.

Meynell, Hugo. *Introduction to the Philosophy of Bernard Lonergan*. 2nd ed. Toronto: University of Toronto Press, 1991.

Meynell, Hugo. *Redirecting Philosophy: Reflections on the Nature of Knowledge from Plato to Lonergan*. Toronto: University of Toronto Press, 1998.

Morelli, Mark D. *Self-Possession: Being at Home in Conscious Performance*, second ed. Los Angeles: Encanto Editions, 2019.

National Park Service, "Chicago's Black Metropolis." https://www.nps.gov/articles/chicago-s-black-metropolis-understanding-history-through-a-historic-place-teaching-with-historic-places.htm

Neary, Timothy B. "Bishop Sheil, the CYO, and Reflections for our Times." *Journal of Religion & Society* 20 (Supplement, 2019): 45-62. https://dspace2.creighton.edu/xmlui/bitstream/handle/10504/123125/2019-36.pdf

Neary, Timothy B. "Black Belt Catholic Space." *U.S. Catholic Historian* 18 (no. 4, 2000): 76–91. https://www.jstor.org/stable/25154746

Peace Corps. "The Founding Moment: President John F. Kennedy's University of Michigan Speech." https://www.peacecorps.gov/about/history/founding-moment/

"Peace Corps Act." http://files.peacecorps.gov/documents/MS-101-Policy.pdf

Picard, Cheryl. "Learning about Learning: The Value of 'Insight'" *Conflict Resolution Quarterly* 20 (2003): 477–84.

______. *Practicing Insight Mediation.* Toronto: University of Toronto Press, 2016.

Picard, Cheryl and Marnie Jull. "Learning Through Deepening Conversations: A Key Strategy of Insight Mediation." *Conflict Resolution Quarterly* 29 (2011): 151–76.

Pius XI, Pope. *Quadragesimo anno.* Encyclical of Pope Pius XI on Reconstruction of the Social Order. May 15, 1931. http://w2.vatican.va/content/pius-xi/en/encyclicals/documents/hf_p-xi_enc_19310515_quadragesimo-anno.html

Porter, Jean. *The Recovery of Virtue.* Louisville, KY: Westminster/John Knox Press, 1990.

Price, James. "Method in Analyzing Conflict Behavior: The Insight Approach." *Revista de Mediación* 11 (no. 1, 2018): 1–9.

______. "Method in Peacemaking." In *Peacemaking: From Practice to Theory*, vol. 2, eds. Susan Allen Nan, Zachariah Cherian Mampilly, and Andrea Bartoli, 610–621. Santa Barbara, CA: 2012.

________. "Explaining Human Conflict: Human Needs Theory and the Insight Approach." In *Conflict Resolution and Human Needs*, eds. Kevin Avruch and Christopher Mitchell, 108-123. London: Routledge, 2013.

________. "Practical Idealism: How Sargent Shriver Built the Peace Corps." *Commonweal* (February 10, 2012): 18–21.

________. "Sargent Shriver, Insight Skills, and Retaliatory Violence." In *Practicing Insight Mediation*, by Cheryl Picard, 149–155. Toronto: University of Toronto Press, 2016.

Price, James and Andrea Bartoli. "Spiritual Values, Sustainable Security, and Conflict Resolution." In *The Routledge Handbook of Religion and Security*, eds. Chris Seiple, Dennis Hoover, and Pauletta Otis, 160–170. London: Routledge, 2013.

Price, James and Kenneth Melchin. "Recovering Sargent Shriver's Vision for Poverty Law: The Illinois Familycare Campaign and the Insight Approach to Conflict Resolution and Collaboration." *Clearinghouse Review* (January–February, 2010): 468–8.

Price, James and Kenneth Melchin. *Spiritualizing Politics without Politicizing Religion: The Example of Sargent Shriver.* Toronto: University of Toronto Press, 2022.

Price, Jamie and Megan Price. "Insight Policing and the Role of the Civilian in Police Accountability." *Clearinghouse Review* (August, 2015): 1–8.

Price, Megan. "Intentional Peace: The Role of Human Consciousness in the Emergence of Peace and Conflict." In *Exploring Spirituality, Emergent Creativity, and Reconciliation*, ed. Gloria Neufeld Redekop, 267–282. Lanham, MD: Lexington Books, 2019.

________. "The Practical Value of Linking the Personal and the Social in Efforts to Change Complex Social Conflict." *Theoforum* 50 (no. 2, 2020): 241–58.

______. "The Process and Partnerships behind Insight Policing." *Criminal Justice Policy Review* 27 (no. 5, 2016): 553–567.

Redmon, Coates. *Come As You Are: The Peace Corps Story.* San Diego: Harcourt Brace Jovanovich, Publishers, 1986.

Rice, Gerard T. *The Bold Experiment: JFK's Peace Corps.* Notre Dame: University of Notre Dame Press, 1985.

Schwartz, Karen. *What You Can Do For Your Country.* New York: Anchor Books, 1993.

Shriver, Sargent. *Point of the Lance.* New York: Harper & Row, 1964.

Shriver, Timothy. *Fully Alive: Discovering What Matters Most.* New York: Sarah Crichton Books, 2014.

"Sisters of Mercy." https://nebo.sistersofmercy.org/west-midwest/history/chicago/

Skerrett, Ellen. "Catholic School System." http://www.encyclopedia.chicagohistory.org/pages/218.html

"St. Joseph's Church." https://en.wikipedia.org/wiki/St._Joseph_Roman_Catholic_Church_(Chicago)

"St. Joseph's Parish." https://stjosephparishchicago.org

"St. Malachy Church." https://johnamallin.com/project/st-malachy-church/

"St. Patrick Academy." https://en.wikipedia.org/wiki/St._Patrick%27s_Academy

Stossel, Scott. *Sarge: The Life and Times of Sargent Shriver.* Washington: Smithsonian Books, 2004.

Szulc, Tad. *Dominican Diary.* New York: Dell, 1966.

Teilhard de Chardin, Pierre. *The Phenomenon of Man.* Trans. Bernard Wall. London: Collins, Fontana Books, 1974.

Tuttle, William M. *Race Riot: Chicago in the Summer of 1919.* New York: Atheneum: 1970; reprint University of Illinois Press, 1996.

U.S. Catholic. "How Mexican Immigrants Changed Chicago's Parishes." *U.S. Catholic*, June 4, 2020. https://uscatholic.org/articles/202006/how-mexican-immigrants-changed-chicagos-parishes/

Winters, Michael Sean. "'Crossing Parish Boundaries' Sheds Light on Chicago Racial History." *National Catholic Reporter* (February 15, 2017). https://www.ncronline.org/blogs/distinctly-catholic/crossing-parish-boundaries-sheds-light-chicago-racial-history

ACKNOWLEDGMENTS

As rewarding as writing can be—and writing this book was truly rewarding—it can also be a long, lonely, solitary affair. Breaking open my solitude with timely and needed assistance was a close circle of friends without whose curiosity, support, and engagement I could not have completed this manuscript. With heartfelt thanks for your care and concern, I give it up for Ken Melchin, Marnie Jull, Barbara Waldeisen, Stacey Engels, Charles Hefling, Lowell Boyers, and Tim Shriver.

The shortcomings in this work are most assuredly my own. That is clear. Equally clear is the fact that the achievement of self-transcendence is a group affair. So I give thanks to all the friends, colleagues, and family members who read this manuscript at one point or another—or who listened to me read part of it—or who were willing to cheer me on from the sidelines. Your support has sustained me; your insights and critiques made me better, and the manuscript is better too. Thank you Mark Shriver, Megan Price, Steve Edwards, Barbara Kelly, Lucy Di Rosa, Kirby Jones, Patrick Smalley, Bill Josephson, Tyler Ross, Chip Hughes, Andrew Mangini, Audrey Rosenberg, Jeffrey Rothstein, Kahlila Kramer, Devon Price, Jonathan Kramer, Lauri Portz, Sarah Wharton, Anthony Vavasis, Jeff Bond, Martin Maidenberg, Caitlin Price, Jim Portz, Shane Killoran, Jim Price, and Wilma Price.

I needed a place to write this book. Every writer does. So I am thankful for the staff of two coffee bars that hosted countless hours of my efforts with such personable, professional good cheer: Brandon and the baristas at Underline Coffee, which unfortunately did not survive the Covid shutdown in New York City; and the fine team of baristas at Highline, which fortunately did—Gonzalo, John, Joey, Rae, Dro, and Kat. Here's to you.

I also needed support, which I generously received from the board and staff of the Sargent Shriver Peace Institute. I thank you for your patience, your trust, and your steady belief that I would ultimately pull this off. And I did; we did, thanks to the steady, empathetic and knowledgeable David Wilk and his team, who helped prepare the manuscript for publication.

"The last shall be first." And first in my affection and gratitude is Vieve Radha Price, whose husband and partner I have the great fortune to be—who like no other has born the burden of my writing from its beginning to its long-awaited end, and born it with utterly unfathomable love, consideration, and candor. I cannot thank you enough, my darling.

ABOUT THE CONTRIBUTORS

Sargent Shriver (1915–2011) was a graduate of Yale University and Yale Law School, a leading figure in the Catholic Interracial Council movement in the United States, the founding director of the Peace Corps under President Kennedy, the architect of America's War on Poverty under President Johnson, the Chairman of Special Olympics International in partnership with his wife, Eunice Kennedy Shriver, and a citizen diplomat who made signal contributions to the fields of bioethics, nuclear arms control, and interreligious dialog and peacebuilding.

Jamie Price was the founding director of the Sargent Shriver Peace Institute, which he led for its first twenty years. He has also held faculty positions in religion, philosophy, and conflict resolution at Georgia State University, The Catholic University of America, George Mason University, and the University of Chicago, and he is the co-author of *Spiritualizing Politics without Politicizing Religion: The Example of Sargent Shriver* (Toronto, 2022). Jamie lives and works in New York City.

Charles Hefling taught theology, philosophy, and Great Books for thirty years as a professor at Boston College. He has translated and edited works of Bernard Lonergan and served as Editor-in-Chief of *The Anglican Theological Review*. His most recent book is *The Book of Common Prayer: A Guide (Oxford, 2021)*. Charles lives and works in Cambridge, Massachusetts.

Lowell Boyers is an American painter who works in a variety of materials to blend figurative and abstract imagery. He received his MFA from Yale University, and his work has been the subject of exhibitions worldwide, including in Cologne, Abu Dhabi, New York, Los Angeles, Houston, and Dallas. Lowell lives and works in New York City.

CPSIA information can be obtained
at www.ICGtesting.com
Printed in the USA
JSHW020022140423
40328JS00001B/3